MAYDAY
I'M FALLEN

MAYDAY
I'M FALLEN

Survival Strategies for Christians

ROSS CHADWICK

TATE PUBLISHING & *Enterprises*

This title is also available as a Tate Out Loud product. Visit www.tatepublishing.com for more information.

Published by Tate Publishing & Enterprises, LLC
127 E. Trade Center Terrace | Mustang, Oklahoma 73064 USA
1.888.361.9473 | www.tatepublishing.com

Tate Publishing is committed to excellence in the publishing industry. The company reflects the philosophy established by the founders, based on Psalm 68:11,
"The Lord gave the word and great was the company of those who published it."

Cover design by Lynly D. Taylor
Interior design by Kristen Polson

Published in the United States of America

ISBN: 978-1-60247-841-1
1. Christian Living 2. Spiritual Growth
07.10.01

To him who is able to keep you from falling
and to present you before
his glorious presence without fault
and with great joy.

To the only God our Savior be glory,
majesty, power and authority,
through Jesus Christ our Lord,
before all ages, now and forevermore!
Amen.

Jude 24-25 NIV

TABLE OF CONTENTS

MAYDAY I'M FALLEN!

Survival Strategies for Christians

In the fall of 2001, I sat in the darkened Biltmore Hotel's conference ballroom in Phoenix, Arizona, anticipating the sad review of the line of duty death of an eight-year veteran firefighter named Bret Tarver, who had been killed in a structure fire in a supermarket on March 14, 2001. It wasn't something I relished hearing but it really impressed me that the Phoenix Fire Department was willing to share with a group of fire service leaders the tragic details of losing a valued family member. The forum revealed every known aspect of the fatal incident for analysis by other fire service professionals, mostly command level chief officers. But as it turned out, the conference had a tremendous impact on my life.

As the fire chief in a medium size Texas city, I once served on the State Fire Marshal's task force that responded to line-of-duty firefighter deaths in Texas. The task force appointed by the other fire chiefs in the state reviewed all the operational details surrounding any on-duty fatal incident to a firefighter in the state of Texas. After investigating all the details, interviewing witnesses and participants, and collecting all the pertinent information, the group published its findings in an official report–usually exposing all the fatal mistakes made at the incident causing the death of an emergency responder.

So I know that, unfortunately in most line-of-duty deaths, fire departments usually go to the opposite extreme and keep the details as private as possible. Fire departments consider themselves close-knit families, so airing their dirty laundry by admitting to mistakes and sharing the details of a family member's untimely death are neither common nor easy—especially to someone from another department.

Virtually every firefighter death results from one or more common errors committed on their battlefield, the fireground. The mistakes usually result from simply not following standard operating procedures. Firefighting comes with many expected risks, making it one of the most dangerous professions, and every year about one hundred firefighters die in the line of duty fighting an extremely dangerous and real enemy. As a matter of fact, the Occupational Safety and Health Administration (OSHA) labels firefighting as "ultra hazardous, unavoidable dangerous activity." Even though firefighting is very dangerous, almost all firefighter deaths and serious injuries are preventable! Everyone on the discussion panel from Phoenix agreed this fire should never have claimed the life of Firefighter Tarver.

All firefighter line-of-duty death investigations result in mandatory administrative reports to the entire fire service from a federal government agency called the National Institute of Occupational Safety and Health (NIOSH). Furthermore, like Texas, most states in which the death occurs investigate and then release their own reports. Each of these reports condenses the traumatic loss of a firefighter into a few technical pages detailing the tragic events that led to the death.

Scanning over the victims' names on these sterile and impersonal pieces of paper, the fire service community considers the lessons learned and all the professional recommendations, then prays that it never happens in their fire department. But, the investigative reports never really capture the human side of these events and the heart-breaking sequences of events gone terribly wrong or the overwhelming reality that a firefighter will never come to work again and never go home. Getting personal hurts too much and reminds us of our own vulnerability.

At the conference in Phoenix, larger than life size pictures of Firefighter Tarver appeared on both the giant auditorium screens. Supervisors and command staff in charge of the terrible incident presented very emotional overviews of the fire that claimed Tarver's life and forever changed theirs. Fellow firefighters tearfully testified about Bret's life and his value as a loyal team member and the devastation of his death. Bret Tarver's death suddenly became a very real and personal encounter for me. And it did hurt! Bret left behind a wife and three daughters. Along with my son, David, I'm blessed with my lovely wife, Lu Ann, and three beautiful daughters, Margrete, Megan, and Melanie! My emotional reaction surprised me and it seared my very soul with the senselessness of his death and the tremendous loss to both his biological family and his fire department family.

I listened intently with tears in my eyes as the story of Firefighter Bret Tarver's death and forty years of life unfolded. Sadly, the incident exposed many of the familiar fireground mistakes that kill and seriously injure too many firefighters every year. Firefighter Tarver left the safety of his hose line, wandered away from the security of the rest of his crew, became disoriented, lost his way, got trapped by unseen debris, ran out of life-saving air and ripped off his breathing mask, and stood up unprotected into the super heated and highly toxic environment of a burning supermarket. In reality, Bret died needlessly in an old market no one really cared about.

Before you read the following excerpt from the official Phoenix Fire Department report of their line-of-duty death incident, picture this scene in your mind. The visibility is zero, and you absolutely cannot see your hand in front of your face. As the room temperature continues to grow unbearably, your core body temperature climbs from 98.6 degrees to over 104 degrees; your body feels extremely uncomfortable and weighed down in all the protective clothing you're wearing. You run out of air from your self-contained supply, so you rip off your protective mask in an environment filled with heated, toxic, and lethal smoke, exposing your airway and lungs to poison. Many of the tall supermarket shelves have fallen over into the aisles invisibly blocking your exit and rescue. You've become so disoriented that you have absolutely no idea where you are in a large burning structure or how to get out. And, as you expend great effort to breathe your last breaths, you actually suck in more killer toxins from the hot polluted air. You scream out "Mayday–Mayday–Mayday!" Now think about the moment your panic level skyrockets because you realize you are struggling by yourself, without your team and your cries for help are not being answered. "Help me! Somebody please help me!" Physically, mentally, and emotionally you slowly and painfully begin to die–all alone!

> Firefighter Tarver, a member of the Engine 14 crew, told his captain that he was running low on air in his self-contained breathing apparatus (SCBA) and needed to leave the building. The captain gathered his crew together and told them to follow the hoseline out to the exterior. The engineer led the way out, followed by two firefighters with the Engine 14 captain at the back. As the two Engine 14 firefighters, including Firefighter Tarver, turned to leave, they became disoriented and ran into a wall. They got back up, turned in the direction they thought was the correct way to go, and ran into another wall. The Engine 21 captain and two firefighters entered the building immediately and followed the hoseline. Visibility in the supermarket had dropped to zero. They came upon firefighter Tarver. He was disoriented, out of air, standing on his feet, and calling for help. The Engine 21 captain brought firefighter Tarver down to the hoseline and instructed him to follow it to the exterior. Firefighter Tarver had become incapacitated by the smoke and could not follow the instructions of the Engine 21 captain. Firefighter Tarver crawled a short distance, then stood up, turned, and disappeared in the smoke.[1]

Hearing the unfolding tragic story told by the Phoenix Fire Department, I recalled the excellent article written by Battalion Chief John Salka of the Fire Department of New York I had just read a few days earlier on firefighter survival and how to stay out of trouble. I appreciated the valuable lessons he shared from his many years fighting fires for a major metropolitan fire department.

Chief Salka has undoubtedly fought more "big" fires in one year than I have in my entire career. In the article, he expertly turned his professional lessons learned into five simple and basic firefighter survival tips on how to stay out of trouble and how to survive: stay low, monitor conditions and stay oriented, stay together, stay calm, and monitor the radio.

> There are some tactics that all firefighters can take at all fire operations to reduce their chances of being injured in sudden dangerous occurrences or getting into a situation they cannot escape from. There are five basic tactics that if performed at every interior structural fire operation will dramatically increase a firefighter's chances of surviving the operation.[2]

Over the next several days after I returned home to Texas, Firefighter Tarver's death and Chief Salka's survival tactics raced through my mind. I spent many hours contemplating why they were impacting me so drastically. It struck me that Bret Tarver had failed to follow the most basic of firefighter survival guidelines and lost his life in a horrific manner. He got into trouble and he did not survive! But why was this incident bothering me so much?

Finally, during my "quiet time" one early morning as I studied the Gospel of John, the Holy Spirit hit me like an earthquake starting in my heart and seismically moving through my entire soul and spirit! I vividly remembered the apostle's eyewitness description of the night of Christ's betrayal, that Judas had done several things that sounded so very familiar and that now struck me from a whole new perspective. Judas failed to follow the simple and basic survival guidelines that Jesus had talked about and modeled during the previous three years. Judas fell into a situation he could not escape from and then got into trouble fighting an invisible and powerful enemy and he did not survive! Why? I went back and carefully read John chapters 13 and 14 again from a new standpoint on survival strategies.

- Judas had been at the feet of Christ. Jesus had even washed his dirty feet, but Judas did not stay low. Instead, he pridefully stood up into the hostile environment of his ego and breathed in the lethal toxicity of an unseen enemy.

- Judas had sat in a place of honor next to the very Creator of the universe at the last supper with an intimacy and security that even some of the other disciples did not have. Yet, Judas left the safety of his eternal Life Line, got lost, wandered off on his own, and died.
- Judas had lived in a close relationship with the other disciples during three years of fellowship, miracles, and teachings from the Messiah. But when he needed them most, Judas became separated from his crew's fellowship and safety and hopelessly faced the enemy completely by himself.
- Judas had been with the Good Shepherd who had led him on the right path and clearly given him directions to eternal life. Amazingly, Judas still became disoriented and took the wrong road as he stood up, turned, and disappeared into the darkness of night to be consumed by an unseen, powerful, evil enemy.
- Judas betrayed the Son of God and became physically, emotionally, and spiritually distressed—even to the point of death. In the ultimate moment of stress, Judas could not stay calm and he hung himself!

Over the next few weeks, I compared the survival strategies of firefighters to those of Christians. The concept just continued to expand. After serving more than thirty-five years in the fire service, I completely understood the dangers firefighters face every day but I had failed to fully comprehend the constant trouble Christians encounter as they struggle in their daily, spiritual lives. Forces and enemies we cannot even see surround us, creating many of the same dangers that fires do to firefighters. We live in an increasingly toxic spiritual environment that constantly seeks to overwhelm and kill us. So many similarities exist between firefighters surviving fires and Christians surviving "fires" on our spiritual journeys to eternal life that it dawned on me that the Holy Spirit might be trying to tell me something.

Just as firefighters must have survival skills and since Christians have such strong and powerful enemies that do not want us to get to paradise, we need strategies that can help us survive. Daily we are involved in hazardous battles for our very lives. Even though there's a little of Judas in all of us, God has assured those of us who have personally chosen to follow him of the victory in the war, but he expects us to be ready and prepared to fight the battles. However, *when* we get in trouble how do we survive? Notice I didn't say "if" we get in trouble, because in our fallen human nature, we will always manage to get into trouble. Jesus personally gives us clear warning: "In this world you will have trouble" (John 16:33).

THE ROADS TO ETERNITY

It's Always A Personal Choice!

All human beings struggle down troublesome spiritual roads. There are many different roads that will ultimately take us some place—wherever and whatever it is–somewhere on the other side of time. Someday, we all will step out of time as we know it and cross over to the "other side" into what we call eternity. Along the way, most of us will take dangerous detours that get us into big trouble or expose us to great risks. How do we avoid trouble when possible or how do we survive when we get into trouble on our spiritual journeys? Therein lies the questions of this book for Christians–those who have made a personal choice to follow Jesus Christ.

As Christians, we realize that all roads but one lead to death in eternity. The roads to death are usually wide, easy, and fast with few rules. It's the spiritual Autobahn. That's why most people choose these various paths. Jesus says, "For wide is the gate and broad is the road that leads to destruction, and many enter through it" (Matthew 7:13). On the other hand, one path exists to everlasting life but it is narrow and often difficult, with plenty of rules making it much less traveled. Jesus confirms this, "But small is the gate and narrow the road that leads to life, and only a few find it" (Matthew 7:14).

In Texas, we call this narrow road the farm to market (FM)

road. It's no highway with its narrow lanes, curves, and bends that perpetually slow us down. It takes us through areas we would most times rather avoid in our hurry to get somewhere. Then again, we sometimes see wonderful views that folks on the freeway never observe. Very often, obstacles such as slow moving farm vehicles or miscellaneous domestic and wild animals or smashed armadillos in the middle of the road get in our way, interrupting our journeys.

Just like the farm to market road, God's path isn't always the easiest road to take. There are some places we're tempted to take shortcuts via easy access to the freeway. That's when we get into trouble. Since we don't always know God's path, if we just let him be our guide he will take us on the earth to heaven road through great adventures with the most spectacular views ever imaginable. But it will never be easy or fast or pain free!

So many people today, including Christians, are asking, "Why follow the narrow road with all the old fashioned rules and road kill when I could just as easily take a super freeway with no speed limits nor obstructions? Anyway, what's the big difference, since the world preaches that all spiritual roads lead to eternal bliss with some loving divine being?" I guess the increasingly popular notion that all spiritual roads ultimately lead to the same place is actually correct. Well…almost! All roads do lead to eternity–but either eternal life or eternal death.

All roads have a beginning and an ending, so time directly impacts our journey to eternity. We choose the route based on our desires to do good or evil. Adam and Eve's original choice thousands of years ago drastically clouds our ability or desire to choose the right way. How do we avoid the troubles we bring upon ourselves when we stray from the road God has divinely mapped out for us to get home to him? All we have to do is acknowledge the truth and obey the one who created all life. Jesus makes it very clear: "I am the Road, also the Truth, also the Life. No one gets to the Father apart from me" (John 14:6, MSG). God's road is always better than our ways, and he makes several key points in his Word about our journeys on the roads to eternity and how to survive!

- God always shows us the right road to life just as David confirms. "You have made known to me the path of life" (Psalm 16:11).
- We are surrounded by the invisible–the eternal. "So we fix our eyes not on what is seen, but on what is unseen. For what is seen is temporary, but what is unseen is eternal" (2 Corinthians 4:18). Most of us are oblivious to the invisible, but we'll see that's where our troubles originate and where the key survival battles rage!
- We most often only see the temporary, so that's where we live our lives–substantially restricted by time and space and the world. "Live life then, with a due sense of responsibility, not as men who don't know the meaning of life, but as those who do. Make the best use of your time, despite all the evils of these days. Don't be vague, but grasp firmly what you know to be the will of the Lord" (Ephesians 5:15–17).
- The wide roads begin with life and lead to death.
- The narrow road begins with death and leads to life.
- We are all born with internal maps of these roads. The Holy Spirit inside us provides the directions to life, but we must pay close attention. We must never be afraid to ask for clarification when we feel lost and God provides the Bible as our navigation system and map book.
- Satan is the tour guide on the roads to death. He's happy to take us on one of many freeways to get us there. But his goal is to make sure we get to his same destination! Amazingly enough, these directions come very naturally to us so we don't usually need any clarification. "Although they know God's righteous decree that those who do such things deserve death, they not only continue to do these very things but also approve of those who practice them" (Romans 1:32).
- God loves us to life! We walk in heavenly light on his road. "This is the message we have heard from him and declare to you: God is light; in him there is no darkness at all" (1 John 1:5). God's Word illuminates our way. "Your word is a lamp for my feet and a light for my path" (Psalm 119:105).
- Satan hates us to death! We walk in the false light of worldly

darkness on his roads. "If we claim to have fellowship with him (God) yet walk in darkness, we lie and do not live by the truth" (1 John 1:6).

- Death is the wages of sin, and life is the free gift from God. If that's true, why would anyone choose the road to death instead of to life? Even as Christians, we sometimes travel with everyone else on a wrong road. But every so often, we see a signpost that points us back to the right road. Why do so many still choose to stay on the wrong road and ignore God's directions? John 3:19–20 gives the tragic answer: "This is the verdict; Light has come into the world, but men loved darkness instead of light because their deeds were evil. Everyone who does evil hates the light, and will not come into the light for fear that his deeds will be exposed."
- God does not choose your path for you! Even though God will set and map the right path, all humans still must choose their own spiritual path–either to life or to death. God knows before you do which path you will ultimately choose, but it's still your choice.
- Christians often seek God's will, but many times we think we know the best way on our own so we seek shortcuts to "help" God out. Without exception, shortcuts always disorient us and we quickly lose our way. Becoming disoriented is a spiritual killer and usually very painful. When called upon, God in his wonderful grace and mercy rescues us and brings us back to the correct road.
- The best news of all is that up to the very last second before you cross from time into eternity, no matter that you have traveled the evilest possible roads to death all your life, you can instantly change your direction to the road to life. Jesus makes this very clear, "I tell you the truth, whoever hears my word and believes him who sent me has eternal life and will not be condemned; he has crossed over from death to life" (John 5:34).

INCIDENT & LIFE PRIORITIES

Make Sure You Follow the Incident Commander's Commands!

At an emergency, the incident commander (often referred to as the "IC") must always have clear incident priorities to successfully accomplish the fire department's mission. These priorities become the most important functions that drive the management of the emergency incident and are constantly evaluated and re-evaluated until the incident is terminated and the mission effectively completed. In all firefighting operations, incident commanders always have three key priorities: life safety, incident stabilization, and property conservation.

The top priority always involves all the survival activities needed to reduce the threat of death and injury to firefighters and civilians. The IC resolves the emergency incident and makes sure all the firefighters survive the incident without injury or death. The next main concern is to stabilize the incident as quickly and safely as possible with the least risk to all exposures. The third priority requires the actions necessary to reduce the property loss caused by the event.

To successfully accomplish these incident priorities, the incident commander must be at the scene and personally giving the commands. The firefighters' survival depends on constantly paying attention to the strategic instructions of the IC. Being commanded to go into a dangerous and life threatening environment, firefighters must trust that the incident commander clearly knows what's going on and is always watching out for their well-being. Firefighters constantly place their lives in the IC's hands and entrust their ultimate survival on the IC's skillful and experienced strategies and tactics.

As the Supreme Commander, God also sets clear life priorities for his true followers. As Christians facing an evil enemy in a temporary world, we must follow God's commands as we confidently march toward our eternal home in heaven with him. As followers of Christ, we must trust that our Life Commander knows exactly what's going on and believe he is intimately involved and concerned about our survival. He promises to be personally at the scene and in charge of every disaster in our lives. Oftentimes, just as in firefighting, failure to follow the commands results in death or serious injury. Our heavenly IC will never let us down, but his commands must be understood and followed in order to survive. "Trouble and distress have come upon me, but your commands are my delight. Your statues are forever right; give me understanding that I may live" (Psalm 119:143–144).

As Christians, our eternal life priorities are similar to firefighting's three incident priorities. As Jesus was going home to prepare an eternal place for us, our Incident Commander said his top priority was for us to go into the world and make disciples (eternal life safety). He then told us to baptize them in his name (stabilize the life situation). Once that was done, Jesus said we should teach these new disciples to fully obey all the commands he had given (reduce further loss). And our eternal and ever present Commander unmistakably told us he would personally be on the scene with us, constantly watching out for our well-being until our mission is accomplished. "And be sure of this: I am with you always, even to the end of the age" (Matthew 28:20).

Just as a good incident commander uses survival strategies to assure that the incident priorities are satisfied, God gives us spiritual survival strategies. From a military standpoint, strategy is the science (or art according to some commanders) of using all your resources to bring about a desired result. Essentially, strategy deals with the big picture–the overall plan for winning the war. Ten basic strategies in this book form the framework to spiritually move toward the priorities necessary for Christians to stay out of trouble, if at all possible, and to survive when we so often get in trouble.

"MAYDAY"

I'm in Trouble and I Need Help!

Ships and aircraft in trouble traditionally use the word "mayday" as their call for assistance. This international distress signal originates from the French word "*m'aidez*," which sounds a lot like mayday and simply means "help me." The fire service cautiously borrows the term mayday and strictly uses it to mean any emergency situation involving a firefighter who is either trapped or lost or missing or otherwise in dire trouble. Mayday on a fire scene indicates that something has gone terribly wrong in the firefighting operation and a firefighter needs help immediately to survive. It's life and death!

A mayday call stops the normal emergency operations in its tracks, and firefighters initiate major efforts to find and rescue their injured comrade as their highest priority. Timothy E. Sendelbach in a *Firehouse Magazine* article "Managing the Fireground Mayday" emphasizes the importance of developing a plan of action for maydays by firefighters to prepare fireground commanders in what might ultimately be the most critical decision of their careers.

> The initiation or transmission of a firefighter distress signal produces more stress and potential chaos than any other singular type of incident we may encounter throughout our careers. As firefighters, fire officers, and trainers we must develop a standard plan of action that permits our fireground strategists to properly manage and overcome these potentially chaotic and unquestionably stressful events. Our lives and the lives of our fellow firefighters depend on our preparatory efforts.[3]

Christians constantly face dangerous situations and fall into serious trouble, exactly like firefighters. Just as it becomes a life and death physical situation for firefighters, Christians often get into life and death spiritual circumstances and sometimes even risky physical conditions. Many times we should be screaming, "Mayday, I'm in trouble and I need help now!" This is especially true in what we call our "fallen condition" caused by the original sin of Adam and Eve. This human state exposes all humans to a toxic and dangerous environment of sin with its relentless attacks and constant deceptive obstacles that have the potential to destroy us and knock us off the road to life.

Unfortunately, Christians are much like firefighters when they get in trouble. Rather than call for help immediately, they foolishly believe they can figure a way out on their own. We really don't like to admit we might need to be rescued. The delay in calling a Mayday may be caused by several factors including the stigma associated with admitting to yourself and letting others know you need help, not knowing the strategies for calling a Mayday, and indecision. When interviewed after a disastrous and deadly fire, a firefighter stated, "I knew I was in trouble, I thought about using the radio, but I thought, 'I found my way in; I can find my way out.'"[4] After the tragic line-of-duty death of a fire captain in a high rise fire in October 2001, the Houston Fire Department determined in its final report, "We have almost completely ignored the most important first step, getting the firefighters to recognize they are in trouble and need to get help, to call Mayday."[5] The culture of the fire service is: Don't call for help–it's a sign of weakness. Does that sound like your Christian walk?

Strategies must be learned and put into practice to keep us out of trouble if possible and help us survive when we inevitably fall into trouble. Our spiritual lives and the lives of fellow believers may depend on our preparatory and response efforts. Just like Chief Salka's admonition to firefighters to stay out of trouble or how to survive when they do get into trouble, there are strategies that all Christians can practice in our spiritual lives to reduce our chances of being spiritually injured in sudden dangerous occurrences or getting into situations we cannot escape. These ten survival strategies, if practiced and performed, will dramatically improve our survival on the way to eternal life. Following them will make us better disciples of Christ!

And when Christians get into trouble, we need to call out immediately for assistance. Our lives and possibly the lives of fellow believers, or even future believers, depend on our survival efforts. When in extreme trouble, the firefighter shouts to the incident commander, "Mayday, I've fallen!" and the Christian cries out to the Savior, "Mayday, I'm fallen!"

STRATEGY 1

STAY ORIENTED!

Know Where You Came From

Disorientation ranks high as one of the major factors killing firefighters in fires. Survival strategy emphasizes the critical importance of knowing where you came from during the firefight and staying constantly aware of that orientation because it provides your way out if you get into trouble. Your orientation represents what you know to be true and safe. Many of the firefighters killed inside structural fires simply became disoriented and then lost their ways. Constantly staying oriented saves lives. Jerry Smith, a former Los Angeles City Fire Captain with many years working for one of the best fire departments in the world, considers disorientation a firefighter's worst nightmare.

> Fire service veterans will tell you disorientation means you have lost your sense of direction and that's enough to cause panic when you feel trapped while wanting to retreat to safety. Many of us have experienced a variety of dangerous atmospheres inside a burning building where any one mistake might have been fatal...Unfortunately for firefighters, disorientation remains a high risk anytime you enter an unfamiliar building where fire conditions deteriorate quickly and you're unable to track a way out.[1]

In today's world, Christians also must stay oriented to answer the three most fundamental questions in life: Where did I come from?

What am I doing here? Where am I going? Yet, when it comes to spiritual survival, how many people can firmly and confidently answer any of these crucial orientation questions? Losing track of where we came from and where we are affects our sense of direction to the point that it can kill us spiritually and sometimes even physically. And, most importantly, our orientation always determines where we're going.

Just as physical circumstances in a fire, spiritual conditions change for Christians without warning. What was safe one minute ago can rapidly evolve into a life and death situation. An unsafe and hostile environment combined with zero visibility will cloud our ways making it easy to lose our orientation and get lost. Losing our way can be disastrous and almost always starts by losing our point of reference. Christians must, therefore, maintain constant awareness of their environments and their ever-changing situations along with the ability to use this information appropriately for survival.

With this in mind, the first survival strategy of staying oriented and knowing where you came from builds the foundation for the other strategies. The beginning point where one comes from eventually influences the critical decisions in the choice of an eternal road. Simply put, our journey to eternity starts with creation. Where did I come from? Not just from my mother and father, but where and how did everything I see around me get its beginning? Was there a design or does everything exist by some fluke or accident? If a master creation plan existed, who or what was the creator or designer? Were my ancient ancestors something less than humans or did the human race somehow commence with pure and individual human DNA?

Why is this orientation of where you came from so vital for a Christian's survival? Until you know where you came from, how can you really know where you are or where you're going? When you know what direction you're traveling, only then can you know where you're headed. People's beliefs on their origins directly impact their present viewpoints of where they are and ultimately influence their hopes for their endings, since the answers to these questions directly influence the road we take to our final destination–either life or death.

Many religions rely on the first three chapters of Genesis in the Holy Bible for their origin of life answers. They believe that a supreme being of some sort made everything and ultimately created man. But, in the last one hundred years or so with the introduction of many scientific theories, religious and non-religious people alike have been inclined to disregard or severely compromise portions of the Old Testament, especially Genesis 1 through 11. Arguments always include some or all of the following:

- The Genesis account appears too similar to the mythological literature of the ancient Middle East to be true. It sounds suspiciously like a spinoff of other old fables and comparable myths. Literary accounts such as the Bible just can't be considered literal anyway.
- The Creation story in the Bible happened such a long time ago no one can really know if it's factual. It can't be historical because there were no witnesses to actually see it happen.
- The Creation account in Genesis requires a supernatural and preexisting creator so it can't be scientifically correct because it's based on faith rather than facts.
- Evolutionary presuppositions, geologic periods, and the scientific community's unwillingness to accept the young earth chronology significantly influence modern interpretations of Genesis.

THIS ANCIENT FABLE CAN'T POSSIBLY BE TRUE!

...But It's a Very Nice Story

Many just accept the Genesis account of creation as a nice story with some spiritual significance. Somehow it evolved into one of those religious yarns to help humans deal with their internal need to know where they came from and who they are. And because no one really has any absolute, firsthand knowledge of our beginnings, scientists advise us that without solid scientific evidence, this ancient fable can't possibly be true. Since it's based on something other than nature, the Genesis account just isn't reliable!

Many modern scientists insist the factual and scientific evidence proves that a theory called evolution naturally and logically answers our constantly pressing desire to know where we came from. They theorize that simple stories, such as the Genesis account, only originate from some burning inner human yearning to know who we are and how we got here. Humans have always struggled finding their orientation of where they came from. Interestingly enough, scientists can't adequately explain why we have this intrinsic longing within us and evolution can't answer that nagging question either. But scientists still believe only science and science alone can provide the answers as to the *how* of all origins.

Sadly, even contemporary theologians have bought into the "it's a nice story with a good message–just not a scientifically correct" interpretation. The following direct quote from an actual sermon preached from a Christian pulpit in 2001 entitled "Created in God's Image" illustrates and echoes the current liberal understanding of Genesis by many people who claim to know and understand God.

> Now, the seven days of Creation is a very nice story–especially to tell children. They love to hear about God creating new things each day, until finally everything is ready, and God creates people to live in that beautiful, new world. For the little ones, it doesn't matter whether it really happened that way or not. The message they get is that God made everything, and that it is all "very good." For adults though, the story presents some problems. It seems that instead of being about six thousand years old, as the Bible's chronology would have it, the earth is actually several billion years old...Many secular scientists have come to the conclusion that the Bible is simply wrong, and is therefore outdated and not of much use...The fallacy is in thinking that the Bible can be considered "true" only if it is literally true. Vast portions of human literature

> - poetry, novels, fantasy, science fiction, and so on were never intended by their authors to be taken as literally true, and yet they often contain powerful truths about the human condition...Similarly, God has spoken to us in the Bible through many different kinds of "literature," much of which was never meant to be taken literally, either by its original human authors or by God, who is its divine Author. This is especially true of the first eleven chapters of the Bible, where we find great, mythical stories as the Seven Days of Creation, the Garden of Eden, Noah and the Ark, and the Tower of Babel. These are stories about the human condition and about how we humans came to be the mixture of good and evil we are today.[2]

THE REAL STORY HAS A DIVINE PURPOSE!

My Point of Reference Really Needs a Who, a What, and a Why!

This liberal sermon points out our human desire to create a god in our own image, based on our own limited knowledge. Unfortunately, this theology in effect says that if some accidental fate from an infinite unknown eternal past (billions and billions of years) caused a human to evolve, then random chance will ultimately determine a person's final destiny. If this is true, an eternal outcome for people after death becomes a mute point if evolution really happened. On the other hand, only if some supernatural intelligent designer uniquely and specially created us in his or her image does it make any sense that the image-bearer might have some eternal destiny as promised or provided by the image-maker.

If our first orientation strategy is to know where we came from, why is it so important Christians believe and fully accept the Genesis story of creation? Obviously, most modern scientific theories of our origins remove any supernatural process, thereby eliminating any need for God and his revelation that we were created with a perfectly designed plan in his very image. Scientists feel content and confident to answer the *how* question but avoid the more difficult *why* or *who* questions. This avoidance severely distorts any true orientation of where we came from.

Two well-known atheist scientists, Richard Dawkins and Peter Atkins, advocate that the universe has no purpose and that the question "Why are we here?" is indeed a very stupid question. For them, the only appropriate question to ask of nature is the *how* question. But without a purpose, the very existence of humans makes no sense! Too many Christians miss this crucial point and fail to see why the first few chapters of Genesis are so extremely significant to their survival. Genesis explains that the universe has a definite purpose, answering not only the *how* and *what* questions but addressing the even more important *who* and *why* questions.

If man evolved as a product of chance (as commonly taught and believed–even by many Christians), then does the concept of good and evil really make any sense? If the world didn't need a supernatural creator, then why would it eventually require a supernatural savior? Phillip E. Johnson, a senior professor at the University of California at Berkeley, says this crucial debate fundamentally comes down to: "Is God real or imaginary? Did God create man or did man create God?"[3] Although Christians may overlook this critical point, atheists obviously recognize the significance of the Genesis record as the following comments from the *American Atheist Magazine* indicate:

> The whole justification of Jesus' life and death is predicated on the existence of Adam and the forbidden fruit he and Eve ate. Without the original sin, who needs to be redeemed? Without Adam's fall into a life of constant sin terminated by death, what purpose is there to Christianity? None...Without Adam, without the original sin, Jesus Christ is reduced to a man with a mission on a wrong planet.[4]

If we reject or compromise the Genesis account of where we came from, we undermine the entire Bible and it becomes just another big history book based loosely on facts from an ancient culture.

On the other hand, if we accept it as factual, the book of Genesis stands alone as the absolute foundation of all true human history. One of the very important keys to survival should be the knowledge that the inspired writers of the Bible, and even Jesus Christ himself, considered Genesis as their orientation of where they came from. After all, the New Testament refers to Genesis more than 200 times, over 100 of which are from Genesis 1–11.

Clearly, neither Jesus nor any New Testament writer viewed these wonderful Genesis stories, most likely written by Moses, as anything other than pure history and truth. Jesus confronted the Pharisees by telling them, "If you believed Moses, you would believe me, for he wrote about me" (John 5:46). The question for Christians today is: If Genesis cannot be believed exactly as written, then why should we believe Jesus or anyone else who accepted it? Jesus asked the Pharisees that exact question, "But since you do not believe what Moses wrote how are you going to believe what I say?" (John 5:47). If we hesitate to accept the Genesis creation account as our orientation, then Jesus could just as easily ask us that very same question.

Without the true point of reference that the special creation in Genesis gives, we face the danger of determining which stories in Scripture are real and which are just nice yarns. The only accurate and chronological account of the divine beginnings of all things comes from the first few chapters of Genesis. Along with the *when*, only it truthfully answers the *how* and the *what* and the *who* questions! The rest of Scripture confirms it and keeps us oriented with a beginning point on the map on God's road to eternity. Knowing where we came from gives us our divine purpose and lights our paths to eternity.

Therefore, the first words of the Bible, "In the beginning God created the heavens and earth" arguably represent the most important truth in all of Scripture. None of the words that follow make any sense without the beautiful and amazing creation by God the Creator and Image Maker. Believing this unconditional truth can't be emphasized enough. But why do today's Christians seldom take their beginnings seriously? Maybe they believe it's too controversial or they just think it just doesn't matter anyway–only the future really matters. However, this starting point of absolute truth establishes the foundational purpose of our lives. Accepting this remarkable and fantastic certainty, in spite of our inability to fully fathom its reality, causes us to live our lives in a specific manner and ultimately it keeps us oriented and gives us clear eternal directions.

THE CREATOR MUST BE ETERNAL!

Some "Thing" or Some "One" Existed Before Our Origin

Atheists and other skeptics often ask Christians: "Where did God come from?" And, Christians logically respond back with an equally probing question, "Where did the life building blocks of evolution come from?" Neither question can be easily answered. The creation theory needs an eternal intelligent designer and the evolution theory requires eternal random matter. Those are really the only choices we have. Actually, if you think about that dilemma, is it really surprising that the created or evolved beings have extreme difficulty understanding the preexistence and eternality of their creator or their life building matter?

In order to create everything we see today, that person, place, or thing must have existed prior to the creation or the evolution or anything else. And, the originator or original matter of our beginning had to exist preceding the creation or evolution whether it took place six thousand years or several billion years ago. The philosophy of a "beginning" requires the concept of time, which begs the question, "Has time always existed, was it created, or did it just evolve too?"

God's creation of the universe ("the heavens and earth") as described in Genesis 1:1 had a specific start ("in the beginning") that set in motion time as we know it and started the clock ticking. Evolution apparently does not have as clearly a defined beginning because it requires almost infinite amounts of time. Many suggest the "Big Bang" as the beginning of evolution's time. But where did the energy creating the matter come from and when and why and how did all the stuff go bang?

With the supreme guidance of the Holy Spirit, the Apostle

John recorded one of the most profound passages on the Creator and creation in the entire Bible. In addition to amplifying the account in Genesis, John 1:1–14 presents the gospel's fundamental reality that a supernatural force with intelligence, a plan, and a purpose made all things. The first chapter of John's gospel clarifies the significance of the eternal God and his eternal relationship to Jesus Christ, the "Word" who John writes created everything. "In the beginning was the Word, and the Word was with God, and the Word was God. He was with God in the beginning. Through him all things were made; without him nothing was made that has been made" (John 1:1–3).

The eternal nature of God - the Intelligent Designer - completely counters evolution's unspecified claim of random eternal matter. The special creation of the Bible simply states that the all-powerful God created everything out of nothing (theologians call this *ex nihilo*). Nothing, including space, matter, and time, existed before creation! Vines says in a word analysis of Genesis 1:1, "The writer uses scientifically precise language to demonstrate that God brought the object or concept into being from previously nonexistent material."[5] Although more complex than we can ever imagine, God simply spoke it into existence and it was so. As created beings, we can never fully grasp this supernatural accomplishment, but the writer of Hebrews confidently says not to worry, it ultimately comes down to a faith issue. "By faith we understand that the world was made at God's command, so that what is seen was not made out of what was visible" (Hebrews 11:3).

Conversely, also by faith, evolutionists scientifically understand that the world was made from some stuff that was naturally made out of something from somewhere with absolutely no design or plan or thought over billions of years of seemingly infinite time so that what is seen evolved from what was always visible–apparently just in a different state. Obviously, those who espouse such a creation theory deny the existence of a god and particularly the need for a supernatural designer and creator. Nature categorically denies that something can come from nothing! It's so much easier to understand the visible than the invisible. Consequently, many scientists just assume that the visible material world is all that exists and for no known reason or purpose continues to randomly evolve.

Why should Christians be so concerned about evolution and their survival? A relationship with eternal matter isn't possible so our propensity to do bad things (we call it sin) presents no issues and our behavior shouldn't concern us. With no absolute truth naturally advocated by evolution, humans have learned to do their own thing. It's survival of the fittest! As the world more and more turns to that worldview, should we wonder why things are going as they are?

And when Christians say it doesn't really matter anyway, I wholeheartedly agree with Michael Ruse, a Florida State University professor and ardent ally of Darwinism who adamantly rejects any thought of a creation by intelligent design. Listen very carefully to his words when he says that the fight over our orientation of where we came from is extremely important because it's a "struggle for the hearts and souls of people, with deep implication for the ways in which we live our lives and regulate our conduct. It is a religious or metaphysical battle, not simply a dispute about scientific theory."[6] That's why it's so critical that Christians take notice of the intense ongoing struggle for our very hearts and souls!

Most people (including many professing believers) accept the cold scientific deceit of evolution as the only reliable explanation of where we came from, making it a risky and dangerous orientation with bad directions leading down a very hazardous road. But here's the key question, can they answer *what*, *who,* or *why*? If they can't answer these crucial survival questions, their starting point ultimately ends up impossible to establish. Their evolutionary *how* does not give directions to eternity. It only disorients, distracts, and confuses the sojourner, especially Christians.

WHAT DO CREATION'S RESULTS DECLARE?

It is Indeed Very Good!

As completed on the seventh day, the universe was exquisitely beautiful and free from defects or flaws. All aspects of his creative handiwork pleased the Creator so much after its completion that six times in Genesis 1 God inspected his handiwork and declared it "good." And at the end of his six days of creative activity, God looked over everything he had done, with mankind as the crowning jewel, and said, "It is indeed very good!" God's proclamation triumphantly exclaimed that he had completed everything flawlessly and that this paradise needed no evolutionary improvements or enhancements.

Perfection separates the supernatural from the natural and that notion should tremendously impact every Christian's orientation. The evolutionary process can only be natural as scientists define it–never supernatural. Evolutionists don't see a need for a god, and God certainly doesn't need evolution over any period of time to create anything. If a God so powerful and mighty could actually create this unimaginable universe from nothing, why would he need additional time or chances?

Unmistakably, evolution requires ongoing change to make it keep working. There can never be total satisfaction with the state of the universe. It just keeps changing and changing and changing. It's never "very good" because it's just one mistake and correction after another. The end is never in sight because there is no end. Time continues, change happens, and eternity never occurs. How can the evolutionist ever speak of perfection or completion? Since it's a constantly moving target, how would an evolving being even recognize it? Will the evolutionist ever be able to say, "Wow, this is great - finally!"?

If evolution orients us to where we came from, how can it possibly provide a point of reference as to where we are and especially show us where we're going? It doesn't even know or care where it came from. Christians who accept evolution in any form must recognize and accept this severe disorientation quandary. And just like firefighters in a raging fire, disoriented Christians often lose their ways and have extreme difficulty surviving.

And yet, various Christian compromises attempt to harmonize evolution theory with their biblical beliefs because six literal days to create everything appears utterly impossible. So, they reject the atheistic evolution hypothesis but instead blend God's supernatural power with an evolutionary process. Many believers justify the scientific theories by extending the six literal days of creation into six long evolutionary periods that more closely match up with modern scientific thought and religion. Evolution remains the *how* but now God is the *who* and supposedly provides some *why*, but obviously without a plan or purpose. The three most popular ways in which Christians have incorporated the extensions of time into the Bible are the "gap theory," "theistic evolution," and "progressive creationism." All three views seriously compromise and blur the Christian's orientation of where they came from.

The gap theory proposes a gap of several million or even billions of years between Genesis 1:1 and 1:2. This theory's proponents translate some key Hebrew words to mean that one creation was made and then many millions of years latter a re-creation took place. Most serious Hebrew scholars have declared this translation wrong but the false theory continues as a method of compromise. Many versions of the gap theory exist, but most agree that the time required by modern science can be neatly and conveniently inserted into the "gap" because God needed evolution and more time to slowly create the universe.

The most liberal compromise theologically is the deception often called theistic evolution. Unfortunately, this is also one of the most popular beliefs among Christians and non-atheists today. This theory often rejects most or all of the creation account in Genesis and simply states that God made the "Big Bang" or something similar in nature and occasionally stepped in during the natural evolutionary processes over millions or perhaps billions of years. Nevertheless, any use of evolution forfeits God's "very good" confirmation! This compromising concept even bothers serious evolutionists.

> While it is nothing less than scandalous that creationist beliefs have survived into the Twentieth Century, we must also express our embarrassment at the fact that there are many people who, despite the fact that they are relatively well schooled in evolutionary science, believe in something known as theistic evolution. This is the view that evolution has, in fact, occurred, but it has been directed by a super-

> natural power...The best thing that can be said about the theistic evolution idea is that it is not contradicted by the facts of nature.[7]

Progressive creationism opposes both atheistic evolutionism and historic Christianity's belief in a literal biblical creationism. This has recently become a very popular teaching among Christian scientists and university students. Generally, they believe: (1) the "Big Bang" was most likely God's way of starting the creation process; (2) natural processes (sounds like evolution) over twelve to seventeen billion years have gotten us to where we are today; (3) the days of creation were overlapping periods of millions and billions of years; (4) death existed from the beginning of creation long before Adam's sin; and, (5) man was God's "Special Creation" but only after the vast majority of earth's history including ape-men as evidenced by fossils had occurred. Although progressive creationists present their views as being based on a literal interpretation of the Bible, their teachings at times strongly indicate a belief that scripture and nature have equal authority in explaining a supernatural God. Scientific "facts" trump the first eleven chapters of Genesis.

Any compromise of the literal view of God's special creation just to match current theories of science dangerously weakens our orientation of where we came from. However, let me stress this very important point. If believers clearly know the *Who* resulting in an unambiguous *why,* even with some misunderstanding and confusion and compromise of the *how* and *what,* then the *when* becomes less critical. As Christians, we can only find the *why*, *what*, and *how* when we know the *Who* in a personal relationship with our Lord and Savior! In Christ, I lovingly embrace those harmonizing and compromising Christian creationists as long as their *Who* is absolute. Certainly, God accepts them if they have a personal relationship with him. But sadly, their compromises may sabotage or weaken their points of reference on their roads to eternity. It places an incredible obstacle in that narrow path that may ultimately jeopardize their eternal survival, and their teachings may even bump someone else off this path. Here's the key survival principle: compromise is always a very risky orientation at best.

Our orientation as Christians must constantly recognize and celebrate that in six literal days, the great Creator, King, and Image Maker shaped a complete universe bigger than people can ever imagine with earth as an incredible living paradise for the human race to personally enjoy with him. In God's special creation, there were no accidents, no mistakes, no random chances, and no changes necessary until the Maker of the universe finally somehow got it right. Solomon, one of the wisest men to ever walk the earth, humbly states in Ecclesiastes 3:14, "I know that everything God does will remain forever, there is nothing to add to it and there is nothing to take from it, for God has so worked that men should fear Him." Unlike evolution, God never changes! He got it right the first time. Our true orientation as Christians is perfection and never confusion, compromise and chaos.

WHAT YOU SEE IS WHAT YOU GET

Image is Everything!

Image signifies many different things to people, especially in the media-loving fantasy world in which we live. The media bombards us constantly with the image the world thinks we should have. It promotes the impression that the "right" image means everything. And then it defines what right is! Others constantly judge us and relate to us based on that acceptable image. We too often fall in a trap believing that our self-worth comes from that artificial representation. Unfortunately, too many Christians, especially young people, chase after that right image and quickly lose their orientations and all too often crash on some dangerous detour on their spiritual roads.

As we struggle daily, remembering where we came from, we need only recognize our image represents a living mirror to that origin. The deception of evolution throws rocks at that mirror and continually tries to shatter the mirror into a million pieces. Without doubt, God tells us that he made us in his image. "Then God said, 'Let us make man in our image, in our likeness, and let them rule over the fish of the sea and birds of the air, over the livestock, over all the earth, and over all the creatures that move along the ground.' So God created man in his own image, in the image of God he created him; male and female he created them" (Genesis 1:26–27). When it comes to the value and worth of created things, humans stand above all creation, making us the most significant of all God's creative acts.

Paul tells the Ephesians, "We are God's workmanship" (Ephesians 2:10). As God's masterpiece, we must never forget that manifest truth when dealing with our troubles. Great pictures did not evolve from some colored paints and pieces of canvas over a long period of time all by themselves. Great artists created them, and every work of art points back to the artist. Our image is everything because it represents our eternal Artist's image!

Our orientation as Christians ought to be the constant awareness that we alone bear the Creator's true image. Human beings stand on a different level, separate from all the other creatures upon earth. Only people can reason with an intellect, can feel with emotion, and can choose with a free will. We reflect God in personality and only we can communicate and fellowship with him. A note in my NIV Study Bible says, "Because we are created in God's image, (1) we have a spiritual thirst, (2) we have eternal value, and (3) nothing but the eternal God can truly satisfy us."[8] No other created being enjoys those attributes, and evolution can't account for those internal feelings. Think about it–a human is a creature who is unlike any other living thing.

Among all other humans, how do Christians keep from becoming disoriented and getting lost? Even though all people are created in God's image, only Christians stand unique and unlike other human beings because of Jesus Christ! We originate from God's express image. Paul declares that Jesus exactly represents God by reflecting and revealing God to us. Christ reigns supreme over all his creation, and only he holds it all together. "Christ is the visible image of the invisible God. He existed before God made anything at all and is supreme over all creation. Christ is the one through whom God created everything in heaven and earth. He made the things we can see and the things we can't see–kings, kingdoms, rulers, and authorities. Everything has been created through him and for him. He existed before everything else began, and he holds all creation together" (Colossians 1:15–17, NLT). When Christ's image becomes everything to us, then and only then does our image truly reflect our orientation!

IT'S ALL SO AMAZING!

Look Up at the Glory of God and Listen to The Cheers!

"The heavens declare the glory of God;
the skies proclaim the work of his hands.
Day after day they pour forth speech;
night after night they display knowledge.
There is no speech or language where their voice
is not heard." (Psalm 19:1–3)

On a clear, dark night without any modern metropolitan lights diffusing the starlight, a young shepherd boy looked at the heavens and recognized that the exceptional and intricate design and orderliness of the multitude of stars he was seeing could only come from God, the Creator. The boy grew up to be a king and even though David didn't have all the astronomical and cosmological knowledge we have today, he certainly understood the divine display of awareness of the vast universe staring down at him. And in spite of all we have learned since David first gazed in amazement at the heavens, modern cosmologists really have no idea of the total magnitude of the heaven's declaration of God's glory, not even peering into their giant telescopes from earth and space! When David sang about the amazing vastness of the heavens, he stated what most scientists still can't fully explain or understand.

Thousands upon thousands of unbelievable facts point out God's power and transcendence relating to what David saw on that starry night and repeated every night since. We should all stare in awe and be overwhelmed by the magnitude of God's seemingly infinite universe. Day and night, these facts constantly scream out in a universal human language the absolute impossibility and absurdity of any random formation of the heavens. Contemplate for a moment the following marvelous constants with absolute astoundment that a person standing on earth actually moves in at least four different directions at unbelievable speeds–all at the same time.

- The earth spins on its slightly tilted axis daily at a speed of about 1,000 miles an hour. Yet it travels around the sun once a year and stays tilted in the same direction no matter where the earth is in its path near the sun.
- The earth orbits around the sun at a speed of nearly 67,000 miles per hour.
- Besides its movement on its axis and around the sun, the earth, along with our entire solar system whirls around the center of the Milky Way Galaxy at 487,353 miles per hour.
- Our solar system is 26,000 light years (one light year is the distance light travels in a year or 5,880,000,000,000 miles) away from the center of our galaxy so it will take our sun approximately 225 million years to make one trip round the galaxy.
- Our Milky Way Galaxy, one of the millions of other galaxies that exist in our universe, spans over 100,000 light years, about 7,000 light years thick and contains 200 billion stars and moves about 185 miles per second or 666,660 miles per hour.

Modern science has no viable explanation for the thousands of cosmic factors that exist in just the right way for humans to stay alive, other than an intelligent designer. Where does the incredible power and immense energy come from to keep it all going? The working of our vast universe day after day proclaims that a Supreme Creator had an unbelievable design (not to mention tremendous and unknowable supernatural powers) to put it all into place and more importantly for us, to somehow keep it there. Who else but God can say: "To whom will you compare me? Or who is my equal? says the Holy One. Lift your eyes and look to the heavens: Who created all these? He who brings out the starry host one by one, and calls them each by name. Because of his great power and mighty strength, not one of them is missing" (Isaiah 40:25–26).

IT'S ALL SO AMAZING!

Look In The Microscope and See the Glory of God!

And if you think outer space is the only amazing evidence of God our Creator, think about inner space. The microscopic world of atoms and molecules displays complex design, purpose, order, and arrangement. God's amazing fingerprints of design are clearly evident as discoveries about cells and DNA reveal powerful evidence of a designer's role in creation.

On December 16, 2004, *The Dallas Morning News* printed a story with a headline that caught my eye: "The supreme science - Academics viewing the universe through a narrow scope should rethink assumptions." It reported that the most famous and best-known atheist in the academic world, Professor Antony Flew of England's University of Reading, had apparently changed his mind about the need for an intelligent creator shocking the entire scientific world–especially fellow atheists. After years and years of insisting belief in God was a mistake, Professor Flew now concludes that some sort of intelligence must have created the universe.

> Now, in a remarkable reversal, Mr. Flew holds that the universe was brought into being by an infinite intelligence. "What I think the DNA material has done is show that intelligence must have been involved in getting these extraordinary diverse elements together," he said. "The enormous complexity by which the results were achieved look to me like the work of intelligence." Given the conventional wisdom of some psychologists that people rarely, if ever, change their worldview after the age of 30, this radical new position adopted by an 81-year-old thinker may seem startling.[9]

The human race has made some incredible strides in understanding the intricacies of life. Scientists in Darwin's day imagined the living cell as a very simple organism that had a nucleus and some liquid around it, inside a membrane - a "simple lump of protoplasm" as they called it. However, we now understand that the cell is a complicated system with hundreds of parts and thousands of functions so complex that man cannot come close to replicating it. There is no such thing as a simple cell. The more we learn, the more we realize that cells, just like the universe, remain totally beyond our human capacity to fully comprehend.

"You made all the delicate, inner parts of my body
and knit me together in my mother's womb.
Thank you for making me so wonderfully complex!
Your workmanship is marvelous–and how well I
know it." (Psalm 139:13–14, NLT)

DNA exists in the core of life itself. According to geneticists and molecular biologists, DNA speaks a language to the cell as a molecular communications system. Since a code in the DNA provides instructions for every living structure, we now fully appreciate the role the DNA molecule plays in providing the blueprint for constructing the majority of life on earth. Christian philosopher and popular author Ravi Zacharius asks, "How does the universe, which itself developed from nothing, impart into every human strand of DNA enough specific information to cover 600,000 pages of information from nothing?"[10] Dr. Kelly Hollowell believes that our growing understanding of the genetic code makes it very difficult to think that life evolved as a result of chance.

> Suppose you discover on a beach not a watch but the instructions for making the watch. Are there any natural forces like wind and rain capable of creating these written instructions? Evolutionists say DNA molecules originated by purely physical, natural, chemical forces. That is like saying the instructions for making a watch were written spontaneously by chemical reactions between the paper and ink. Are we really supposed to believe this? The truth

is that the DNA code provides the most powerful and scientific evidence that life is the product of intelligent design. By the way, in all our experience, only intelligent agents write messages.[11]

A NOTE TO THE DISORIENTED:
You Have No Excuse Getting Lost!

Because the amazing outer and inner spaces plainly declare God's invisible qualities–his eternal power and divine nature - Paul tells us in Romans that those who ignore God's evident truths have absolutely no excuses. Their disorientation as to where they came from puts them in extreme danger of God's anger. "The wrath of God is being revealed from heaven against all the godlessness and wickedness of men who suppress the truth by their wickedness, since what may be known about God is plain to them because God has made it plain to them" (Romans 1:18–19). Godlessness means to disregard God, just as if he doesn't exist. This is the prevalent attitude and philosophy of our world today. Not necessarily that there is no god, but that any god out there is most likely an illusion created in man's image. So it makes God mad when disorientation causes people to lose their ways. "For since the creation of the world God's invisible qualities–his eternal power and divine nature–have been clearly seen, being understood from what has been made, so that men are without excuse" (Romans 1:20).

The fact of God's existence can be understood through the existence of his visible creation, but I find it very interesting that Paul says the evidence of God's invisible qualities is also "clearly seen." The plain truth constantly surrounds us. No one who really wants to find God can miss him. Yet, in their blindness to the invisible realities, scientists lead the charge to suppress the existence of a supernatural being of eternal power and majesty, missing or avoiding the greatness of God. "People knew God perfectly well, but when they didn't treat him like God, refusing to worship him they trivialized themselves into silliness and confusion so that there was neither sense nor direction regarding life" (Romans 1:21, MSG).

Does that sound remarkably like the disorientation so prevalent in our culture today?

DISCOVERING YOUR TRUE ORIENTATION

So That's How God Did It!

Atheists, skeptics, and the scientific community actively promote the false impression that any credible scientist must believe in evolution and a creator-less beginning. In 1990, several reputable world-class scientists founded the Center for Science and Culture as a secular think tank to challenge various aspects of the theory of evolution, as well as support the work of scholars and scientists who are working on the scientific theory known as intelligent design. Intelligent design holds that certain features of the universe and living things are best explained by an intelligent cause, not an undirected process such as natural selection. Although it is not a religious organization, the Center for Science and Culture represents a variety of religious traditions including mainline Protestant, Roman Catholic, Eastern Orthodox, Jewish, and agnostic.

Doctoral scientists, researchers, and theorists at a number of universities, colleges, and research institutes around the world support the intelligent design theory. These established scholars have directly challenged Darwinian evolution on a scientific basis. Over 300 prominent scientists have signed a document called the "Scientific Dissent from Darwin." Scholars from various scientific arenas, including biology and chemistry, have voiced their skepticism over the central tenets of Darwin's theory of evolution. The following full statement signed as a living testimony by these recognized and renowned scholars displaces the popular notion that all reputable scientists support Darwinian evolution: "We are skeptical of claims for the ability of random mutation and natural selection to account for the complexity of life. Careful examination for the evidence for Darwinian theory should be encouraged."[12]

Dr. Henry F. "Fritz" Schaefer III is an outstanding scientist who believes the Genesis account of creation and signed the "Dissent from Darwinism." This renowned scientist is the Graham Perdue Professor of Chemistry and the Director of the Center for

Computational Quantum Chemistry at the University of Georgia. He was nominated for the Nobel Prize and cited as one of the most quoted chemists in the world. Dr. Schaefer once told the U.S. News and World Report, "The significance and joy in my science comes in the occasional moments of discovering something new and saying to myself, 'So that's how God did it!' My goal is to understand a little corner of God's plan."[13] This world-renowned scientist who has discovered many notable chemistry finds gave this testimony on his most important discovery.

> If you were to ask the average Ph.D. chemist what Professor Henry Schaefer's most important discovery was, he or she would probably say "the structure of methylene." From time to time, people actually do ask me, "What is your most important discovery?" And I respond that the most important discovery in my life occurred during my fourth year on the faculty at Berkeley. This was not a time of professional turbulence in my life. Although I was still an assistant professor, I had been told that the chemistry department was going to recommend my promotion to tenure. Nor was it a time of personal turbulence, since I had already been married for seven years to the most wonderful woman in the world. At the time of my discovery, my students and I were doing some very interesting theoretical work on the identification of the interstellar molecules hydrogen isocyanide and protonated carbon monoxide. However, the most important discovery of my life was the discovery of Jesus Christ. In 1973, I discovered the Jesus Christ of history, the Jesus whose life is described on the pages of the New Testament.[14]

GOD IS GOD
...And I'm Not!

We are not and cannot be God as he states: "I am the Lord, and there is no other; besides me there is no God" (Isaiah 45:5). He preexisted creation and caused creation. He made us from the substance of his creative thought and energy. As difficult as it is for us to grasp, God was not created. He told Moses that he is the "I AM," the Existing One (Exodus 3:14) because he exists and has always existed and will always exist, and he made us. Although we were made in his image, he is God and we are not God or a god. Never have been and never will be! God, through his prophet Isaiah, makes this perfectly clear:

- "I am the Lord; that is my name! I will not give my glory to another or my praise to idols" (Isaiah 42:8).
- "Before me no god was formed, nor will there be one after me" (Isaiah 43:10).
- "I am the first and I am the last, and there is no God besides me" (Isaiah 44:6).

I love the story in Exodus 3 when Moses confronted the burning bush on Mount Horeb. As the eighty-year-old Moses looked at this unbelievable and strange phenomenon, God personally spoke to him from within the fiery vegetation. If the talking and blazing plant that could not be consumed by the fire was not enough, God called Moses by his name and told him he would lead the nation of Israel from its captivity in the land of Egypt. In his astonished surprise and human resistance, Moses asked God his name so he could tell the Israelites who had sent him. This request may seem a bit unusual to us, but God's chosen people were living as slaves in an ancient culture where the Egyptians worshiped more than 2,000 different gods and goddesses. Moses, who had been raised and educated by the Egyptians, essentially inquired of God, "Which god should I tell them sent me?"

The Creator of the universe directly and simply answered Moses' question in a complex manner we can never fully comprehend: "I AM WHO I AM. This is what you are to say to the Israelites: 'I AM has sent me to you'" (Exodus 3:14). Thus, God revealed himself to Moses in such a way that only God can - as an eternal Supreme Commander with unchangeable character. Will Pounds, in an excellent article entitled "What's Your Name," exquisitely and profoundly writes the following words in what he considers his humble attempt to understand the Infinite.

> "I AM THAT I AM" contains each tense of the verb "to be." We can translate it "I was, I AM, I shall continue to be." He is the eternal "I AM." He is the same yesterday, today, and forever. He announced that Elohim is self-existent, beside whom there is none else. He is without beginning, without ending, from everlasting to everlasting He is...By His name He is eternal, uncaused, unconditioned, independent, and self-sufficient.[15]

Is it any wonder that after receiving direct and personal confirmation from the supernatural God of all creation that I AM was, is, and will forever be his name, Moses was able to say without reservation or explanation that "In the beginning I AM created everything!" Isaiah relays the spoken words of God in Isaiah 44:24, "I am the LORD, who has made all things, who alone stretched out the heavens, who spread out the earth by myself."

My daughter, Megan, and I attended a nationally televised conference in March 2004 at Irving Bible Church in Irving, Texas, called "The Big Change." One of the highly renowned speakers, Louie Giglio, a passionate communicator and innovative speaker and founder of Choice Resources, made a powerfully profound statement that really struck my heart and mind: "If God is 'I AM,' then my name must be 'I am not!'"[16] We are a finite part of an infinite plan. In God's grand story, we are very, very, very small. The story was going on long before we got here. But, naturalists, the evolutionists who are also "I am nots," claim that man does not need a creator and that science has all the answers (except the *what*, *who*, and *why*). But, Giglio's Spirit-inspired words define the eternal difference between Christians and everyone else: "I am not! But I *know* I AM!"[17] Jesus is the same yesterday, today, and forever!

Dr. Schaefer discovered on his personal journey to eternity the vital importance of the orientation of personally knowing I AM.

> I discovered there is no problem too heavy for Jesus. I spent several months at the University of Texas. On a Sunday morning (December 9, 1979, to be exact) I had just returned from church and was tidying up a few things in my office in Austin. My wife called and told me that our five-month old son, Pierre, had just died of crib death, of sudden infant death syndrome. Whatever illusion I had that life was just a bowl of cherries disappeared forever in that instant of time. Without going into the details, I can stand here tonight and tell you that never before, nor since, have I been so overwhelmed with the certainty of the love of my heavenly Jesus. There is no problem in your life that Jesus can't bring you through. I discovered that life with Jesus begins at the moment of conversion, through death, and then on to eternity. Jesus isn't only interested in extracting a prayer of submission from me. He wants to change my whole life. That's a tremendous challenge. Finally, I discovered that the intellectual challenge to fully understand the depths of the Christian faith is quite comparable to that required to plumb the depths of molecular quantum mechanics.[18]

Think about it, with this point of reference, how can we ever get lost even in the most hostile and evil environments? It's a divine road map that absolutely cannot and will never change! Personally knowing I AM must be our constant orientation because I AM is where we are. I AM is also where we're going. But our first survival strategy requires believing and accepting by faith the visible and invisible evidence that I AM is where we came from and always exists as our only starting point to eternal life.

STRATEGY 2

KNOW & UNDERSTAND YOUR ENEMY

That's Where the Trouble Comes From!

Many similarities exist between firefighters and soldiers because their basis for existence always remains the presence of an enemy that they must constantly recognize and fight for survival and victory. There's a war going on and firefighters and soldiers signed up to battle an opposing foe, often putting their lives on the line! Karl von Clausewitz, a nineteenth-century Prussian officer and philosopher who wrote the classic military warfare book, *On War,* said, "Combat means fighting, and in this the destruction or conquest of the enemy is the object, and the enemy, in the particular combat, is the armed force which stands opposed to us."[1] One of the difficulties that wars pose for commanders is that they require knowledge of the enemy, and Clausewitz warned leaders "to remember that it is a slippery path he is treading on, one which the god of war may surprise him, and to keep his eye always on the enemy..."[2]

Heat, smoke, and other products of combustion are the life-threatening enemies of the fighters called to combat fires. Gary Seidel in "Ultimate Firefighting" says, "To synergistically mitigate fire requires that we have a sound knowledge of those enemies, so we can make a safe, coordinated, and effective attack and effectively control the incident."[3] Good firefighters do not fear fire if they know and understand their enemy and respect it for what it is and what it can do. But taking your enemy for granted can kill you!

Successful military leaders and fire incident commanders never go into their battles without carefully studying their opponents. Without this foreknowledge of the enemy, they would have a difficult time defeating it. When an army goes into battle, the commander will seek to know everything about the nature, capability, capacity, and intentions of the enemy. When firefighters go into a raging fire, the incident commander will seek to find out everything about the fire: where it is, what's burning, and what exposures the enemy may threaten.

In our spiritual battles, Christians must recognize an evil enemy named Satan and how he operates. To be effective against our spiritual adversary, we have to know and understand him because that's where our troubles originally came from. Survival requires knowing this enemy's character, strengths, and weaknesses, and understanding his tactical methods and schemes. Sun Tzu, the famous sixth-century Chinese general, emphasized the importance of knowing the enemy in his famous book, *The Art of War*.

> If you know the enemy and know yourself, you need not fear the result of a hundred battles. If you know yourself but not the enemy, for every victory gained you will also suffer defeat. If you know neither the enemy nor yourself, you will succumb in every battle.[4]

Satan, the deceiver, never likes to be revealed for who and what he is and especially how he operates. That's been his primary strategy for thousands of years and one we must be constantly aware of. Satan deceives us into believing no spiritual enemy really exists. And if there's no enemy, then there's no war! This strategy seems to be working since most people, even Christians, have serious doubts about an invisible war going on around us. It's not something they even want to think about! That's only something they see in scary movies or that extreme cults deal with. However, the great evangelist Billy Graham, who has probably reached more people with the gospel than any other person on earth, identified the real life, spiritual, invisible, fight-to-the-death struggle going on around us all the time.

> We live in a perpetual battlefield–the great War of the Ages continues to rage. The lines of battle press in ever more tightly about God's own people. The wars among nations on earth are merely popgun affairs compared to the fierceness of battle in the spiritual, unseen world. This invisible spiritual conflict is waged around us incessantly and unremittingly.[5]

Think about our battle with evil in modern terms. Compare Satan to the very worst terrorist who operates in secrecy and is tremendously hard to see or catch, yet continues to create great destruction, dysfunction, and havoc. As the extremist Muslim terrorist swears to a holy war, or jihad, and plots to destroy all infidels, how much more do you think Satan has declared a true holy war against every person who follows his ultimate enemy–Jesus Christ? Our enemy is not human but an invisible powerful spirit terrorist with an army of ruthless soldiers who also hate all followers of Christ. Since Christians live in a high state of war, they must be constantly alert of this ongoing daily battle in a heavenly realm we can't even see. "For our struggle is not against flesh and blood, but against the rulers, against the authorities, against the powers of this dark world and against the spiritual forces of evil in the heavenly realms" (Ephesians 6:12).

But the belief in a literal spiritual enemy causes most people–even Christians–great consternation. According to a poll by George Barna of the Barna Research Group, even though two-thirds of all Americans claimed to believe the Bible, only one-third of all Americans surveyed believed in the literal, personal existence of Satan.[6] For most, Satan or the devil only symbolizes evil, and they refuse to believe that he is a real personal being currently at work in the world. In 2004, Barna Research found that 60% believed that the devil, or Satan, was not a living being at all, but only a symbol of evil. Barna also discovered that 50% of born again Christians denied Satan's existence.[7] Furthermore, surveys showed that 65% of teenagers are now much more inclined to deny the personal existence of Satan as compared to adults.[8]

An article in *The New York Times* states that people "have an easier time personalizing religious concepts of good than evil," and that this is "a nation inclined more to theological optimism than to pondering literal representations of faith's dark side."[9] Does that conclusion surprise you with the increasing number of horror and evil movies on television and the big screen depicting so many figures of wickedness? With this in mind, consider the late great Christian songwriter Keith Green's prophetic words of our enemy in his classic song about the devil, *"No One Believes in Me Anymore."*

> Oh, my job keeps getting easier as time keeps
> slipping away,
> I can imitate the brightest light and make your night
> look just like day,
> I put some truth in every lie, to tickle itching ears,
> You know, I'm drawing people just like flies, cause they
> like what they hear,
> I'm gaining power by the hour, they're falling
> by the score,
> You know, it's getting very simple now cause no one
> believes in me anymore.
> Oh, heaven's just a state of mind, my books read
> on your shelf,
> Or have you heard that God is dead? I made that
> one up myself!
> They dabble in magic spells, they get their fortunes read,
> You know they heard the truth, but turned away and they
> followed me instead,
> I used to have to sneak around, but now they just open
> their doors,
> You know, no one's watching for my tricks, since no one
> believes in me anymore.[10]

God's Word clearly teaches the reality of Satan as a personal entity. The Bible vividly presents Satan as an evil enemy who directly and indirectly affects humanity by his malevolent actions. Seven Old Testament books teach of his existence and every New Testament writer affirms that reality. Jesus clearly believed in the personal existence of the devil. In fact, in twenty-five of the twenty-nine passages that refer to Satan in the gospels, Christ is the one speaking.[11] Since Scripture declares Satan as our enemy as well as God's, we must find out as much as possible about him as our survival strategy because we can't be ignorant of his destructive methods and devices.

Army Lieutenant General William Boykin, the Deputy Undersecretary of Defense for Intelligence charged with finding high-profile terrorist targets, confidently declares the war on terror to be a spiritual battle. Often appearing in Christian churches around the country and usually in uniform, he asserts the real enemy is not the terrorists themselves, but actually an enemy who has been around for thousands of years–Satan!

> We are a nation of believers. We were founded on faith. And the enemy that has come against our nation is a spiritual enemy. His name is Satan. And if you do not believe that Satan is real, you are ignoring the same Bible that tells you about God. [12]

Not surprisingly, General Boykin's remarks have stirred up the liberal national media. Columnist Cynthia Tucker responded to General Boykin's beliefs: "His foolish, bigoted remarks will be repeated ad nauseam on Arab TV and used to buttress the view of Islamic extremists."[13] Bill Berkowitz added, "I don't have a problem with people traveling about the country dishing up slide shows to fundamental Christian audiences telling them that Satan is behind terrorism–other than it's a ridiculous dumbing-down of some very serious business."[14]

NBC news even televised a national news story about this greatly respected general on their nightly news program. Although NBC called this highly decorated military officer who was twice wounded in combat a "warrior's warrior," they only focused on his fundamentalist Christian beliefs and highlighted them as very extreme and dangerous. When asked by NBC, "Why are terrorists out to destroy the United States?" Boykin honestly and simply responded: "They're after us because we're a Christian nation."[15] NBC news military analyst Bill Arkin investigated Boykin and critically commented about the General's view that the war on terror is really a religious war against a spiritual enemy: "I think… it is a dangerous, extreme and pernicious view that really has no place."[16] And the devil sings on!

> Oh, my job keeps getting easier, as day slips into day,
> The magazines, the newspapers, print every word I say,
> This world is just my spinning top, it's all like child's play,
> You know, I dream that it will never stop, but I know it's
> not that way,
> Still my work goes on and on, always stronger
> than before,
> I'm going to make it dark before the dawn since no one
> believes in me anymore.[17]

That's why the survival strategy of knowing your enemy is so important. The Apostle Paul warns us not to be outwitted by Satan because we should already have some knowledge of him based on history, "For we are not unaware of his schemes" (2 Corinthians 2:11). When we believe in Christ as our personal Savior, powerful evil forces led by Satan become our personal enemies, and they employ every strategy to turn us away from God and back to sin. Never underestimate this diabolical creature because he seeks to kill and destroy us. Based on his personal experience, the Apostle Peter exhorts us to be alert to the enemy and his deadly tactics. "Be self controlled and alert. Your enemy the devil prowls around like a roaring lion looking for someone to devour" (1 Peter 5:8).

THE SUPREME COMMANDER GIVES THE FIRST COMMAND

Defeating Our Enemy Always Depends on Obeying the Commander!

In a fire, someone must establish and assume command so everyone knows who's in charge and to whom to listen. Because their lives may ultimately depend on the commands given, firefighters must fully obey the Incident Commander to survive. Still, many firefighters die every year in fires because they ignored or chose not to totally obey their Incident Commander. They thought they had a better way of fighting their enemy. Here's an important survival lesson: In ignorance, they perished doing it their way! The success of the entire mission rests on fully complying with the orders given by the Commander.

> And the LORD God commanded the man, "You are free to eat from any tree in the garden; but you must not eat from the tree of the knowledge of good and evil, for when you eat of it you will surely die.
>
> Genesis 2:16–17

Lovingly, God tells the perfect human being he's created, "I freely give you everything you can see. I created the whole world for you, the entire planet! You may eat the fruit from any of the thousands of beautiful trees in this living paradise." Then, God issues his sovereign command: "But because I want your complete obedience, let me make this perfectly clear, do not eat the fruit from that one tree–the Tree of the Knowledge of Good and Evil. Since I created you, I know what's best for you!" And along with the command, the Supreme Commander clearly warns man, "If you disobey me, the consequences will be more severe than you can possibly know, and you will die!"

God's warning actually translates, "dying thou shalt die." The personal consequences for disobedience would not immediately annihilate the human race, but death would occur agonizingly over time and forever. The consequences would come from disobedience, not from eating a piece of poisonous fruit. God's original command set the stage for the appearance of our ageless enemy and his declaration of war on the human race.

DISOBEDIENCE CAUSES "THE FALL"

Genesis 3: There's Trouble in Paradise!

Genesis 3 may well be one of the most important chapters in the entire Bible. The story of Adam and Eve's disobedience and eviction from paradise packs tremendous meaning for current earth dwellers. It reveals the strategy and tactics of a created being who had already fallen from grace and now strives to take all humans with him. Genesis 3 exposes the deceptive enemy for the first time and explains the spiritual and physical trouble we find ourselves in today. It introduces a powerful, evil, spiritual being into the history of the human race, the "ancient foe" whom Martin Luther warns about in his classic hymn, "A Mighty Fortress is Our God."

> For still our ancient foe
> Doth seek to work us woe;
> His craft and power are great,
> And armed with cruel hate,
> On earth is not his equal.[18]

Sadly, as we learned earlier about the first two chapters of Genesis, most people today simply write off the third chapter as a myth. And just like the creation story, they interpret the fall of the first humans as symbolic and just another religious fairy tale—a legend that may have some spiritual significance but never actually happened. Interpreting the Adam and Eve story as a literary description of the rise, not the fall, of humanity, liberals teach that humans, in fact, advanced from animal-like creatures with no moral sense into full, glorious beings. However, even these skeptics recognize the extreme importance of Genesis 3 to Christians.

> Take the snake, the fruit-tree, and the woman from the tableau, and we have no fall, no frowning Judge, no Inferno, no everlasting punishment–hence no need of a Savior. Thus, the bottom falls out of the whole Christian theology.[19]

Watering down or removing Genesis 3 dramatically takes away meaning from the rest of scriptures. Ignoring the divine teachings of this chapter in the history of humanity makes the concept of human nature impossible either to understand or to explain. This monumental event produces all the problems and troubles in our universe. The significance of the story of the fall of humankind explains the reason for all the imperfection and death we find in our world. It is absolutely vital to Christians today because, "dying we continue to die!"

THE ENEMY EXPOSES HIMSELF FOR THE FIRST TIME!

A Serpent By Any Other Name?

"Now the serpent was the shrewdest of all the
creatures the LORD God had made.
'Really?' he asked the woman.
'Did God really say you must not eat any of the
fruit in the garden?'" (Genesis 3:1, NLT)

Is this simply a talking snake, or is it Satan himself? The writer of Genesis 3 uses the definite article ("the") throughout this chapter to designate this serpent as a specific created being, suggesting much more than some eloquent reptile that can speak. The definite article seems to indicate a very specific serpent. Who is this being? The Apostle John clearly identifies the serpent in the last book of the Bible: "The great dragon was hurled down–that ancient serpent called the devil or Satan, who leads the whole world astray" (Revelation 12:9). So, there should be no question about the true identity of the "ancient serpent" who suddenly appears here in the lush and beautiful Garden with Eve and Adam.

The Hebrew word rendered "serpent" in Genesis 3:1 is *nachash*, which can mean "to shine" or "a shining one." The Apostle Paul tells us that Satan often appears as an angel of light, counterfeiting the appearance and activity of God.

For such men are false apostles, deceitful workmen, disguising themselves as apostles of Christ. And no wonder, for even Satan disguises himself as an angel of light. So it is not strange if his servants also disguise themselves as servants of righteousness. Their end will correspond to their deed.

2 Corinthians 11:13–15

This evil "angel of light," the "Shining One," was apparently far more subtle, more cunning and crafty than any other living creature that the Lord God had made. He "was the shrewdest of all the creatures God had made."

It's difficult to conceive of Eve holding a conversation with a snake, but easier to understand her being fascinated by a glorious shining being who seemed to possess some superior knowledge. We could even imagine that the devil came to Eve in some human form counterfeiting the God who regularly walked and fellowshipped with Adam and Eve in this beautiful Garden of paradise. No matter the form, human or dragon or reptile, this magnificent creature must have been very beautiful, appealing, and alluring. What is clear, a created being took some bodily form other than a common variety garden snake. This serpent, by any name and form, remains our constant evil enemy and is Satan himself!

WHERE DID OUR ENEMY, THE "ANCIENT SERPENT," COME FROM?

A Good Angel Gone Bad!

So who is Satan and where did he come from? Although scriptures give a great deal of information regarding what he is doing and where he is ultimately going, many mysteries remain about where our great enemy came from. Not much about his beginning is perfectly clear, at least not as obvious as we might like it to be. But Scripture explains that there are many things humans will never fully understand about their Creator and his creation unless he reveals them to us. Deuteronomy 29:29 says: "The secret things belong to the Lord, but the things revealed belong to us and to our children forever, that we may follow all the words of this law."

For whatever secret reasons, the sovereign God chooses not to reveal much about Satan's background. I believe a detailed description of Satan's origin might give this evil creature way too much credit. Our need is to dwell on the riches of Christ rather than on the lies of Satan and his evil followers. God does not want to glorify the being that he created perfect but, because of arrogance and free will, chose evil and defiantly declared war against his creator. A lengthy discussion of his origin and fall might create an environment of pride that far too many people would dwell on. As we'll see, pride was the primary reason for his downfall. Even with limited knowledge, too many people already dwell on and even worship this counterfeit god. He runs the world's system!

The Bible is the historical and spiritual journey of the human race–not the angels. God's relationship with man is the primary focus of the Holy Scriptures. Do you remember where we came from? Men and women—not the angels—were created in God's image. Humankind was created to represent God on earth and to rule the earth. David tells us:

> What is man that you are mindful of him, the son of man that you care for him? You made him a little lower than the heavenly beings and crowned him with glory and honor. You made him ruler over the works of your hands; you put everything under his feet.
>
> Psalm 8: 4–6

Satan desires to rule the earth, and he hates competition from Christians.

Jesus came to earth to be a man and not an angel. He lived as a human being, and then he died and rose again to save humans–not angels! He provides for the redemption of mankind–not angels! Is it any wonder that Satan hates us so much because of this love relationship his Creator has for us? We are God's treasured possession, and he has chosen us to be his bride and live eternally with him. God loves us so much his enemy hates us, and that much we clearly know from the Scriptures and history.

Many details about our greatest enemy are available in God's

Word, but the facts have to be searched out. What is absolutely certain is that Satan temporarily reigns as God's adversary and evil enemy. The very word *Satan*, used fifty-two times in the Bible, comes from the Hebrew meaning "adversary" or "opposer." *Devil*, used thirty-five times in the Scriptures, comes from the Greek word *diabolos*, meaning "slanderer, accuser."[20]

For starters, we do know God created Satan. "For by him (God) all things were created: things in heaven and on earth, visible and invisible, whether thrones or powers or rulers or authorities; all things were created by him and for him" (Colossians 1:16). So Satan has not always existed. Even though this enemy appears more powerful and crafty than any human and in spite of what he wants us to believe, his limitations as a created being absolutely prohibit him from manifesting any divine attributes like his eternal Creator.

Satan knows a lot, but he is not all-knowing (omniscient). God knows all things past, present, and future, but Satan has limited knowledge of the past and present and cannot know the future.

Satan is very powerful, but he is not all-powerful (omnipotent). He has no power other than what God has given him. Read the book of Job. He can do nothing outside God's approval, which severely limits his authority and power over Christians.

Satan gets around quickly, but this enemy of ours is not everywhere present at the same time (omnipresent). Thus, he cannot be everywhere at once like the eternal Living God is.

Without any divine attributes, how does Satan accomplish so much in so many different parts of the world? The answer is in his army of helpers. Paul called them "principalities in high places," or an organized force of demonic creatures that assist Satan in his attacks against believers and deadly influence of non-believers who involuntarily and unknowingly work for the enemy. He must operate through his fallen angels and especially the fallen world system (those "rulers of darkness of this world and wicked spirits in high places") he now so greatly influences. But our key questions still remain unanswered, how and why did all this start?

Two passages in the Old Testament may shed some light on the mystery of Satan. However, a considerable debate exists as to whether either of these passages, Isaiah 14 and Ezekiel 28, even describes Satan at all. Although both writings are in the context of prophecies about earthly kings and Satan is not named in either passage, many conservative theologians and scholars believe that the very nature of the wording describes someone with superhuman powers and aspirations that go far beyond the human kings of Tyre and Babylon. For this reason, they say that the verses must refer to Satan's original, perfect state and then refer to the rebelliousness that led to his downfall. Still, some scholars, especially those who completely reject the concept of the existence of a personal, "real" devil, hold that these passages refer only to earthly kings. Enough evidence exists in scripture and the whole body of biblical revelation to make it likely that Satan is the intended subject of both Ezekiel 28 and Isaiah 14.

In Ezekiel 28, many commentators think we find a vivid description of a beautiful and powerful angelic being before he sinned. Early in this chapter, Ezekiel gives a word from God to the prince or ruler of Tyre. Tyre was an important ancient city on the Mediterranean coast and a major city of trade at the time. However, because of the things said about this king, it appears that God is no longer speaking to a mere man, starting in verse 11, because no human being fits this description. God now addresses some great spirit being whose existence both pre-dates and dwarfs any human ruler.

- Satan is a created being (vs. 13:"on the day you were created;" vs. 15: "from the day you were created") which means he had a definite beginning.
- Satan is a powerful angelic creature, "You were anointed as a guardian cherub for so I ordained you (14). " The term "cherub" refers to a class of powerful and awesome angels. God never uses this term to describe any human.
- Satan was privileged to stand in his unfallen state in the very presence of God in heaven. "You were on the holy mount of God; you walked among the fiery stones." (14) These words could apply to no one except Satan.
- Satan was not always evil as we learn in 28:12 and 15 that he was

"the model of perfection, full of wisdom…" and "…blameless in your ways from the day you were created."

- Satan must have been one of the most beautiful of God's creatures, for he was "perfect in beauty" (12). His beauty was illuminated with precious stones. "Every precious stone adorned you: ruby, topaz and emerald, chrysolite, onyx and jasper, sapphire, turquoise and beryl " (13). Satan pridefully ignored the fact that his perfect beauty only came from the one he reflected–the Lord God Almighty!
- Satan became extremely proud, "Your heart became proud on account of your beauty; you corrupted your wisdom because of your splendor" (17).
- This evil and violent king sinned through his "widespread trade." The word rendered "trade" means "merchandise" or "traffic." A closely related word means "slanderer." The New Testament calls Satan the "devil," which also means "slanderer." This fast talking, powerful angel apparently went around to the other angels, seeking to build support for his assertion that the angels were much better qualified to run the earth than humankind.

In Isaiah 14, the prophet Isaiah speaks in the form of a lament, an exclamation of mourning over a great loss, to give a prophetic warning to the wicked "king of Babylon." Just as in Ezekiel 28, the statements made in this passage seem impossible for a mere earthly king. Isaiah 14:12 states that this angel of brightness was thrown to earth: "How you have fallen from heaven, O morning star, son of the dawn! You have been cast down to the earth, you who once laid low the nations!" The original Hebrew word for the being in this verse means "brightness" or "shining one." The language again seems to have a greater spiritual reference, and many biblical scholars believe Jesus Christ referred back to Isaiah 14:12 in Luke 10:18, when he told his disciples: "I saw Satan fall like lightning from heaven."

The key survival lessons to be learned from Isaiah 14 revolve around the five times this evil being pridefully says: "I will." This shining one was not satisfied with the glory with which he was created. As one of the highest and most beautiful beings ever created, he wanted to become equal to or even higher than God. Here's an important survival fact to always keep in mind about our enemy: God is the Creator of the imitator, and Satan is the imitator of the Creator!

- "I will ascend to heaven." As the "anointed cherub" and the guardian of God's holiness, Satan had access to God's abode, but Satan desired to occupy heaven as a sovereign one equal with God.
- "I will raise my throne above the stars of God." Even though Satan apparently ranked as one of the top angels in heaven, he desired to rule over everything. His pride kept him from being content standing in God's glory and majesty.
- "I will sit on the mount of the assembly, on the utmost heights of the sacred mountain." Satan expressed his determination to rule over the affairs of the created universe. This mountain is the center of God's kingdom where he controls the affairs of the entire universe.
- "I will ascend above the tops of the clouds." "Clouds and thick darkness surround him" (Psalm 97:2). Satan foolishly desired to seize the glory that belonged only to God.
- "I will make myself like the Most High." This was the culminating desire of Satan's heart, "I will be just like Him!"–an impossible, foolish, and eternally fatal desire. God leaves absolutely no room for other competing gods! "Before me no god was formed, nor will there be one after me" (Isaiah 43:10). "I am the first and the last; apart from me there is no God" (Isaiah 44:6).

LET THE FALL OF THE HUMAN RACE BEGIN!

Our Enemy Asks the Woman a Loaded Question

The slippery wording of Satan's inquiry to Eve in Genesis 3:1 is extremely significant. "Did God really say, 'You must not eat from any tree in the garden'?" Does the enemy directly ask the first woman, "What did God actually say?" That would be a justifiable and appropriate question, "Hey Eve, what did God tell you, I'd really like to know!" Instead, he deceitfully asks her this loaded question: "Are you positive God really told you not to eat from any tree in the Garden?" With just one simple-sounding question, he shrewdly plants a seed of doubt in the woman's heart and sets her and her husband on a fatal course that will forever change human history.

The serpent's question cunningly inquires, "What do you think about what God said? Don't you think he's being a little unreasonable? Why would he deprive you if he loves you so much? Surely a good God would not have said this, would he?" He deliberately distorts the command of God, but in such a clever and crafty way as to imply, "Are you *really* sure that's what your God meant? Maybe you misunderstood him or perhaps he didn't really say that at all!" By his question, Satan not only engages Eve in discussion, but he also deflects her eyes off the generous provisions of God and causes her to focus only on God's prohibition.

That same foe still asks each of us the same question hundreds of times a day, and we still listen and converse with evil. Satan's initial approach to humans is simply to deceive and raise doubts. This wicked strategy of deception always leads us toward disobedience if we listen. God's Word still makes clear what's right and wrong and gives the consequences for our bad answers to the loaded question. But can you hear the questions hissing through your mind, "That's *really* not what the Bible says, is it? Are you absolutely sure?" In debating the extremely divisive issue of consecrating avowed homosexuals and lesbians into the ministry of his denomination, the United Methodist Church, Pastor Curtis Bond courageously points to the dangers of changing or reinterpreting the unarguable Word of God.

> The latent goal of Satan is to cause the church to reinterpret–question–what God has said. To make a behavior that is clearly wrong by scripture and nature right and to silence the righteousness of God. When the church reinterprets the Holy Scripture and gives its blessing to

unions between avowed homosexuals and allows them into ordained ministry, what happens to the holiness and righteousness of God and his Word? It can only mean one thing: God doesn't mean what he said in his Word! God is a liar! At this juncture, it is just a short leap to there is no heaven or hell, no punishment or reward, no good or evil, no afterlife, no nothing!!! The Bible just becomes another book with some fairytales to read and a few to live by. The chilling words of Luke 17:32 ring in my ears: *Remember Lot's wife.*[21]

THE BIG LIE

"God Really Is a Liar! Isn't He?"

"The woman said to the serpent,
'We may eat fruit from the trees in the garden, but God did say, "You must not eat fruit from the tree that is in the middle of the garden,
and you must not touch it, or you will die."'
'You will not surely die,' the serpent said to the woman. 'For God knows that when you eat of it your eyes will be opened, and you will be like God, knowing good and evil.'" (Genesis 3:2–5)

Did you notice that Satan never mentions either the Tree of Life or the Tree of the Knowledge of good and evil to Eve! With one deceitful question, Satan not only engages Eve in conversation, but he brings the forbidden tree to the center of Eve's thinking. Picture the first woman standing in a pristine and wonderful paradise of exquisite beauty and complete abundance. "And the Lord God made all kinds of trees grow out of the ground–trees that were pleasing to the eye and good for food. In the middle of the garden were the tree of life and the tree of the knowledge of good and evil" (Genesis 2:8–9). Focusing only on the prohibited tree rather than the unlimited number of beautiful and pleasing trees, Eve never brings up the most beautiful tree in the garden–the

Tree of Life! Here's a critical survival tip: Satan never wants us to think about the abundant grace of God but only to meditate in our hearts upon God's limited prohibitions.

Here's the scene I visualize. This beautiful and attractive, shining being casually leans up against the Tree of the Knowledge of good and evil, reaches up and plucks a piece of the forbidden fruit, and then eats it. Smacking his lips, he looks over at his now captive audience and turns up the deceitfulness another notch. "Hey, Eve, you're joking! He actually said you would die if you ate this wonderfully delicious fruit? Do I look like I'm dead? No way will you die! You can't be stupid enough to believe that! It's the best fruit in the Garden. Why doesn't he want you to eat the best stuff? He's lying to you because he doesn't want you to be a god like me or him! Don't you want to be just like me?"

With his malicious lie, the enemy introduces a fog of doubt into Eve's mind. He accuses God of holding something back from Adam and Eve. While Satan casts uncertainty into his deceitful mixture, he cunningly stirs in a portion of misunderstanding. Instead of listening to their Creator, Adam and Eve turn their attention to the enemy's seductive lie–if you eat, you will be like God, knowing good and evil. They didn't actually have to do anything to be like God–they were already like him because they were created perfect in his very image. Adam and Eve quickly find out that disobedience to the Sovereign God and the resulting knowledge of good and evil is fatal, just as the Commander said. But it's not the knowledge that gets you; it's the consequences of the sin of disobeying God that kill you every single time!

As unbelievable as it might seem, Satan calls God a liar! But who's lying? Since this is the first recorded lie in the Bible, the title "father of lies" would seem a proper description of the being doing the lying to Eve. Remember how Jesus responded to some Pharisees who were trying to kill him?

> You're from your father, the Devil, and all you want to do is please him. He was a killer from the very start. He couldn't stand the truth because there wasn't a shred of

truth in him. When the Liar speaks, he makes it up out of his lying nature and fills the world with lies.

John 8:44 (MSG)

Jesus was referring back to this exact moment in the Garden at the beginning of human history when the enemy told the first recorded lie to kill Eve and her husband.

THE BIG LIE WORKS: MISSION ACCOMPLISHED?

Let The Fall Begin!

"When the woman saw that the fruit of the tree
was good for food and pleasing to the eye,
and also desirable for gaining wisdom,
she took some and ate it.
She also gave some to her husband who was
with her, and he ate it." (Genesis 3:6)

Eve quickly finds the temptation leading to sin a very appealing process, as we all do. Sin always looks good, otherwise why would we be so easily deceived? Eve takes her eyes off all the other trees, even though they were all pleasing to the eye and good for food. But there is something different about this tree. The tempter suggests that it will give her wisdom about things God doesn't want her to know. Eve desires to know these things even though she doesn't know what they are. Isn't that exactly what we do when we disobey God? He always knows what's best for us, yet we think with some wisdom we can make needed changes. He always knows what's right! Nonetheless, we still believe the Creator of the universe somehow can't get it done without us crafting our own personal rules for what's right and wrong.

It's amazing to me that Eve so typifies humans today. God speaks his Word clearly to Adam and Eve in the Garden and gives his Word to us in the Holy Scriptures. David tells us in Psalm 19 about the greatness of God's Word: his law is perfect, his statues are trustworthy, his precepts are right, his commands are radiant, and his ordinances are sure and righteous. According to David, God's Word revives us, makes us wise, gives joy to the heart, gives light to the eyes, warns us, and rewards us. Eve's eyes wandered away from God to the worldly tree of gold, honey, and wisdom. Eve looked past God's Word when she saw the fruit pleasing to the eyes (gold), good to eat (honey) and would make her wise (wisdom). She took the easy route and the quick gratification of sin and missed the really good stuff. Sound familiar?

What did Eve (and the rest of us) miss by not obeying God's Word? "They (God's law, statutes, precepts, commands, and ordinances) are more precious than gold, than much pure gold; they are sweeter than honey, than honey from the comb" (Psalm 19:10, author's emphasis). Just like Eve, Christians face these two same issues in the world today—materialism and hedonism. David says that obedience to God's Word satisfies us in ways far above our immediate, worldly acquisitions and pleasures. He also tells us, "The statutes of the Lord are trustworthy, making wise the simple" (Psalm 19:7). God's Word makes us wise in ways we can never fully appreciate until we get to heaven. Eating of the world's fruit gives us the glitter and wisdom of temporary pride, leading to death, but God's Word gives us eternal wisdom that lights our paths to life. That's why the enemy relentlessly pushes us to dwell on the world and not the World Maker!

According to liberal theologians like Rabbi Harold Kushner, the wise serpent actually enlightened man who wasn't quite up to normal human capacity yet. So Adam's excused! Eve really didn't sin when she ate the forbidden fruit; rather, she boldly opened up the full possibilities of human life on this earth. Rabbi Kushner blesses the woman, "I see Eve as being terribly brave as she eats the fruit...She is boldly crossing the boundary into the unknown, venturing to discover what lies beyond the limits of animal existence, and reaching back to bring Adam after her."[22] So Eve is excused! Thanks to the valiant snake, the human race is now ready for the great rise, not the great fall! The snake shines as the real hero of the story. Poor Adam and Eve, their Creator maliciously stacked the decks against them, and they really had no other choice after they received the real truth and moved toward enlightenment and true freedom. The hissing of this "hero" still deceives us today with his "enlightenment."

MY EYES ARE FINALLY OPEN!

Hand Me Another Fig Leaf So I Can Cover Up!

"At that moment, their eyes were opened,
and they suddenly felt shame at their nakedness.
So they strung fig leaves together around their hips
to cover themselves." (Genesis 3:7)

Have you ever been going along, feeling great about where you are and how you're doing, and then you're tempted and you give in and all of the sudden you feel so humiliated and exposed and you just can't believe you did what you did because you absolutely know you did wrong? Most times, we even feel bad when we don't get caught. Have you ever done something wrong and realized it was wrong and suddenly became afraid that somebody would find out? That's when cover-ups become necessary. Just look at human history or read your daily newspaper. Verse 7 reminds us that sin has its consequences of shame and separation, even before God's punishment.

SWEET FELLOWSHIP NO MORE!

The Big Lie Leads Adam and Eve To the Big Die!

"Then the man and his wife heard the sound
of the LORD God as he was walking in the garden
in the cool of the day, and they hid from the LORD
God among the trees of the garden." (Genesis 3:8)

God comes walking in the "cool of the day," which literally means "the breeze of the day," and according to Hebrew geography and culture occurs in late afternoon or early morning. This passage suggests that God fellowshipped regularly with Adam and Eve when it was most pleasant for the humans, not because it was the best time for the Creator. Up to this point, the Lord apparently had an ongoing fellowship with Adam and Eve in a very natural, close, and intimate way.

Now it's the cool of the day, time to be together again, and God comes looking for his own beloved children. Yet for the first time, they are afraid of him and hide because of their disobedience. This new feeling of guilt and shame impacts Adam and Eve for the very first time. Instead of running toward him for help, they run away and hide from him in fear. Hiding becomes an instinctive reaction and remains the human response to guilt.

Isn't it astounding that the spiritual death of Adam and Eve occurs immediately upon their disobedience–that is, there is now separation from God, a split in their relationship? "You will surely die." Understand this very important survival point. God does not initiate the separation–Adam and Eve do, and they die! Isn't this exactly what sin still does today? We always have the opportunity for sweet fellowship with God, but when we sin, that intimate friendship immediately disappears until we deal with the wrong-doing. We choose (by sinning) to separate ourselves from God! Why do we think we're going to succeed at being someplace he won't find us? Separation from God kills us! Listen closely, can you hear the enemy's cheers and snickers?

HIDE AND SEEK
Where Are You?

"But the LORD God called to the man, "Where are you?" (Genesis 3:9)

If people are lost and you're seeking to help them, the first question you might ask is, "Where are you?" God asks Adam that exact question. The first man and woman shamefully hide, and the Lord graciously seeks them. The first obvious result of the fall is man's self-consciousness and sense of shame. Some things never change. Most of the time, we're just like Adam and Eve hiding from God because of our "nakedness." He always knows what has happened and where we're hiding. Just as God takes the initiative to find Adam and Eve in their hiding place in the Garden, he does the same in our secret places. He still asks every human being, "Where are you?" even though he knows exactly where we are.

Do you see the life-changing difference between God's question here and Satan's before? God asks, "Where are you?" as the heartfelt cry of a sorrowful father to his lost children not as an angry interrogation by a heartless and powerful sovereign seeking to destroy the first humans who willfully disobeyed him. On the other hand, Satan's deceitful question maliciously and hatefully attempts to bring about the eternal downfall and death of man. Much to the enemy's dismay, God's question lovingly seeks Adam and Eve's reconciliation and restoration. Notice that God never asks the serpent any questions. For reasons we just do not understand, God gives no grace or forgiveness to this evil enemy because his fate has already been sealed in another paradise in another time.

I WAS AFRAID!

I'm Fallen and I Can't Get Up Because I'm Naked!

> "He answered, 'I heard you in the garden, and I was afraid because I was naked; so I hid.'" (Genesis 3:10)

Adam tastes fear for the first time, stumbling to truthfully answer God's question. Interestingly enough, no one tells Adam that he's naked but somehow he now figures it out. He's still lost and doesn't know where he is but now he knows why. "I'm naked, God, and I just can't face you!" An evil knowledge that he never had before has come to man, adding confusion and chaos to his life, just as God said it would. This new-found knowledge causes Adam to be afraid.

The consequences of eating from the forbidden Tree of the Knowledge of good and evil strike Adam deep within his soul and spirit. A new voice inside Adam that he's never heard before tells him about his shameful condition. All these thoughts stir their evil turnings in his heart and mind. A few thousand years later, Jesus tells his disciples about the evil results of the fall. "For out of the heart proceed evil thoughts, murders, adulteries, fornications, thefts, false witness, blasphemies. These are the things which defile a man" (Matthew 15:19–20, NKJV). Here, in Genesis 3, we get an ugly glimpse why.

Disobedience of God's commands always defiles us starting within our hearts and killing us one sin at a time. "Dying we shall die!" But since Adam and the fall of humankind, the enemy constantly reminds us and we continue to listen: "You will not surely die but now your eyes are wide open and you will be like God and know good and evil. You are fully capable of deciding what's right and wrong for yourself. Do whatever is good, pleasant, and desirable! Don't worry, be happy!"

YES, I DISOBEYED YOU!
But You Know It Wasn't Really My Fault!

"And he said, 'Who told you that you were naked?
Have you eaten from the tree that
I commanded you not to eat?'
'Yes,' Adam admitted, 'but it was the woman
you gave me who brought me the fruit,
and I ate it.'" (Genesis 3:11–12, NLT)

God immediately asks Adam two more penetrating and soul-piercing questions directly to the original command receiver. God seeks an admission of wrongdoing from Adam, but he answers, as we all do, by pushing the blame to someone else. "Well, God, remember who gave me this woman in the first place. You really need to share part of the blame with her. It was the woman you put here with me that gave me the fruit. I was fine without her! I didn't even talk to that snake." Since Satan is the great accuser, blaming others remains an inherited evil trait from the fall. We now call this human nature. "All the ways of a man are clean in his own sight, but the Lord weighs the motives" (Proverbs 16:2). Blame destroys our most intimate relationships–especially with our Heavenly Father.

I find it very interesting that Adam never speaks to the enemy, but somehow he blames God! Adam in no way charges the serpent with any wrongdoing but plainly implies that both Eve and

God must share the responsibility for his disobedience. Is it any wonder to whom the Lord assigns the ultimate responsibility for the fall? "For as in Adam all die, so in Christ all will be made alive" (1 Corinthians 15:22). Because he received the command directly from the Life Commander, Adam knew better and had absolutely no excuse! There is some good news for Adam, once he finally admits he ate the fruit, there are no more questions for him.

YES, I DISOBEYED YOU!
But I Was So Deceived By That Dazzling Serpent!

"Then the LORD God said to the woman,
'What is this you have done?'
The woman said, 'The serpent deceived me,
and I ate.'" (Genesis 3:13)

God now turns to the woman and only asks her one simple question. It seems to me that God puts the question much more softly and gently to Eve. Even though she casts some blame to the deceitful serpent, Eve gives God the most honest answer. At least she identifies the true culprit! She simply states the same answer most of us should when we sin, "I was deceived." She doesn't blame her husband, and she never blames her Creator. Paul explains in 1 Timothy 2:14: "And Adam was not the one deceived; it was the woman who was deceived and became a sinner." At first glance it may appear that Paul casts the blame mostly on the woman. To the contrary, Paul says the woman has some excuse because she was deceived and became a sinner, but Adam had no excuse because he was not deceived and still sinned. Paul clarifies the issue in Romans. "Therefore, just as sin entered the world through one man (Adam), and death through sin, and in this way death came to all men…" (Romans 5:12).

Just as with Adam, as soon as Eve says these repenting words, "Yes, Lord, I sinned," the Father asks her no further questions. Do you see how God graciously leads the first man and woman to the place where each, in his and her own way, ultimately gives God the answer he desires–"and I ate." In spite of excuses and finger pointing, and with two completely different responses, Adam and Eve eventually admit to disobeying their Creator and his command. Neither human attempts to lie his or her way out of the disobedience. As we'll see, God forgives them but the severe consequences remain.

GOD IDENTIFIES AND CURSES OUR ENEMY

War is Declared!

"So the LORD God said to the serpent,
'Because you have done this, you will be punished.
You are singled out from all the domestic and wild
animals of the whole earth to be cursed.
You will grovel in the dust as long as you live,
crawling along on your belly.
From now on, you and the woman will be enemies,
and your offspring and her offspring will be
enemies. He will crush your head, and you will
strike his heel.'" (Genesis 3:14–15, NLT)

Judgment begins and the serpent comes first. Observe that the serpent never speaks to God and the conversation is absolutely one sided, with God doing all the talking! The great, shining serpent loses his sparkle and roar in God's presence. The Judge warns of great conflict and foreshadows the perpetual struggle for all generations to come from this moment until the last moment of time. The enemy of both God and man is not offered any forgiveness or any possibility of redemption. God directly addresses the serpent here, not the humans.

The words depict complete humiliation and utter degradation of the "Shining One." It paints the picture of Satan's ultimate disgrace. To this day, one of the most humiliating things that anyone can be forced to do is to lie on his belly in the dirt. Clearly from this passage, the devil will always end up as the defeated one, the humiliated one, fallen flat on his belly in the dust, eating dirt in total dishonor. The idea of "groveling in the dust" illustrates the concept of total defeat. God judges his most prideful and powerful creature with complete destruction and degradation.

God tells Satan that a personal animosity will always exist between Eve and him: "And I will put enmity between you and the woman." "Enmity" comes from a Hebrew word, which means "to hate." It is only fitting that since Satan originally attacked humankind through the woman, God would bring about salvation and Satan's eventual destruction through her. But this opposition will broaden even further: "And between your seed and her seed." God refers to the centuries-old battle between the people of God and the followers of the devil. An ongoing war will continuously be fought between these enemies.

God reveals to the still-gloating enemy the personal confrontation between the seed of Eve, the Messiah, and Satan: "He will crush your head, and you will strike his heel." In this confrontation, Satan will be mortally wounded while the Messiah will receive a painful, but not fatal wound. How beautifully God's prophecy portrayed the coming Savior, who as a human seed of Eve single-handedly reversed the events of the Fall with great finality. God keeps his promise of verse 15 and sends his only Son to fix the evils caused by Adam. Christ is called the "second" or "last" Adam. "For as in Adam all die, so in Christ all will be made alive" (1 Corinthians 15:22). And always remember, the Savior loves humans so much he laid down his life for them to keep God's everlasting promise.

Satan's evil plan to eliminate the humans fatally backfires for the being who would be god. The sovereign God places a lasting animosity between all humans and Satan but confidently declares final victory, even before the war begins. From that point forward, the "Shining One" becomes the enemy of all humanity. That's why our survival strategy requires Christians to always know and fully comprehend that Satan remains our hated adversary, and he will do everything he can to knock us off our path to life.

PUNISHMENT IS NOT A CURSE ON THE WOMAN

But The Consequences of Sin Will Be So Very Painful!

"To the woman he said, 'I will greatly increase your pains in childbearing; with pain you will give birth to children. Your desire will be for your husband, and he will rule over you.'" (Genesis 3:16)

The Lord God clearly curses the enemy "because you have done this." He does not curse the woman, but rather he tells the woman there are extremely painful consequences coming to her life and every woman who follows. However, God does not charge her with being totally at fault. We see why in the next verse when God gives the true blame resulting in more severe consequences to Adam, because "you listened to your wife." But there is no such charge of responsibility to the woman. No curses are forthcoming to Eve from the Supreme Commander for her disobedience, only harsh consequences and the fulfillment of God's promise—death!

First, there is the penalty of pain and danger from childbirth, which women alone can experience. No man knows what a woman goes through in the birth of a child, but every mother understands perfectly. Commentators believe the word goes much further here than mere physical pain. The Hebrew word used for pain universally means sorrow and comes from a root that means "to toil," i.e., "heartbreaking toil." That's probably why we describe birth pains as "labor."

God tells Eve that her pain in childbearing will go way beyond just labor and birth. A mother's heart breaks over rearing her children to a degree that most men will probably never fully appreciate or comprehend. The heartbreak associated with raising children frequently causes women more pain than the actual birth. It means that a mother's sense of success or failure in life is often related to her children, a relationship that will bring sorrow along with joy. A threat to a child is a stabbing pain directly to a mother's heart. Only a mother can fully comprehend what Mary experienced in the birth, life, death, and resurrection of her Son.

DISOBEYING THE SUPREME COMMANDER LEADS TO DEATH

The Consequences of Sin Will Make Life so Hard!

> "To Adam he said, 'Because you listened to your wife and ate from the tree about which I commanded you, "You must not eat of it," Cursed is the ground because of you; through painful toil you will eat of it all the days of your life. It will produce thorns and thistles for you, and you will eat the plants of the field. By the sweat of your brow you will eat your food until you return to the ground, since from it you were taken; for dust you are and to dust you will return.'" (Genesis 3:17–19)

Adam did not misunderstand his Supreme Commander. Adam knew perfectly well what God had told him, yet he still chose to follow his own desires and he listened to his wife, even though he knew she was wrong. When Adam sinned he was not deceived, but rather sinned willfully and knowingly in total disobedience to God. I believe Adam stood behind his wife and witnessed the entire conversation between Eve and the snake without ever coming to her aid and then willfully followed her into disobedience. That's a strong message for husbands.

Notice that while the serpent is cursed, it is only the ground that is cursed here and not Adam directly. God curses Satan because he does not intend to rehabilitate or redeem him. But the purpose of God to save humans has already been revealed in verse 15. Spiritual death for the first humans occurred with the first bite. Now physical death begins for Adam and Eve, just as the Creator warned. Not only will Adam have to battle the ground to earn a living, his physical body will eventually return to dust.

ONE PROMISE COMES TRUE AND ANOTHER BEGINS

The Knowledge of Good and Evil is Really Good and Evil!

"And the LORD God said, 'The man has now become like one of us, knowing good and evil. He must not be allowed to reach out his hand and take also from the tree of life and eat, and live forever.'" (Genesis 3:22)

Liberal scholars interpret this verse as a confirmation that the serpent continues to be the story's hero and offers enlightenment to the evolving human race with this newly found knowledge. What the snake told the humans was really true, and now his prediction has come to fruition. For all intents and purposes, a jealous group of gods (notice the plural: like one of *us*) does not want the humans to know what he knows or to live forever. These commentators would have us believe that Adam and Eve had now developed a moral sense, previously possessed only by the gods and the hero snake.

Does it sound like Satan's promise has now actually come true? Adam and Eve had, in a sense, become like God in the knowing of good and evil. Both man and God now know good and evil, but clearly not in the same way. Satan's deception always neglects to distinguish that critical difference! A very good analogy that I've heard to show the difference is the knowledge of a deadly disease by physicians and the disease's patients. Doctors can know of the life-threatening sickness by virtue of their education and experience as physicians. That is, the doctors have researched the illness, heard lectures on it, and observed the terrible results in their patients in order to treat them and hopefully heal them. Patients, also, can know of the malady, but as its suffering and often dying victims. While both certainly know of the disease, patients wish they had never heard of it because they and their loved ones directly suffer its consequences. Such is the knowledge that Adam and Eve now possess. God's promise of "dying thou shat die!" suddenly becomes painfully manifest to the first humans.

Humankind rejects God's way of love, and thereby chooses evil with all its awful consequences. The power of evil could never have been active in our world had Adam and Eve not rejected the God who is all good all the time. Do you remember our orientation of where we came from? God created everything perfectly good. So we understand that God didn't create evil. But we've seen the first humans become influenced by an evil source, causing them to lose some of their goodness and pass the evil on to all future humans. God did not create Adam and Eve with evil in them, but he did create them with a moral free will.

If God knew that Adam and Eve might choose evil rather than good and if he really loved them, why did he give them free will, which could be abused and ultimately bring about so much suffering? We can get an answer to why God would create human beings with the full awareness of potential suffering and sin by asking why we have children ourselves. As a father, I completely understand James Emery White using his relationship with his teenage daughter to poignantly answer the question, "If God knows how things will turn out from cancer to concentration camps, why would He ever create us?"

> But let me–the one who loves her more than anyone, the one who would lay down his life for her in an instant–tell you what has never entered my mind: Never having her. Never bringing her into the world. Never going through life with her. Even though she can reject me and tear out my heart by hurting herself as well as others, if someone were to say, "Why do you even bother?" And having known fathers who have endured far more anguish than I have, suffering through prodigal years, chronic illnesses, and even untimely death, I can say confidently that no matter the cost, the value of bringing our children into the world goes without question.[23]

Today, the source of evil continues to deceive humans by confusing us with the very existence of evil itself. Our knowledge of good and evil has created one of the most argued aspects of the source of our existence by skeptics and atheists. Deceived by evil, they question the very existence of God using the "problem of evil" as their evidence. Their supposed explanation for why the God of the Bible cannot exist is simply based upon the fact that evil does exist. Over the years, skeptics have defined the "problem of evil" as follows: (1) If God is good, he would destroy evil. (2) If God is all-powerful, he could destroy evil. (3) Evil is not destroyed. (4) Hence, there is no God.

Focusing on the presence of evil within God's creation, skeptics ask, "How can God be both good and all-powerful and still allow evil to continue to exist?" We should clearly see that God did not create the evil and does not cause the evil. It is brought forth by the free choices of fallen angels and fallen human beings. But our enemy continues to use his age-old argument of the problem of evil to confuse and deceive. Interestedly enough, those that argue the problem of evil and mistakenly assume humans to be basically good have no explanation of the source of evil. We get so easily swayed by philosophers and secular theologians who confuse the issue with endless intellectual arguments on the problem of evil. Paul wisely warns us of these folks.

> Watch out for people who try to dazzle you with big words and intellectual double-talk. They want to drag you into endless arguments that never amount to anything. They spread their ideas through the empty traditions of human beings and the empty superstitions of spirit beings. But that's not the way of Christ. Everything of God gets expressed in him, so you can see and hear him clearly. You don't need a telescope, a microscope, or a horoscope to realize the fullness of Christ, and the emptiness of the universe without him. When you come to him, that fullness comes together for you, too. His power extends over everything.
>
> Colossians 2:8–10 (MSG)

Christians must understand that the problem of the presence of evil in a world where a good and powerful God exists really presents no problems when we know and understand our enemy. The cosmic conflict between good and evil fought its greatest battle in all of human history at Calvary with Christ's crucifixion. But Jesus was not destroyed by death and, instead triumphed over evil, demonstrating that he has the power. God's warning to the serpent came to fulfillment at the cross once and for all.

Humans do not have an exact understanding of how this victory took place, but we still receive the amazing and life-changing benefits of it. In the midst of all human suffering and ever-present evil from our enemy and his allies, God continues his redemptive work. No evil, no matter how great, can thwart God's sovereign purpose. In bringing forth salvation from the core of great evil, God's absolute goodness shines forth through Christians.

But the nagging question continues, why does evil continue to operate so effectively in this world? Because the story is not over! The victory has been won on the cross, but we live during the interval between the lawlessness of the war-torn completion of the great cosmic battle and eternity. In spite of the wickedness obvious in the world, Paul tells us that Christ alone is the ultimate authority over everything, and his goodness and light will always triumph over all evil and darkness. "And having disarmed the powers and authorities, he made a public spectacle of them, triumphing over them by the cross" (Colossians 2:15).

When we know and understand our enemy, we quickly discover that's exactly where all our troubles originate. But as Christians, we survive because Christ's power extends over all things, including our enemy and all his demons!

STRATEGY 3

BE PREPARED!

Get Ready!

Suited up in their personal protective clothing and emergency equipment, firefighters use certain practiced strategies to keep them safe while at the same time extinguishing their enemy—fire. They get ready for the fight with extensive and comprehensive training and preparation for the fires that may happen at any minute. Those who are not trained and properly prepared will do whatever they need to do to save themselves–they will run out or die! Either way, their mission fails.

Fire service experts state that firefighter survival depends on 75% preparation and 25% actual response. They call it the 75/25 rule. It's three times more important what firefighters do before the emergency than during the actual firefight that keeps them safe. Experience and history clearly show that readiness determines response capability, reaction, and ultimately survival.

Firefighters train seriously in many areas and must always be ready to suit up for emergencies at all times, especially fires. They actively prepare to engage an enemy and respond to any emergency when the call comes. Since fireground survival begins with training and preparation, firefighters learn in their recruit academy the importance of preparation and readiness before they even get to the actual combat response. The City of Los Angeles Fire Department's training motto sums up this philosophy very well: "We need to train as though our life depends on it, because it does." Their slogan holds particular truth for Christians.

In the same manner and with the same concern for survival and success, Christians must know ahead of time exactly what to do when trouble strikes. Survival strategies for Christians and firefighters assume that you have practiced and mastered the tactical basics beforehand. As Christians, how often do we go over and over the basics? In the fire service, knowing the basics saves us from injury and death. In sports, practicing and excelling in the basics makes us champions. In war, soldiers win battles with the basics mastered. And in Christ, believers stand victoriously on the basics. But they have to be learned and practiced prior to their use.

The Apostle Paul describes the Christian life in terms of daily spiritual warfare. We know our enemy will do everything possible to destroy the true followers of Christ. The Christian journey will never be easy; rather, it's an ongoing, difficult fight and a lifelong struggle. Christians must prepare for the battle that they know will come. As we've discussed, it's not a matter of "if" but "when," as Paul verifies in Ephesians 6:13, "so that when the day of evil comes, you may be able to stand your ground." He stresses that trouble is on its way, so if we want to survive we better be prepared and get ready for it!

> Be prepared. You're up against far more than you can handle on your own. Take all the help you can get, every weapon God has issued, so that when it's all over but the shouting you'll still be on your feet. Truth, righteousness, peace, faith, and salvation are more than words. Learn how to apply them. You'll need them throughout your life. God's Word is an indispensable weapon.
>
> Ephesians 6:13–18 (MSG)

Too often we are oblivious to the extreme danger around us. Remember, that's the constant deception of the enemy's commander. An invisible battle in our world rages between the armies of God and the armies of evil forces. Until Christ puts down all rule and authority in the final day, this war will continuously create an extremely hostile environment.

Firefighters and soldiers are very much alike because constant readiness is imperative. With their mission established, soldiers recon the area, locate the enemy, and report back vital information to the commander before the fight. Firefighters search for the location of the fire, determine tactics to extinguish the fire, and then act only under the direction of their incident commander. Both must perform at peak mental and physical levels with little or no notice at any time, night or day. Accomplishing their mission must be their constant focus, but striving to stay alive remains the key goal for success. Christians can learn from both because survival allows victory.

It doesn't do to have all the strategies of survival down if we aren't really ready for the trouble at hand. Without being ready, we risk injury and death and fail to accomplish the mission that we have been called to do! God calls us to battle, but he does not want unprepared soldiers because they may not survive. With firefighters and soldiers, it means possible physical death or injury, and with Christians, it means possible spiritual death or injury, all mean the mission fails!

The old song says, "the battle belongs to the Lord," but when Christians enlist in God's army they accept responsibility to actively participate in that battle. They are called to enter a dangerous battlefield, or the "hazard zone" as firefighters call it. This highly dangerous area represents a battleground that one only enters when fully prepared in the proper protective safety equipment. While the firefighter's hazard zone encompasses that area around the emergency scene where danger constantly lurks, the Christians' hazard zone covers the entire world in which they live. God will not allow the believer to sit idly outside the hazardous area and watch him and others do the fighting. On the other hand, he does not want fighters on the frontline unless they are in a full state of readiness.

According to David Dodson, a firefighter's readiness is "a mental process that answers a few questions. A negative answer to any of these questions may set a firefighter up for an injury."[1] How firefighters answer these questions ultimately determines their survival.

1. Am I in a position to respond?
2. Is my protective gear available?
3. What is my relationship to the response?
4. Physically, can I respond?
5. Mentally, can I check out of my current thoughts and focus on response?

For eternal survival, Christian "fire" fighters need to be able to answer all these preparation questions positively from a spiritual perspective. If we are out of position, the enemy will completely run us over. All our protective gear (or armor) should be available and in place, and we must use it. Our personal relationship to Christ is a life and death response to the spiritual battle raging around us. Spiritually, we respond to the battle knowing that the ultimate victory is assured. Since we've been recruited and drafted by the Supreme Commander of the universe, our thoughts must be the same as his, along with our other company members. Paul warns the soldiers of God's army to be mentally alert and spiritually focused. "And as Christ's soldier, do not let yourself become tied up in the affairs of this life, for then you cannot satisfy the one who has enlisted you in his army" (2 Timothy 2:4, NLT).

PERSONAL PROTECTIVE EQUIPMENT (PPE)

Don't Turn Out Without Putting Them On!

The fire service calls their armor "turnouts" for the obvious reason that when highly trained firefighters get the call, they first must turn out from the safety of their fire station and then respond, fully protected, to the raging and ever growing fire awaiting them. Manufacturers design and construct these turnouts to insulate firefighters from a fire's intense and life-threatening heat. Just as body armor allows a soldier to go into battle, firefighters' personal protective equipment (PPE) permits them to advance into a fight against their unrelenting enemy.

PPE protects them from the harsh and toxic environments that they constantly enter to save lives and property. The specialized protective ensembles of firefighters consisting of fire coats and pants, helmets, hoods, boots, gloves, suspenders, and self-contained breathing equipment guard them in their dangerous job. Designed and manufactured under the strictest national standards, each PPE component protects the wearer from the extreme temperature, cuts, thermal injuries, impacts, and hopefully anything else that firefighters might encounter in the hazard zone.

When Paul wrote about our spiritual battles in Ephesians 6, he envisioned a Roman soldier dressed in full armor, ready for battle. Roman soldiers had conquered the first century world so Paul had acquired familiarity with these fearsome men. During Paul's life, no army had more power and military genius. The Roman Empire came to power because of its highly trained, dedicated, and well-equipped warriors. Therefore, it must have seemed natural for Paul to compare the Roman soldier's armor to fight the physical battle with the believers' readiness to fight spiritual opponents.

Paul had also been imprisoned so many times that he must have acquired a vivid picture and intimate knowledge of how these awesome soldiers dressed and trained, so he used military metaphors several times in his writings. Preparation and readiness made the Romans physically and mentally tougher than any other army, because their ultimate survival depended on it. As a matter of fact, Paul most likely wrote this passage while confined in Rome and personally chained to a soldier.

Being prepared in these days of evil is a crucial survival strategy for Christians. The Holy Spirit tells us very clearly in Ephesians 6 to be prepared and details precisely how to get ready before the battle. Just like firefighters and soldiers, well-prepared Christians do not face their enemies without a comprehensive knowledge and understanding of their protective equipment. God gives us divine PPE and commands us to wear it all so we can stand, survive, and thereby serve him!

BELT OF TRUTH

Cinch It Up!

"Stand firm then, with the belt of truth buckled around your waist." (Ephesians 6:14)

The belt formed the foundation of the Roman soldier's armor. In the ancient dress of Paul's time, this girdle about the loins held in place every other part of the uniform. Because everything else connected to it, including the breastplate and the sword, the belt was foundational and absolutely essential. Without his belt, a soldier couldn't keep himself together. The belt also kept the tunic, which served as an outer garment of the soldier's primary clothing, from getting in the way during combat, especially in hand-to-hand fighting.

Paul describes the foundational PPE for the Christian as the belt of truth. He emphasizes the importance of the soldier's belt to illustrate how significant truth is to the warfare fought by the Christian. Without truth, the Christian cannot stand firm and fight properly. Many consider the belt as the most vital of all the pieces of protective equipment we possess. Why? Because if it fails, so does the rest of the armor. Since Satan's primary weapon is the lie, our best defense against him will always be the truth.

That is why Jesus told the Jews who believed in him: "Then you will know the truth, and the truth will set you free" (John 8:32). That is why Jesus prayed to his Father these words specifically for his disciples just before he went to the cross, "My prayer is not that you take them out of the world but that you protect them from the evil one...Sanctify them by the truth; your word is truth" (John 8:15, 17). That is why Jesus told a cynical Pilate when the Roman ruler asked Jesus if he was in fact a king, "You are right in saying I am a king. In fact, for this reason I was born, and for this I came into the world, to testify to the truth. Everyone on the side of truth listens to me" (John 17:37).

In his darkest hour, Jesus courageously testified to the truth of God. But Pilate's response to Jesus' claim was amazingly similar to how most of the world still views truth. "What is truth?" he asked Jesus as he stared into the face of the Ultimate Truth. Today's society thinks and teaches truth to be relative. People quickly toss away the concept of an objective standard of truth because the world preaches that what is true for one is not necessarily true for everyone. We live in a world that has a tough time with the truth, so the belt of truth remains even more imperative today than ever before.

In our fallen state, the truth does not come easily or naturally for the human race. The world actively shuns the concept of absolute truth. Barna Research Group reported in 1991 that 67% of all adults agreed that there was no such thing as absolute truth. In a 1994 survey, the figure had climbed to 72%. Remarkably, 62% of those who called themselves born-again Christians said they doubted the existence of absolute truth.[2] Then, I truly wonder if they have ever fully understood that Jesus is "the way and the truth and the life." That sounds pretty absolute!

Exactly what truth does Paul tell us to use as our belt that holds everything else together? When Paul compares truth to a soldier's belt, he stresses the absolute and unchanging truthfulness of God's Word in its entirety and emphasizes it as the foundation of our armor and our primary defense. The psalmist describes the Word of God as truth. "Your righteousness is everlasting and your law is true" (Psalm 119:142). "All your words are true; all your righteous laws are eternal" (Psalm 119:160).

The Lord Jesus Christ told the devil that "man does not live by bread alone, but by every word that comes from the mouth of God" (Matthew 4:4). Every word means the entire Bible–every scripture! Jesus lived daily by God's Word to combat the enemy and used scriptures to defeat Satan and overcome temptation. We need to know God's truth because the devil is a liar. Remember Genesis 3? Satan thrives on lies and deception and actually attacks believers with his lies, half-truths, exaggerations, innuendos, and distortions. What can we learn from that? We can only live by every word of God's Word if we read every word of God's Word.

Deception and disobedience remain basic to evil, and truth and obedience stay basic to godliness. A lie is a conscious act of disobedience, and we humans seem to be addicted to lies. Most people today in their fallen state are easily deceived and do not always see a lie as wrong. Therefore, in their minds it is not disobeying anything or anyone, it's just not exactly the truth. And the more we perpetuate that lie, the more that lie evolves into an acceptable "truth." "A lie told often enough," Lenin said, "becomes the truth."

So in order to cover up the lie or feel better about it, we adjust the definition of truth to justify it and pacify ourselves. Columnist Doug Thompson from the *Capitol Hill Blue* writes about the "disposable commodity called truth."

> Early in our lives, we are taught that "honesty is the best policy" and then we immediately forget it as we lie to our parents about where we've been and what we've been up to or lie to teachers about whether or not we really read the assignment. We learn there are "degrees" of truth, that "little white lies" are not as bad as big, bad, blatant misstatements. As kids, we worry about getting caught when we lie. As we get older, the lies get more complex but the worry subsides in an environment where truth is an expendable commodity.[3]

The devil will constantly beat you down if he finds you without your belt of truth! Without a real and objective truth, his deception and deceit become so much easier to swallow. Not acknowledging a truth standard makes the devil's job a slam dunk. Since we know Satan is a liar, the primary way we can expose him and defeat him is with the truth. Once a lie gets into the life of a believer, everything begins to fall apart. When we lie, we take up the very weapon the devil would use against us and commit spiritual suicide with it!

When we sacrifice the truth with a lie, we might as well rip our belt off and throw it in the dirt along with everything else attached to it, including our sword. Without truth, we do not stand a chance in spiritual battles–Satan wins and we lose! Without the belt of truth, we soldiers of the cross may fall into the hands of the enemy. In fact, we become spiritually powerless and some of us may even end up as prisoners of war.

God hates any and all deception from Satan and us. Lying is a sin! We often lie to cover up other sins. The embarrassment of sin causes our hearts and lips to lie. We can't stand as representatives of God's truth in our spiritual battle if we are not truthful ourselves. As Christians, we are obligated to tell the truth and as believers in Christ, not only do we need to know the truth, we ought to practice it in all that we do. Paul speaks of this earlier in Ephesians. "Therefore, each of you must put off falsehood and speak truthfully to his neighbor, for we are all members of one body" (Ephesians 4:25). What did one of the wisest men to ever live on the planet have to say about God's attitude regarding truth and lies?

- "The Lord hates a lying tongue" (Proverbs 6:16–17).
- "My mouth speaks what is true, for my lips detest wickedness" (Proverbs 8:7).
- "A truthful witness gives honest testimony, but a false witness tells lies" (Proverbs 12:17).
- "Truthful lips endure forever, but a lying tongue lasts only a moment" (Proverbs 12:19).
- "The Lord detests lying lips, but he delights in men who are truthful" (Proverbs 12:22).

Christians get into big trouble when they ignore God's Word. We cannot overcome our enemy if we are not rooted and grounded in God's truth! As the foundation, the Word of God's truth enables the Christian soldier to use every other piece of armor. Get girded—put your truth belt on and cinch it up tight!

PUT ON THE BREASTPLATE OF RIGHTEOUSNESS

Be Your New Self!

"Stand firm then...with the breastplate of righteousness in place." (Ephesians 6:14)

In A.D. 60, when Paul presented this survival strategy to the Ephesians, a Roman soldier would never consider going into battle without his breastplate. This piece of armor, made of metal plates or chains, covered the body from the neck to the waist. Usually the breastplate had a back piece too, protecting the body from hits from behind. Because the soldier's breastplate was attached to the belt by leather strips passed through rings on the bottom to keep it secure, the belt had to be put on first before the breastplate. In her wonderful article "The Armor of God," Melinda Lancaster vividly describes this breastplate:

> The breastplate was the shiniest most glamorous piece of weaponry that the Roman soldier possessed. It was the first thing noticed. Running from the top of his neck all the way down to the knees it was composed of two different pieces of metal. One piece went down the front, the other down the back. It was usually made of bronze or brass and covered with scale-like pieces of metal similar to the scales of a fish. These pieces of metal rubbed together when the breastplate was worn and this process caused each piece to have a beautiful luster. When the sun would shine on it, it was a dazzling sight. The more the soldier walked in it and used it, the more beautiful it became. Walking down the road in the afternoon sunlight it gave off the colors of the rainbow. When a whole army walked out in the sunlight it was blinding.[4]

During a battle, the breastplate protected a critical part of the Roman soldier's body. It covered his heart, lungs, and the viscera (his "guts" as we might say today). Even in the ancient days, these were considered vital organs. And in hand-to-hand combat a sword thrust to the area between the head and belt would quickly and painfully take a soldier out of the battle and probably kill him.

God unmistakably defines righteousness as obedience to him. If righteousness means obeying God, why does Paul say righteousness as a breastplate should cover our most vulnerable inner areas? Obeying God, or holy living, protects Christians from spiritual damage to the heart (mind and affections) and the bowels (emotions and feelings). A spiritual wound to any of these areas may be fatal to the Christian's walk before the Lord and especially the world.

We can easily and quickly eliminate our own self-righteousness as the breastplate Paul has in mind. It would be absolutely useless protecting us from any attacks from the enemy. For soldiers or firefighters, using worthless armor and protective clothing would quickly result in physical injuries or deaths. And even worse, using our own useless righteousness as justification to get us into heaven and stand in God's presence would just as swiftly bring us the ultimate spiritual death. Survival in our own righteousness is impossible! As a matter of fact, Isaiah describes self-righteousness: "We are all infected and impure with sin. When we proudly display our righteous deeds, we find they are but filthy rags. Like autumn leaves, we wither and fall. And our sins, like the wind, sweep us away" (Isaiah 64:6, NLT).

Can you imagine relying on a piece of body armor made up of dirty rags to protect your most vulnerable areas from attacks from an enemy trying to kill you? Isaiah said that in our own righteousness our sins "sweep us away." It should be clear that no one has the natural ability to live righteously. Adam and Eve saw to that. God is perfectly holy and, by his divine nature, demands a perfect righteousness from all those who stand in his presence. Since Adam, we have all been born into this world incapable of standing before God in our own righteousness. "As it is written: There is no one righteous, not even one" (Romans 3:10).

The theological term "imputed righteousness" means the righteousness of Christ, which is given to all Christians at the time of salvation as a free gift from God. If you know Jesus Christ as your Savior, not only were your sins forgiven, but Christ also gave you his perfect righteousness. Jesus came to this world and lived his life perfectly in accordance with God's laws. Because he was without sin, Jesus fully satisfied his Father's righteous demands that you and I have no chance at achieving on our own. It's not our righteousness (remember ours is absolutely worthless!), it's Christ's–and his is absolutely perfect.

But, if Paul were referring to this imputed righteousness to wear as our breastplates, would we be told to put it on? Not likely, since God has already put it on all believers in Christ at our spiritual birth. Paul assumes in his epistle that his readers are already saved (he writes to "believers everywhere"), so the breastplate of righteousness signifies our "practical" righteousness. As Christians, it's our responsibility to put into daily practice what is already true of us in Christ. As we put on the breastplate of practical righteousness each day, we have protection against Satan and his demons, because these enemies can't hang out in an environment of righteousness. Keep in mind that imputed righteousness forms the foundation for what theologians call practical righteousness. We can't practice righteousness if we don't already have God's imputed righteousness.

Actually, the Supreme Commander of the Christian army commands his soldiers to be like him in righteousness. What is Paul really getting at? God expects us to put off our old ways (our own righteousness) and to behave everyday in the holy image of our Lord (our true righteousness in Christ Jesus). "You were taught, with regard to your former way of life, to put off your old self, which is being corrupted by its deceitful desires; to be made new in the attitude of your minds; and to put on the new self, created to be like God in true righteousness and holiness" (Ephesians 4:22–24). We can only do that by putting on the breastplate of righteousness.

Sometimes that old self creeps back into our lives. Why do we hear such awful stories of Christians living in sin and going their own ways just like non-believers? Christians who do not put on their breastplate are capable of all kinds of sin and wickedness. As we wear the breastplate ordered by our Commander, we fortify ourselves against Satan's devious attacks in every battle. Satan can never fight our God-given imputed righteousness, but he can certainly attack us when we don't daily practice righteousness. Satan is the accuser, but he cannot successfully indict the believer who is living a godly life in the power of God's Spirit. On the other hand, if we disobey orders and leave the breastplate hanging on the wall, our vital organs become exposed and extremely easy targets.

God's imputed righteousness gives us the ability (actually, the responsibility) to be righteous in a practical manner, yet sometimes we still fail. But the Commander's imputed righteousness never fails! Melinda Lancaster describes the exciting significance of the breastplate to the believer's righteousness: "As we walk in righteousness, just as the Roman soldier's breastplate became more beautiful with each step, we become more beautiful and we also become more and more dangerously blinding to the eyes of the enemy."[5] Jesus provides his righteousness, but we can only practice it when we put on the breastplate of righteousness daily.

WEAR THE SHOES OF THE PREPARATION OF THE GOSPEL OF PEACE

Oh Those Beautiful Feet!

> "...and with your feet fitted with the readiness that comes from the gospel of peace." (Ephesians 6:15)

During battles in Paul's time, enemies would try to kick you or trip you until you fell down. Here's the really bad news. Once you were down and defenseless, they unmercifully cut off your head! With this potential fatal consequence in mind, soldiers needed sure footing and a firm stance with stable shoes. A slip in a battle, fighting with a sword was probably your last. As funny as it seems, that's why some historians consider the sandals worn by the Roman Army as one of the reasons they were so successful.

Roman soldiers were equipped with special shoes made of soft leather with studded soles. The one to three inch spikes on the soles provided the soldiers the balance that gave them a superior gripping stance during battles on hills and uneven terrain. Their footwear allowed Roman soldiers to march farther and faster than other armies of the day, as well as move better in battle. They could dig in and hold their ground without falling, even in deadly hand-to-hand combat. Nike would have been anxious to endorse these sandals, and I can just image their commercials.

Do you really believe that Satan will ever fight a fair fight? He will do everything possible to knock us down by tripping us up with tricks and obstructions. And if we fall down, the devil will kick, stomp, and trample us until he kills us. He will never show us mercy because his goal is to not let us back up before he destroys our walks, our stands, and our testimonies. Paul constantly urges us to *"stand"* and *"withstand."* This military term means to resist the enemy and hold your position. When we stumble and fall, our enemy quickly unleashes his army to finish us off. That's why Paul declares that our survival shoes must give us the same balance and strong stance Roman soldiers had with their footwear.

What kind of shoes does Paul want us to wear to help us stay standing and steady? He tells us to fit our feet "with the readiness that comes from the gospel of peace." This refers to the Christian's willingness and readiness to proclaim the gospel of Christ to the world. As part of being prepared and getting ready, Paul says put on these special shoes. Our full armor requires shoes of the gospel. "How, then, can they call on the one they have not believed in? And how can they believe in the one of whom they have not heard? And how can they hear without someone preaching to them? And how can they preach unless they are sent? As it is written, 'How beautiful are the feet of those who bring good news'" (Romans 10:14–15).

Each day we should be prepared to share the gospel of peace and good news with a lost world. Satan detests the gospel of peace and has declared a perpetual war on Christians because of it. The good news doesn't get anywhere unless we bring it, so we need our feet to move. That's why the devil will do everything he can to trip us up or stomp on our toes to slow us down, and when we're down, guess what? Without hesitation, he goes for the kill!

This "gospel of peace," the good news of Christ Jesus, not only brings truth and righteousness, it brings peace of heart. We can stand firm in our God shoes with peace, even in mortal combat. Christians survive the battle both with the inner peace Christ has already given us and the desire to introduce that same peace to the hearts of others through the Holy Spirit. "How beautiful on the mountains are the feet of those who bring good news, who proclaim peace, who bring good tidings, who proclaim salvation, who say to Zion, 'Your God reigns!'" (Isaiah 52:7).

TAKE UP YOUR SHIELD OF FAITH
Extinguish Those Flaming Arrows From the Enemy!

"In addition to all this, take up the shield of faith, with which you can extinguish all the flaming arrows of the evil one." (Ephesians 6:16)

Now that we've "put on" the belt, the breastplate and the shoes, it's time to "take up" our shield. Exceptionally tough and durable, the Roman soldier's shield was large, usually about four feet long by two or two and one half feet wide. Made of wood and covered with one or more layers of very tough leather, this shield often had an iron frame. It looked like a door because of its size and shape.

Warfare in Paul's time normally involved flaming arrows–usually dipped in tar or pitch and ignited. These fiery darts were especially fearsome weapons. Enemies made the flaming arrow or fire dart of cane with a flammable head that was ignited and then shot so as to set fire to wooden shields, cloth tents, and anything else that would burn. It flew through the air like a comet seeking its target. Not only did it engulf and injure the person it hit with an inferno, but bits and pieces of flaming sticky substance often splattered and painfully injured others standing nearby. The soldier held his large shield out in front of his body and moved it around to protect himself from spears, arrows, and especially those flaming projectiles. Sometimes the leather of the shield would even be soaked in water to help extinguish the flaming arrows that struck the shield.

The size of the soldier's shield, Paul visualizes, gave the most protection when used collectively with the shields of other troops. These shields interlocked together into an impenetrable wall around the soldiers. When used in formation, connecting the shields together gave the whole company more protection, and they could maneuver as one body. Combining our varying levels of faith and sharing it together tremendously improves our collective faith. As we'll find out in the survival strategy of staying together, there is truly strength in numbers, hooking our shields of faith together in spiritual battles.

What is the "faith" Paul metaphorically connects to the shield? The word faith is translated from the Greek word *pistis*, which means "trust, confidence, or belief in."[6] In this case, Paul is not talking about saving faith or specific faith in the Word or the gospel. Rather, he refers to a living faith, an ongoing day-by-day trust in the promises and the power of God. This daily faith protects us like a big shield! For Christians, this means complete reliance on God because he makes it very clear that if we lack faith and confidence in him, we cannot please him. "And without faith it is impossible to please God, because anyone who comes to him must believe that he exists and that he rewards those who earnestly seek him" (Hebrews 11:6). God expects and demands unwavering faith, and he gives us a shield to help us to survive.

Satan shoots fiery darts at our hearts and minds. When the enemy, the ruler of this world, sends his flaming arrows of lies, temptations, doubts, hate, revenge, lust, despair, problems, blasphemous thoughts, and trials into our lives, we must hold up our shields. The devil can fire these darts furiously, one after another, until one finds its mark. How often does the enemy try shooting a fiery dart into our feelings? Time after time and day after day, these attacks can quickly throw our emotions into confusion, rage, anger, anxiety, unbelief, or worry.

If we do not block and quench these fiery darts by faith, they will ignite burning sinful desires within us, leading to disobedience. Therefore, we must keep the shield of faith up and moving. These arrows are deadly and can do tremendous damage to us and even those standing close to us. Fiery darts often come out of the blue, so we must constantly be ready and walk by faith and keep those shields up! Faith gives us the strength to stand against Satan with firm courage, even when he uses one of his most fearsome weapons.

Just as a Roman soldier, when I take up my shield of faith, I need to saturate it in water to put out those fires. As a Christian, I can soak my shield in the living water. Christ himself is the source of this precious living water as he told the Samaritan woman at the well, "but whoever drinks the water I give him will never thirst. Indeed, the water I give him will become in him a spring of water welling up to eternal life" (John 4:14). I have to maintain all my equipment daily, and that includes keeping my shield of faith saturated in living water so it will extinguish those fiery darts.

The writer to the Hebrews describes a "cloud of witnesses" who took up their shields of faith. However, the results of their faith cause me considerable consternation.

> Some faced jeers and flogging, while still others were chained and put in prison. They were stoned; they were sawed in two; they were put to death by the sword. They went about in sheepskins and goatskins, destitute, persecuted and mistreated–the world was not worthy of them. They wandered in deserts and mountains, and in caves and holes in the ground.
>
> Hebrews 11:36–38

Given a choice, I would rather be doing great things for God with my shield held high instead of being eaten, armor and all, by some starving lion. However, in the temporary life on earth, faith does not promise Christians a life without problems or free of serious troubles. God does not guarantee physical survival, but he does promise eternal spiritual survival. When we properly use the shield of faith, we can confidently and faithfully say, "No matter what happens to us, this temporary world is not our eternal home."

Our problem is that we often forget to take up that faith. Or we lay our shields down because they get too heavy or we're embarrassed by what people think of our shield or they make fun of us. But, it's our shields of faith that extinguish these fiery arrows of the enemy. It can also provide refuge for those closest to us without a shield of their own or a broken shield or a dropped shield to momentarily duck behind our shields for protection. We must believe in his protection as we march into battle representing our Commander. We must remain confident of our Heavenly Father's eternal care as we faithfully follow his will for our lives, even when that brings hardships, persecutions, and difficulties, even physical pain or death. In a time of very great trouble and running for his very life, David survived on his faith behind God's shield. "But

You, O Lord, are a shield around me, my glory, and the One who lifts my head" (Psalm 3:3 NASB).

TAKE THE HELMET

When God Lifts Your Head, Protect it!

"Take the helmet of salvation..." (Ephesians 6:17)

The helmet protected the Roman soldier's head and the mind, the major command and control center of the body. A soldier's helmet absorbed blows to the head preventing as much brain and nerve damage as possible. Without adequate medical treatment in ancient wars, major head injuries were most often fatal or, at the very least, caused considerable mental confusion with the loss of thinking and physical capacities. On the battleground, this put the soldier in a very vulnerable position.

As with the majority of their armor, Roman soldiers wore the best helmets of the ancient world. Many other armies used helmets of cloth wrappings, animal hides or bones, or hooves. But the Romans used thick leather, sometimes covered with metal plates, sometimes with a molded bronze or iron shell, at times with extended cheek plates. It was intended to protect the head and face and even the eyes.

Paul says the helmet of salvation protects our minds. It protects us from Satan's relentless attacks on our thought lives. In the midst of spiritual conflict, Satan will hurl thoughts of doubt and discouragement our ways. It's often been said that the greatest battlefield for Christians is our minds. This is the area that the enemy loves to attack the most. These assaults by Satan can prove fatal to the Christian's spiritual life and testimony, if we fail to wear the helmet of salvation.

Without the hope of salvation that the helmet brings, we might ask ourselves whether or not this spiritual warfare is even worth fighting. Putting on the hope that one day we will see Jesus face to face makes it all worthwhile. But, Satan is the master of deception and trickery, especially in the area of our minds. Satan always attempts to deliver fatal blows to our heads, and he knows exactly where and how to strike. Paul gives some excellent advice in Philippians 4:8. "And now, dear brothers and sisters, let me say one more thing as I close this letter. Fix your thoughts on what is true and honorable and right. Think about things that are pure and lovely and admirable. Think about things that are excellent and worthy of praise."

In the Bible, there are many aspects to the term "salvation." It can mean saved from sins, delivered from enemies, or set free from physical harm. Since God has saved us from our sins, Christians confidently believe that the blood of Christ cleanses us and gives us everlasting joy as we live out our Christian lives. The Lord has also delivered us from our enemies, our trials and all the other daily dangers we face. The specific Greek word used in Ephesians 6:17 for salvation is *soterion*, which means "deliverance or salvation from." Paul also uses this same word in 1 Thessalonians 5:8; however, he adds one very important key word, the "hope" of salvation: "But since we belong to the day, let us be self-controlled, putting on faith and love as a breastplate, and the hope of salvation as a helmet." This hope is a certainty–believers have complete assurance that God will do all that he has promised.

In the ancient days, a dressed warrior would take his helmet and sword from his armor bearer. Believers are to take this helmet of salvation from their Armor Bearer. A beautiful picture that constantly encourages me in this area is that God himself stands as my Armor Bearer. When I'm suited up in my armor and ready for battle and as he lifts my head, I take the helmet of salvation personally from him and cover my head; then the majestic King of the universe, in all his power and strength, hands me his sword to use.

USE THE SWORD OF THE SPIRIT

Cut and Thrust!

"Take the...sword of the Spirit, which is the word of God." (Ephesians 6:17)

During the reign of the Roman Empire, a new and improved

offensive military weapon helped the Romans conquer the world. In Paul's time, the common sword was long and often curved, sharpened only on one side and used with a hacking or full swinging motion. But the Romans perfected a short sword of eighteen to twenty-four inches, which was sharpened on both sides and used successfully in a thrusting motion for close fighting: hand-to-hand and face-to-face. The Roman soldier wore this sword on his belt. Winning battles and crushing their enemies using these short swords earned the Roman army the name of the "short swords."

The sword's double edges made it ideal for "cut and thrust" tactics. It inflicted much more damage than the other swords, especially in close combat, where the short sword brutalized the enemy. Not only was it intended to kill, but also to shred the enemy's internal organs. The dual edged sword became one of Rome's greatest military innovations. The writer to the Hebrews compares the Word of God to this sword, because it is sharp and is able to penetrate to the spiritual core of the inner man just as a soldier's sword pierces the body's physical heart.

> For the word of God is living and active. Sharper than any double edged sword, it penetrates even to dividing soul and spirit, joints and marrow; it judges the thoughts and attitudes of the heart.
>
> Hebrews 4:12

Our *Sword of the Spirit* is the Word of God. However, the term Paul uses for "word" in Ephesians 6:17 does not refer to the Bible as a whole, which is God's written Word. Remember, we identified the entire Word as the truth represented metaphorically by the soldier's belt in the armor and the foundation for all the other armor. But now, Paul refers to the Word of God in its powerful parts, the Greek word *rhema*, the spoken Word of God. This is the small portion of Scripture that the Holy Spirit supernaturally uses in Christians as a cut and thrust tactic.

Rhema refers to specific sayings that go straight into hearts and minds at specific times for special purposes by the power of the Holy Spirit. In other words, the Holy Spirit gives us scripture when we really need it to help us fight immediate and raging battles, hand-to-hand and face-to-face and word-to-word. The Spirit makes the Word of God come alive as we speak it and receive it. God's Spirit gives the Word its thrusting power and deeply penetrating edge. We use the Bible as our swords by taking specific sayings, statements, or teachings of scripture and applying them to the current conflicts in our lives. In Romans, Paul gives an example of *rhema*. "Consequently, faith comes from hearing the message, and the message is heard through the word (*rhema*) of Christ" (Romans 10:17, author's emphasis).

With the Holy Spirit within, Christian soldiers have the constant reminder of God's Word to use against Satan's temptations. When the enemy tempts us to do evil, we have the power to send him away with the Word of God. Jesus promises in his own words that the Spirit will bring the words to mind: "The Counselor, the Holy Spirit, whom the Father will send in my name, will teach you all things and will remind you of everything I have said to you" (John 14:26). Martin Luther in his classic hymn, "A Mighty Fortress is Our God," sang of the power of "one little word."

> And tho' this world, with devils filled,
> Should threaten to undo us,
> We will not fear,
> For God has willed His truth to triumph thro' us:
> The Prince of Darkness grim,
> We tremble not for him;
> His rage we can endure,
> For lo, his doom is sure.
> *One little word shall fell him.*

Jesus personally illustrated the greatest example of how *rhema*, or the Words of God in Scripture, should be used as a sword. Following his baptism by John, Jesus went into the wilderness for the purpose of being tempted by the devil. When Satan tempted him in the wilderness, Christ used the sword of the Spirit and defeated his powerful enemy. Jesus responded by quoting from a specific passage that totally destroyed each temptation Satan threw at him. Three times Jesus said, "It is written" (Luke 4:1–13). He didn't argue or carry on a long conversation, he simply used the Word and victory was his. A great survival strategy!

It is interesting that on the second temptation of Jesus in Matthew 4:5–6, Satan actually attempted to use the *rhema* of Scripture himself by quoting an Old Testament passage found in the book of Psalms (Psalm 91:11–12). Note that Satan echoed Jesus words: "For it is written" (Luke 4:10). But did the enemy quote it completely or accurately? Not hardly. Remember, he used the same trick with Eve in the garden. Satan will use the Word of God to confuse us, so it is important that we know every word that God has given us. It's sad but true, Satan knows the Word better than most Christians.

The lesson we must absolutely learn here is the utter and despicable deceitfulness of Satan. Never underestimate his counterfeit knowledge and use of God's Word. He and his followers will not hesitate exploiting God's Word against us. By subtle distortions or misapplications, they will seek to trip every Christian with what might appear to be the truth. How many cults have begun that way? The better you know the Word of God, the easier it will be for you to detect Satan's lies and reject his offers. That's why the sword is attached to the belt. When you are tempted of Satan and you use the sword of the Spirit, the *rhema* of God, he is powerless to overcome you.

We must train in the use of God's sword. God expects us to be in his Word on a consistent daily basis. The Roman soldiers didn't just strap on their swords and wait for the battle. They sharpened them and practiced with them daily, preparing for the fight because they understood it was a matter of life and death. If we don't constantly train with this spiritual weapon and keep it sharp, our minds won't be able to call appropriate scripture needed to fight a temptation or guide us in a questionable situation. Remember, we train like our lives depend on it! A dull sword is worthless in our daily spiritual battles and the slightest hesitation in the heat of the battle may be fatal.

SUIT UP
Put It All On!

Now that we better understand our protective equipment and armor, let's look at God's requirement for total protection. Any time firefighters go into a hazardous area, they must put on the "full" array of their personal protective equipment. They must put on their whole ensemble; otherwise, they are unprotected. Every bit of flesh must be covered so their vulnerability is not exposed in any manner. They wear all appropriate personal protective clothing and equipment while working in a hazardous area, until such time the incident commander determines that protection is no longer required. Firefighters are actually commanded to put on their full armor by law. The National Fire Protection Association's (NFPA) Fire Department Occupational Health Program has been adopted as a requirement through the Occupational Safety and Health Administration (OSHA) and makes several "commandments" that must be followed.

1. The fire department shall provide each member with the appropriate protective clothing and protective equipment to provide protection from the hazards to which the member is or is likely to be exposed.
2. Such protective clothing and protective equipment shall be suitable for the tasks the member is expected to perform.
3. Protective clothing and equipment shall be used whenever the member is exposed or potentially exposed to the hazards for which it is provided.
4. There shall be no exposed flesh to the hostile environment.

God freely provides believers with all the appropriate armor and equipment to provide protection from any hazard Satan can come up with. All we have to do is put it on! God's armor gives us supernatural protection from the hazards to which we will be exposed or are likely to be exposed to every day. OSHA labels the firefighting profession "ultra hazardous, unavoidable dangerous activity." When believers stand according to Ephesians 6, they are exposed to a spiritual battle because they live in a spiritually ultra hazardous, unavoidably dangerous environment. Just as regulations order firefighters to wear their full protective clothing and equipment, God's standard operating procedures command Christians to put on their whole armor. The Holy Spirit considers it so important that Paul says it twice for emphasis!

> *Put on the full armor of* God so that you can take your stand against the devil's schemes... Therefore *put on the full armor* of God, so that when the day of evil comes, you may be able to stand your ground, and after you have done everything, to stand.
>
> Ephesians 6:11, 13

When we put on the whole armor he provides, God expects us to stand and fight because we're protected from head to toe with no flesh exposed. The whole armor that Paul describes, the *panoplia*, means "complete equipment, head-to-toe protection, both defensively and offensively."[7] When facing our enemy, we must put on all our PPE. In a raging fire, none of the PPE can be left off or the firefighter may not survive the physical fire. Standing our ground in these troubled times, believers cannot leave off any of their armor or they may not survive the spiritual fires.

When King David took off his armor, hung it on the wall of his palace, and walked out onto his balcony unprotected, he exposed himself to a greater danger than when he stood on the battlefield (2 Samuel 11). We can never escape Satan's devices, so we must never be without all the armor God provides. As Christians, every day of our lives we must put on our armor so that it becomes a normal part of who we are.

In addition to its defensive nature, full PPE defines a firefighter's offensive firefighting capability. The need to follow safe procedures and to wear protective clothing during fire control operations cannot be over emphasized in the safety and welfare of the firefighter. While helmets, gloves, turnout gear, boots, breathing devices, and personal alert safety system alarm devices protect firefighters from injury and death, they also permit the firefighters to apply streams of water from offensive positions closer to the fire. Full protection gets them closer to their enemy so they can use their offensive weapons safely! The PPE allows firefighters to move into a position to extinguish the fire and stop the enemy from further damage.

Likewise, wearing the full armor of God allows believers to use their swords as offensive weapons and to advance into the enemy's territory. The first five pieces of armor are basically defensive in that they protect Christians in their advancement of the kingdom of God, but the sword will stop the devil in his tracks and extinguish his evil and sinful flames. As God's army moves in a forward march proclaiming the good news of Christ Jesus, their PPE protects them as they lift their swords high in victory.

Most often we struggle trying to use our own power to solve the problems we face. As a fire chief, I wield considerable power–five bugles on my gold badge represent the highest rank in the fire service. But my power in the earthly realm does me no good in the heavenly realm–it means absolutely nothing. Satan laughs at our bugles and titles, at our positions, at our wealth and influence, at our beauty or strength, and at our denominational affiliations. These temporary "things" really mean zilch in the world where the battle is actually being fought. "For though we walk in the flesh, we do not war according to the flesh. For the weapons of our warfare are not carnal but mighty in God for pulling down strongholds" (2 Corinthians 10:3–4 NKJV).

We face an enemy who is much stronger than we are. Wearing all my firefighting protective gear will do me no good against the dark forces of the spirit world, even though they may protect me in a thousand degree fire. Since we are fighting against powerful enemies in the spirit world, we need supernatural spiritual protective equipment both for defense and offense. In ourselves, we cannot provide them; we can only accept them from God. By his grace, God provides the full armor we so desperately need, but we cannot disregard any part. The devil constantly looks for a foothold in every aspect of our lives as believers. Any exposed area not covered by our armor becomes vulnerable and a prime target.

Christians must be prepared for each day's conflicts with the forces of evil. What is the "day of evil" Paul mentions in Ephesians 6:13? That's the day, when things have gone from bad to worse. There will be a day when that evil comes and unleashes the forces of hell on us. When that time arrives, we better have all our armor on because partial protection will never be enough to withstand the attacks of Satan. We must utilize the whole armor of God if we are to be good and effective soldiers of Jesus Christ. God calls us to stand up to evil, but how will we ever be able to do that if we are not fully equipped and protected?

Wearing all the armor for firefighting often takes firefighters out of their comfort zones. In a fire, the very physical nature of the hostile environment creates great discomfort and putting on an additional eighty pounds of protective clothing and equipment just adds to the pain. When the atmosphere becomes extreme and severe, it's uncomfortable wearing all that protective equipment: it's heavy, it's hot, it's confining, it's suffocating. But without it, firefighters die!

Wearing all the armor of God sometimes feels like a heavy burden, especially when the fiery arrows are coming from all directions and retreat seems like our best option. The extreme spiritual nature of the attacks creates hostile discomfort. Sin and evil can generate heat of a higher temperature and greater destructive force than any fire. So if your PPE gets too burdensome, keep asking yourself the question, "How would it be without wearing my armor?"

What do all the pieces in our spiritual armor have in common? They all come from God. I struggle constantly with the truth, so it's not my truth that sets the foundation for my spiritual protection. I'm certainly not righteousness on my own merits, but by wearing his breastplate I move slowly toward holiness and look forward to meeting him face to face. Faith in myself is not very likely to protect me from any enemy, but thanks to God for his shield, those flaming arrows don't have a chance. I can't save myself or give myself eternal hope, and without his helmet I would sustain an eternal headache. My feet have fungus and my shoes have holes in the worn-out soles, providing very poor traction. His shoes give my feet beauty and provide me the firm and balanced footing to live a victorious and abundant life to take his mighty gospel forward. My words are too dull to advance even an inch against Satan, but his Word utterly destroys the evil one. Paul sums up our preparedness survival strategy: "Finally, be strong in the Lord, and in his mighty power" (Ephesians 6:10).

STRATEGY 4

STAY ORIENTED!

Know Where You Are

Battalion Chief John Salka of the Fire Department of New York believes firefighters who continue to bravely but blindly charge into burning buildings without always staying oriented put themselves needlessly into life-threatening situations. Chief Salka says, "Instilling in firefighters the importance of knowing exactly where they are inside a burning structure is paramount in assuring their survival when things go bad."[1] On the other hand, not knowing where they are significantly increases their risks and reduces their survivability. It puts them in harm's way!

In firefighting, it's absolutely a life and death struggle always knowing where you are at any given moment and paying close attention to what's going on around you. Maintaining awareness of their present status in a fire determines the firefighters' ultimate survival in many cases. Rapidly deteriorating conditions usually happen with very little warning, and their chances for survival may depend on if they bothered to locate and mentally map the situation they're in.

Getting lost in terrible conditions becomes very possible when you set your mind and emotions on the wrong things that take away your attention from what's really important. Firefighters die and get seriously injured all the time by this mental and emotional confusion. When their surrounding conditions overwhelm them and they lose sight of where they are, firefighters often lose their orientations and stumble or crawl blindly until rescued or recovered. Gary Seidel emphasizes this important point in an article titled "Ultimate Firefighting."

> Again, be constantly alert and aware of any changing conditions on the fireground...Actions, position, and timing are keys to safety on the fireground. Slow down, and look. Make sure you truly see what you are looking at. Identify the situation, define it, and then act.[2]

Spiritually if you stay oriented, you will know the way things actually exist, even if they appear otherwise. Orientation means keeping in mind what you're sure of and reminding yourself of what you know to be absolutely true no matter how things appear at any given moment. Allen Levi, a great contemporary Christian songwriter and poet, wrote *"The Moon is Round"* to illustrate what, if anything, a Christian can be certain of in this most uncertain world.

"The Moon is Round"
Allen Levi

It is full, then it's quarter, it's fingernail, then gone
At times the clouds will hide it from my sight
The only thing that changes is my partial point of view
But I know the moon is up there every night
When the light cannot be seen,
when the circle can't be found
The moon is round, the moon is round,
the moon is round
At times, it's wrapped in shadows, dark and gray
On another it's a halo shining bright
It wraps itself in swaddling clothes some days
And the next it's in a gown of silver light
Just a tiny string of thread,
then a bright and golden crown
The moon is round, the moon is round,
the moon is round

Like the ocean floor and the air I breathe,
the moon is round
I will trust in things that I cannot see, the moon is round
I believe there is love watching over me,
the moon is round
So I'll write it down on paper,
I just might carve it in a stone
To help me when my faith is losing hold
Something to remind me of the Truth
that does not change
When the eclipse of the moment steals my gold
There's a Light that is sweet and pure
There's a Love that is strong and sure
The moon is round, the moon is round,
the moon is round.[3]

And yet, on every night this past week, as I have watched the moon diminish and disappear, I have known at all times that (1) the moon is up there, and (2) the moon is round. At the darkest moment of the stormy night, I always knew it was there. God seems like the moon at times, one day being clearly seen and the next nowhere in sight. For every major character in scripture, including Jesus, there were times that God seemed covered in darkness. There are periods in my life, probably yours too, where the Lord's presence is warm, soft, bright, recognizable all around me. And yet, at other times, He, and His ways, can be indistinct, hidden, distant, even frightening. What do we hold onto at and during hard times? For me, it's always "the truth as it is in Jesus." It's always and only the cross. Every trip there is reminder enough that (1) He is up there and (2) He is good.[4]

TIME—IT'S WHERE WE ARE NOW!

So Make the Most of It!

As part of staying oriented and always knowing where we are, we must appreciate the concept of time. Unlike H. G. Wells and his classic time machine, we have no way to move through time. It remains one of the great mysteries of our universe to theologians, philosophers, and scientists alike. No one really understands where it comes from or where it goes. Time flows into and out of us, and we still take it for granted until it runs out.

We human beings live our entire lives bound by the confines of time. Time is exactly where we live our lives–in the present, one heartbeat at a time. That's our true personal measurement of time. C.S. Lewis in *Mere Christianity* writes, "Our life comes to us moment by moment. One moment disappears before the next one comes along: and there is room for very little in each. That is what Time is like."[5] By the time we recognize the moment, it's already the past. We sometimes look to the future and often remember the past, but we can only live and act in the now of each heartbeat.

While we are totally restricted by the present moment, God is not! God created the "In the beginning" of Genesis 1 and John 1. He created time so we might have order in our lives and be able to understand the sequence of events of our lives. St. Augustine suggested that God, existing in "an eternal present, creates chronological time for the benefit of our human minds and existence."[6] God doesn't need time, but we certainly do. Without time, life would be very confusing and chaotic to us.

God lives in the past, present, and future. Remember, his name is "I AM." He is the same yesterday, today, and forever. He is without beginning, and the Psalmist proclaims that God is "from everlasting to everlasting" (Psalm 90:2, 12). Our infinite God exists outside the confines of time and space because he fashioned time in his majestic being. "'I am the Alpha and Omega,' says the Lord, 'who is and who was and who is to come, the Almighty'" (Revelation 1:8). Christian philosopher and scientist Lambert Dolphin explains God's relationship to time.

God is outside of time. He is an eternally self-existing, self-defining, living Being. Since he created time as we know it, we can think of past, present, and future as eternally present before his eyes.[7]

"What is Time?"
David Harsha

Time is a stream which is rapidly bearing us all on the
boundless ocean of eternity!
Let us ask again, with all seriousness,
What is Time?

I asked an aged man, a man of cares,
Wrinkled, and curved, and white with hoary hairs;
"Time is the warp of life," he said, "Oh tell,
The young, the fair, the gay, to weave it well!"

I asked the ancient, venerable dead,
Sages who wrote, and warriors who bled;
From the cold grave a hollow murmur flowed,
"Time sowed the seed we reap in this abode!"

I asked a dying sinner, before the tide
Of life had left his veins: "Time!" he replied;
"I've lost it! Ah, the treasure!" and he died.

I asked the golden sun and silver spheres,
Those bright chronometers of days and years;
They answered, "Time is but a meteor glare,
And bids us for eternity prepare."
I asked the Seasons, in their annual round,
Which beautify or desolate the ground;
And they replied (no oracle more wise),
"Tis folly's blank, and wisdom's highest prize!"
I asked a lost spirit, but oh, the shriek

That pierced my soul! I shudder while I speak!
It cried, "A particle! A speck! A mite
Of endless years, duration infinite!"

I asked my Bible and it said,
"Time is the present hour, the past is fled;
Live! Live today! Tomorrow never yet
On any living being rose or set!

I asked Old Father Time himself at last;
But in a moment he fled swiftly past–
His chariot was a cloud, the viewless wind
His noiseless steeds; which left no trace behind.

I asked a mighty angel, who shall stand
One foot on sea, and one on solid land;
"By Heaven," he cried, "I swear the mystery's o'er;
"Time was," he cried, "but time shall be no more!"

Let us ask again, with all seriousness, What is Time?
Time is the path to Glory, or the path to Hell![8]

As we travel down a road of choices on a timeline to eternity, each step in the present takes us into the future and closer to the end of time, and yet becomes a footprint of the past. In the total scheme of things, we really don't have all that many heartbeats, steps, or footprints! Near the end of his 120 years of life, Moses wrote Psalm 90 as a meditation comparing the eternity of God to the shortness of man's life. Psalm 90:4 says, "For a thousand years in your sight are like yesterday when it is past, and like a watch in the night." Moses looked back over his life and realized how short it had been and that death could occur at any moment. Christians should appreciate the short time they have and wisely do everything to make the most of their days so every step counts. I love this old saying: "It's not so much the days in your life that matter as much as it is the life in your days." I recently heard a song on the radio that says, "And life's like an hourglass, glued to the table."

There's only so much time in our lives and when the sand runs out, we can't turn the hourglass over and start again.

Not only is our time short, but we also live in evil days so we must be very wise in how we spend our time. Since the enemy strives to obstruct every step we take on our road to eternity, Paul urges us to use extreme caution. "Therefore be careful how you walk, not as unwise men, but as wise, making the most of your time because the days are evil" (Ephesians 5:15–16). The apostle says to watch or look carefully at what we do and where we step and, especially, how we use our time.

On April 20, 1999, Cassie Bernall's short life on earth tragically came to an end at Columbine High School. When confronted by the evilest of days, Cassie made the most of her time and courageously stood up for the Savior she loved with all her heart and life. She stayed oriented and knew exactly where she was before she left time and danced into eternity. Michael W. Smith wrote and then sang these powerful lyrics in celebration of Cassie's life at her memorial service.

> This was her time
> This was her dance
> She lived every moment;
> Left nothing to chance.
> She swam in the sea,
> Drank of the deep,
> Embraced in the mystery of all she could be,
> This was her time.[9]

That's the exciting orientation of where we are, even in these wicked days. We need to live every moment like it's our last and leave absolutely "nothing to chance." This is our time! God, who is outside our time and already in eternity, constantly surrounds us in our present time and helps us embrace the mystery of all we can ever be. His frame of reference is without bounds. Clearly, this is our time, not God's. Time has absolutely no bearing on God's will, only ours.

Since we can only live in the present, where we are at any given moment is where we make our important choices. I'm not just talking about the day-to-day decisions we all have to make, like what we will eat and what we will wear, but the moral choices that impact our lives and those around us, especially our spiritual lives. I'm talking about our life and death choices on the path to eternity, just like the critical decisions that firefighters make in a fire to accomplish their mission. Choices that keep them alive so they survive to fight the next fire.

Staying oriented and knowing where you are constantly revolves around our "free will." Free will is intimately tied to the present but ultimately impacts our future. When I say free will, to what am I referring? On our road to eternity, these are life and death moral decisions where we are. Adam and Eve's bad moral choice in the Garden of Eden makes living in the present even more difficult, putting pressure on every moral choice we make. The first humans superglued life's hourglass to the table!

Christians should consider free will to be the greatest power given to us by God because it's the choice between life and death. But, does anyone really choose death over life? C.S. Lewis wisely answers that question: "The choice of ways is before you. Neither is closed. Any man may choose eternal death. Those who choose it will have it."[10] That's why our orientation of where we are is so vitally important. We make the free will choice of our ways to eternity only in the present–never in the past or the future. As a matter of fact, we daily live with that choice!

The idea of free will has been hotly debated by philosophers and theologians, as well as skeptics, for hundreds of years. There's even significant disagreement among Christians. If God is truly omniscient (He knows everything past, present, and future!) and omnipotent (He can do anything and everything!), then how can we possibly have free will? Since God is truly sovereign and omnipotent, everything we do must be God's will. His Word actually confirms this: "The Lord does whatever pleases him, in the heavens and on the earth, in the seas and all their depths" (Psalm 135:6). The fact that God can know the future and yet we still maintain free will at every moment, remains one of the great mysteries of mankind. I agree with Kitty Ferguson and especially like how she answers this age-old question.

> Why should we assume that knowledge of the future robs us of our ability to change the future? Why, in any instance, should knowledge of an outcome determine that outcome? But why should this necessarily hold for God in a regime where time as we know it doesn't exist at all? It isn't difficult to imagine a situation in which I have free will and God might know every last detail of what I'm going to do for the rest of my life. A seventeenth-century Afghan writer expressed it, "All the pages not yet written He has read–and yet I can write on them anything I choose."[11]

God can see everything at once–birth, death, and everything in between. The Jews have long appreciated this mysterious paradox and the Jewish Talmud says: "Everything is foreseen, yet freedom is given to choose" (Pirkei Avot 3:19). God not only knows every path, but he also knows which path we will choose. And despite that, we still have free will to pick our courses–even the wrong ones. How can God be in ultimate control and yet we can still have free will? No matter what anyone may tell us, it all comes back to the simple fact that the limited thinking of our human minds does not bind God in any way. Humans living in a visible world bound by the limits of time just don't have the capability to fully understand this paradox.

I believe that God maintains his absolute sovereignty no matter the choices we make. His will always reigns supreme. Our free will never impacts his perfect and superior will. That's a complete impossibility, so there can never be any question about that! But God's will contains two different characteristics–sovereign will and moral will. In a *Stand to Reason* program, Christian commentator

Gregory Koukl distinguished between these two distinct wills of God.

> Moral will entails all those things God wants us to do, yet we may disobey. God wants us to be saved, yet many are not. God wanted Israel to turn to Jesus, yet most did not. God wants all kinds of things of His people–He wills those things–but they don't come to pass. There's a sense of God's will that can be violated. Yet at the same time, there are other things which are clearly stated about God's will that He intends actually to pass. We see some of those details in the Book of Daniel, and this is why Daniel makes the statement that God's will, in this sense, cannot be violated.[12]

Remember back to the Garden of Eden when God told Adam, "You are free to eat from any tree in the garden" (Genesis 2:16). The Creator, the Image Maker said to his image bearer, "I created you to make choices and you are absolutely free to do whatever you want in the paradise I've given you." But then God, as the Supreme Commander, lovingly but clearly gave Adam this command, "but since I know what's best for you, you must not eat from the Tree of the Knowledge of good and evil, for when you eat of it you will surely die." God explained it was really very simple: "Obey me in your free will and you'll live, but if you disobey me in your freedom you will die." But keep in mind our discussion of Genesis 3 and as Adam and Eve ultimately discovered, free will always has consequences–good or bad. And God knows the consequences of all our decisions, even before we make them.

Adam and Eve freely chose to eat of the tree of knowledge of good and evil, even after their Creator instructed them otherwise. And we've been in trouble ever since! God's moral will was that they not eat of this tree and thereby, continue in a perfect relationship with him. But he loved them so much he still gave them that choice. However, the consequences of their free will absolutely remained God's sovereign will. Promising what the consequences would be if they made the wrong choice, he cursed the serpent forever and evicted Adam and Eve out of the Garden to die. Their free will was divinely trumped by God's sovereign will.

God controls the future and nothing happens that he doesn't see and doesn't allow. There are things in the future that are absolutely certain because God has already told us so in his Word. These things will happen because of his sovereign will and nothing that humans, angels, or demons do can ever change that! God has already willed it to happen. However, I firmly believe that for the most part we set our own futures. Based on the orientations of where we are, our daily decisions impact our future outcomes in life. God knows the paths we will choose, yet we choose them, not him! Philip Yancey writes, "God's terrible insistence on human freedom is so absolute that he granted us the power to live as though he did not exist, to spit in his face, to crucify him."[13]

A key survival lesson in staying oriented is that even though the gift of free will is an act of love by the Creator, God always keeps his promises and does exactly what he says he will do. So, from the very beginning, humans have been given free will by the sovereign and all knowing God. We can choose to obey and stay within God's will or choose to disobey and stay within our own wills. It's always our free will to decide!

LOOK UP AND BE ALERT!
Don't Be So Earthly Minded That You're Of No Heavenly Good

Where is Jesus Christ right this moment? He's sitting at the right hand of God in heaven with full honor and all power. And where are Christians at this moment? Paul tells us in Ephesians, "And God raised us up with Christ and seated us with him in the heavenly realms in Christ Jesus" (2:6). Because Christ was raised physically, we are raised spiritually the exact moment we receive Christ Jesus as our Lord. We become new creations in Christ as spiritually resurrected beings.

> Since, then, you have been raised with Christ, set your hearts on things above, where Christ is seated at the right

hand of God. Set your minds on things above, not on earthly things.

Colossians 3:1–2

Bodily, we reside here on earth but spiritually, as believers of the Lordship of our Redeemer and Savior, we live with him next to God the Father. C.H. Spurgeon, in a sermon called "Following the Risen Christ," preached about our spiritual rising with Christ: "Christ is your life; such a life as you never knew before, nor could have known apart from him. If ye then be risen with Christ ye walk in newness of life, while the world abideth in death."[14] Christians live in two spheres, the earthly and heavenly as described by Paul. The earthly restricts us in our frail human bodies, but the heavenly belongs to the Lord and he is sitting next to his Father, the source of our power and survival if we stay oriented to where we are living with him.

With those facts established, what's our orientation right now? In the present? We are to set our hearts and sights on the things of heaven–those things that influence our journey on the road to life. The King James Version says we are to "seek those things which are above." Seek means having an urgency and a desire and an ambition. Seeking spiritual things brings excitement and adventure to our daily orientation. God wants us to live on earth with a heavenly perspective. This means that as we daily choose to follow Christ, we must desire him more than all earthly things, obey his very life-giving words, and think about the one we love more than life itself. When we do those things in the light of his life, the things of earth really will grow dimmer and dimmer, just as that great classic hymn by Helen Lemmel sings.

Turn your eyes upon Jesus
Look full in His wonderful face
And the things of earth
Will grow strangely dim
In the light of His glory and grace.[15]

Those things of heaven are the things of Christ! Paul tells the

Philippians, "Fix your thoughts on what is true and honorable and right. Think about things that are pure and lovely and admirable. Think about things that are excellent and worthy of praise" (Philippians 4:8). We are to think about the things of heaven–the things of Christ Jesus! How I live in the present is directly proportional to how I think! It's an ongoing process–moment by moment! Christians are in Christ right now. That's our true identity! How we live our lives on earth depends greatly on having a heavenly perspective that becomes our daily orientation. We must stay oriented in our present existence by giving Christ our full attention and first place in everything we do, thereby making him our top priority.

Christians receive the tactical instructions on our daily orientation strategy in Colossians. We are to be compassionate, kind, humble, gentle, and patient. We are to bear with each other and forgive each other. And over all these heavenly virtues, we are to put love! Conversely, Paul sternly warns us to get rid of all our old earthly nature: sexual immorality, impurity, lust, evil desires, greed (idolatry), anger, rage, malice, slander, filthy language, and lying.

> So if you're serious about living this new resurrection life with Christ, act like it. Don't shuffle along, eyes to the ground, absorbed with the things right in front of you. Look up, and be alert to what is going on around Christ–that's where the action is. See things from his perspective. Your old life is dead. Your new life, which is your real life–even though invisible to spectators–is with Christ in God. He is your life.
>
> Colossians 3:1–4 (MSG)

DON'T JUST STAND THERE GAZING INTO AN EMPTY SKY!

Don't Be so Heavenly Minded that You're of No Earthly Good

After his resurrection, Jesus walked and talked with his disciples on many occasions for forty days. This same group of eleven men who had denied him, hid behind locked doors, and for a time was fearfully invisible immediately after his death had now become radically transformed by Jesus' resurrection and living presence among them. As he taught them and encouraged them and prepared them for the period of time they would remain earth dwellers without him, this must have been a phenomenal experience!

And now as he was getting ready to leave them, his disciples anxiously wanted to know how long this period of time would be so they asked the Master one last question. "So when they met together, they asked him, 'Lord, are you at this time going to restore the Kingdom to Israel?'" (Acts 1:6). Here in Acts 1, on a mountaintop as Jesus was saying goodbye to the disciples after forty glorious days on earth in his resurrected body, the Savior answered their final question and gave them very clear and specific instructions. Essentially, they received their living directive from God himself to stay oriented.

> "But you will receive power when the Holy Spirit comes on you; and you will be my witnesses in Jerusalem, and in all Judea and Samaria, and to the ends of the earth." After he said this, he was taken up before their very eyes, and a cloud hid him from their sight. They were looking intently up into the sky as he was going, when suddenly two men dressed in white stood beside them. "Men of Galilee," they said, "why do you stand here looking into the sky? This same Jesus, who has been taken from you into heaven, will come back in the same way you have seen him go into heaven."
>
> Acts 1:8–11

We inhabit a planet called earth at a definite time and in a certain place. Our orientation comes as earth dwellers! Christians have unmistakably been placed here on earth to accomplish a heavenly purpose as we travel toward eternity. Jesus planted the first seeds of his kingdom in his disciples and now the seeds are being watered and told to bear fruit. He gives them a job to do as earth dwellers! "You will be my witnesses!"

Two things are required of good witnesses. First, they must have seen and/or heard something. Secondly, witnesses must tell others what they have seen and heard with truthful testimonies. Jesus tells his disciples to give true testimony as witnesses of everything they have seen and heard. The word here for "witness" comes from the Greek word *marturos* from which we derive our English word martyr. So Christ's witnesses receive a serious assignment in view of the fact that it could well mean being put to death because of their testimonies.

Once in a while, I get called to court to testify concerning a particular fire or emergency incident. The legal system considers me an "expert" witness because, as an authority on fires, I supposedly know what I'm talking about. Even though I didn't personally witness the actual event, my specialized knowledge and expertise still allows me to give a testimony. Based on my education, experience, and personal knowledge of fires, judges and lawyers consider me a person who can give a true account.

In my daily orientation living for Christ, can I consider myself as an expert witness for the God of the universe? Have I educated myself on his very Word, spoken to me by his Holy Spirit and do I know what the life-changing words truly mean? Do I have enough familiarity of God to make me an authority? Could I sit in a witness chair in a packed hostile courtroom under intense cross-examination and truthfully and expertly testify as a witness for the Savior of the world? These are tough questions that I have a difficult time answering positively, especially when I sometimes even find it difficult just telling others about the radical impact Jesus has made in my life.

While some people may regard you as an expert witness on a subject, expect that others will constantly challenge and confront you. Opposing attorneys will actively and intensely dispute the expertness of my witness if it is contrary to what they are telling the jury or want them to believe. The "other side" will persistently question my authority, veracity, and motives! Their job is to somehow bring into question the accuracy of my testimony and make me look inept. If this is true in a professional venue, consider how severe the attack will be when it means eternal life or death and the opposing attorney is a powerful and experienced enemy who hates us so much he will do anything and everything to devour us. Our daily orientations as Christians must prepare us for the opposition's constant challenge and attack on our testimonies. As our testimonies go, so does our survival, and sometimes even the survival of those around us.

Jesus further answers his disciples' question about when the kingdom will be extended to Israel. He expands their vision by telling them that not only will it be extended to Jerusalem (Acts 2–7), but also by their witness it will spread out to Judea (Acts 8:1) and then to Samaria (Acts 8:4–25) and then to the entire world (read the rest of Acts). Jesus directly gives this job assignment called the "Great Commission" to only eleven disciples. The initial fulfillment takes in a great many more believers as Luke describes historically in Acts. But the ultimate achievement goes far beyond those eyewitnesses to whom it was initially given. It's the true job description or orientation of all Christians today as expert witnesses.

Some versions of Acts 1:10 say the Apostles were "gazing" up into the heavens to where Jesus had vanished. Two men described as angels in Luke's gospel (24:4) ask the eleven: "Why are you just gazing into an empty sky?" It almost seems like a gentle rebuke. "Don't just stand there looking where Jesus has gone. Didn't he give you a job to do? Didn't he tell you what to do? And didn't he explain how to do it? So, why aren't you on your way back to Jerusalem to wait where he told you to go?" God sent these heavenly messengers to encourage the disciples and remind them of the job they had been given. Jesus Christ's clear orientation message remains the same for us today. "Even though I promise to come back, don't just stand there waiting, do what I told you to do. Give expert testimony of my life, death, and resurrection and witness faithfully until I return!"

Do you remember the earlier survival admonition for firefighters? "Make sure you truly see what you are looking at–but don't get caught up in it. Identify the situation, define it, and then act!"

Christians should apply that identical caution to their survival struggles, because too many well-intentioned Christians are just standing around, anxiously gazing toward heaven awaiting Jesus' glorious return. They are so heavenly bound that they are of no earthly good. Stay oriented–know where you are! Stop standing around gazing and get busy bearing record of Christ Jesus and serving him daily. Keep your hearts and minds always on Jesus and the eternal things of heaven, but diligently and faithfully accomplish his works in the power of the Holy Spirit while we're temporarily stuck here on earth.

Remember that God loves us earth dwellers so much that he came here to live with us, to touch us, and to die for us in our place, radically changing us forever just like the first disciples. With such transformed lives, should our testimonies reflect anything less as his expert witnesses? It's an awesome responsibility!

SHOW ME YOUR GLORY!

It Starts With a Covenant as a Chosen People

The remarkable book of Exodus recounts the many great adventures—good and bad—of God's chosen people in the wilderness on their way to the Promised Land. Through Moses at Sinai, God established a solemn pact between the Israelites and himself as a covenant. God presented Moses with the Law and promised his people salvation through the faithful keeping of the Law. What laws did God give? The core of the covenant was the Ten Commandments, but God gave many other laws to his chosen people at Mt. Sinai as their orientation to holy living with a perfect God.

The chosen people solemnly agreed to keep all the laws and obey the Lord as their part of the covenant. Christian theologians often call this the "old covenant." These strict laws became part of the oath that necessitated ratification with blood (Exodus 24:6–8). The sacrifice of animals became repeatedly necessary by designated priests to cover the sin of God's people because they could not keep all the laws. Nevertheless, God pledged a very special recognition to the rescued Israelites: "Now if you obey me fully and keep my covenant, then out of all nations you will be my treasured possession. Although the whole earth is mine, you will be for me a kingdom of priests and a holy nation" (Exodus 19:5).

In Exodus 33:18, their God-appointed leader, Moses, makes one of the greatest requests a person can ever make of God. "Now show me your glory." What does Moses mean? In the Old Testament, the word "glory" conveys a sense of something that has "weight" and "heaviness," which gives worth or wealth, preeminence or majesty. But most importantly, in reference to God, the word glory describes his self-manifestation.[16] Glory stresses the presence and the activity of the majestic living God. Here in Exodus, it refers to God's intense, profound, and magnificent presence—his sheer "weight!" With great faith and boldness, Moses implores God to show him the heaviness of his divine presence. Could he have asked for anything greater?

Notice that Moses starts his request with "*Now...*" implying something has occurred prior to his amazing request. What events led up to such a great boldness to ask God a truly remarkable action? Let's turn back the pages of Exodus to get a quick recap. Remember the burning bush and Moses' first conversation with God? And then he personally witnessed and participated in God's miraculous rescue of the Israelites from their captivity in Egypt. They have arrived at the mountain of God, and he has begun preparing an impatient and ungrateful group of more than a million freed captives (some estimate up to two million!) for the eagerly anticipated trip to the Promised Land of milk and honey.

Amazingly, the Israelites had lived daily only by the miracles and grace of God in the wilderness. They continually saw evidence of God's presence every single day. Yet, they failed miserably over and over. God directed Moses to leave Mt. Sinai and continue to the Promised Land, and Moses asked God two remarkable questions: "How will anyone know that you are pleased with me and with your people unless you go with us? What else will distinguish me and your people from all the other people on the face of the earth?" (Exodus 33:15–16).

The distinguishing mark of God's people is his presence—always has been and always will be. And that is the crux of our daily orientation. As Christians, without the presence of God, there is absolutely nothing unique about us. But when we have God's living presence, we truly become unique from all the other people on the face of the earth. No other religion can make that claim! God has always desired a people that, because of his presence in their lives, continually display a living testimony.

As recorded in the Bible, Moses climbed Mount Sinai eight times. I can't even imagine the wonders that Moses had seen and heard up to that point. Most of us would have been very content with the glory we had already experienced. The majesty and presence of God had transformed Moses, but now he boldly asked for even more. Here's the survival principle: The more we orient ourselves to God's glory, the more we change and the more we want. And now, on the eighth time up the mountain, Moses finally makes the big request: "Now that I'm oriented to where I am and personally know I AM, really show me your glory."

Before we see God's response, let's fully understand the reasons that Moses can even make the appeal because his relationship with the Living God has a great deal to teach us about our orientation in our daily walks. Prior to asking God to show him his glory, Moses strategically oriented himself by doing four essential survival tactics.

1. Moses chose to have an intimate, personal relationship with the God of all creation. God told Moses, "I will do the very thing you have asked, because I am pleased with you and I know you by name" (Exodus 33:17). "The Lord would speak to Moses face to face, as a man speaks with his friend" (Exodus 33:11).
2. Moses asked God to teach him the right way to live, according to God's will, so that he could really know him. He understood that God wants those who love him to truly know him. "If you are pleased with me, teach me your ways so I may know you and continue to find favor with you" (Exodus 33:13).
3. Moses believed that God had called him to be different from everyone else on the face of the earth, based solely on his personal relationship with the Living God. Only those who personally have the presence of God can find favor with him.

"How will anyone know that you are pleased with me and with your people unless you go with us? What else will distinguish me and your people from all the other people on the face of the earth?" (Exodus 33:15–16).

4. Moses depended totally upon the Lord.

God agrees to show Moses his glory, and I believe with great pleasure, tells Moses, "I will cause all my goodness to pass in front of you, and I will proclaim my name, the Lord, in your presence" (Exodus 33:19). God's glory is the revelation of his character and presence! However, God warns Moses of the extreme greatness of his glory: "But, he said, 'you cannot see my face, for no one may see me and live'" (Exodus 33:20). And then the Lord makes one of the greatest promises in the Bible.

> Then the Lord said, "There is a place near me where you may stand on a rock. When my glory passes by, I will put you in a cleft in the rock and cover you with my hand until I have passed by.
>
> Exodus 33:21–22

Moses could only see the glory of God while secure in the cleft of the rock. God told him to stand on the rock and be in the rock in order to see such glory! That rock, Paul tells us in 1 Corinthians 10:4, gives us a picture of Jesus. We, too, have the same promise of God's majestic presence. But our orientation must be just like Moses'. Every day we need to stand upon our Rock and dwell in our Rock–the Lord Jesus Christ. That orientation brings us into God's presence every time! In Exodus 34:6–7, we read of God's goodness when it says, "And he passed in front of Moses, proclaiming, 'The Lord, the Lord, the compassionate and gracious God, slow to anger, abounding in love and faithfulness, maintaining love to thousands, and forgiving wickedness, rebellion and sin.'"

When Moses came down off the mountain after his eighth trip, his face glowed from the glory of the presence of God. It was so radiant that when Aaron and the other Israelites saw him, they were afraid to come near him, so Moses put a veil over his face.

Whenever Moses was in the presence of the Lord, he took off the veil. He would leave God's presence with a luminous face and after the people saw that his face was radiant, Moses would then put the veil back on until meeting with God again. As soon as Moses left the Lord's presence, the glory on his face would slowly begin to fade.

Why did Moses keep the veil over his face? Moses wasn't trying to keep the people from seeing the glory; actually, he didn't want them to see the glory fading. He knew the brightness was caused only by his time with Jehovah and would begin fading away as soon as he was absent from his presence. When Moses was in God's presence, he got the radiant glory, but as soon as he left God's presence, the glory started vanishing, so he wore a veil. The old covenant was temporary and faded and was enjoyed by only one person.

TAKE OFF YOUR VEIL!
Reflect the New Covenant!

The glory of the Lord affected Moses physically, but only he experienced it. The New Testament, or new covenant, grants all Christians a vision of God's glory in Jesus Christ. The Apostle John announces the old covenant came through Moses but tells us that Christ, as the new covenant, came expressly to make God known. "For the law was given through Moses; grace and truth came through Jesus Christ. No one has ever seen God, but God the One and Only, who is at the Father's side, has made him known" (John 1:17–18). Paul adds, "It started when God said, 'Light up the darkness!' and our lives filled up with light as we saw and understood God in the face of Christ, all bright and beautiful" (2 Corinthians 4:6, MSG). The glory of God revealed in Jesus Christ makes God approachable for any who call him Lord, just as Jesus told his Father: "I have given them the glory you gave me" (John 17:22).

Jesus represents God the Father exactly. Philip posed a similar question to Jesus just like Moses did to God, "Lord, show us the Father and that will be enough for us" (John 14:8). "Jesus, show me the glory of God!" Jesus leaves no doubt! "To see me is to see the Father" (John 14:9, MSG). Jesus, in this manner, clearly reveals the only possible way to comprehend the glory of God: "The Son is the radiance of God's glory and the exact representation of his being, sustaining all things by his powerful word" (Hebrews 1:3).

In the old covenant, God's presence was evident in his temple, whether it was the portable tabernacle in the wilderness or the permanent temple in Jerusalem. However, the presence was behind a curtain, accessible only by a very select few. In the new covenant, when God redeems you, you become his temple, a dwelling place for his glory and presence. "Don't you know that you yourselves are God's temple and that God's Spirit lives in you?" (1 Corinthians 3:16). Our orientation is that the distinguishing mark of God's people remains his presence. We are God's house, his holy temple, and the presence of God dwells in us as his precious possessions. "For we are the temple of the living God. As God has said: 'I will live with them and walk among them, and I will be their God, and they will be my people'" (2 Corinthians 6:16).

According to Paul, all Christians can, with unveiled faces, mirror the glory of the Lord. "And all of us have had that veil removed so that we can be mirrors that brightly reflect the glory of the Lord. And as the Spirit of the Lord works within us, we become more and more like him and reflect his glory even more" (2 Corinthians 3:18, NLT). There are two important aspects of a mirror in this verse. First, the mirror reflects light. Since ancient mirrors among the Jews, Greeks, and Romans, were made of highly polished metal, it would often happen, especially in strong sunlight, as you looked into a mirror your face would be greatly illuminated by the brightly reflected light. We look in a spiritual mirror, catch the Lord's light, and reflect his glory. When Christians persistently look into the face of Jesus, they brightly reflect his glory like a mirror reflecting light. We can only do that with our veils off.

Secondly, an image is reflected when one looks into the mirror. But the mirror reflects only what it sees. We will become changed into the same image of the Lord if our daily orientation is to look into his face and reflect his image. Ancient mirrors in Paul's time gave a duller reflection than mirrored glass does today. Though we see the glory of the Lord, we can't see it perfectly yet. Even still, we are continuously being transformed into the image we see slowly perfected in us. When you look into a mirror whose face do you see? It all depends on your orientation.

All people exist in God's presence because God is omnipresent. He's everywhere all the time. Unfortunately, most people only exist in God's presence but live in their own presence, shadowed by Satan's dark presence of counterfeit brightness, which takes them down the road to death. However, Christians because of the Holy Spirit living inside us, live in God's presence. When you really think about it, there's a tremendous difference. Everyone exists in the Living God's presence, but only true believers daily live in his presence. I like the way Dr. Phil differentiates between really living and just existing.

> Are you really living or just existing? Existing is instinctual; it is involuntary, reactive self-preservation, with the primary goal of just getting from one day to the next without regard to quality. Living, on the other hand, is the exercise of certain learned skills, attitudes, and abilities that you have acquired and honed to a sharp and focused edge.[17]

My orientation to where I am is that I can never come into God's presence until I get out of my own presence. That's my daily choice. I can really live in the presence of the Creator of the universe or I can die just existing in mine! Now, Lord, show me *Your* Glory!

STRATEGY 5

MONITOR CONDITIONS

Stay Out Of Trouble!

Performing their difficult jobs, firefighters often venture into perilous situations. We've already seen they don't do this without substantial training and preparedness and proper protective attire and equipment. As firefighters tread on such dangerous ground, it's imperative that they pay attention to everything going on around them. They intently listen to their radios and receive vital information from their team, other crews, and most importantly the Incident Commander. Sometimes, the awareness they don't actually see or hear or feel is just as important as those situations staring at or even touching them. Firefighters must constantly be alert to the ever-changing conditions because it's a key strategy for their survival, and it may even keep them out of trouble in the first place. Avoiding trouble to accomplish their mission with the least amount of risk goes way beyond staying oriented.

During a fire, chances are the situation will usually get worse before it gets better. Conditions change so rapidly that firefighters have to monitor what's going on around them–continually evaluating all the warning signs. Even the most ordinary seeming circumstances can quickly turn into serious trouble and escalate into disaster. They can never let their guards down too soon or take off their protection before the Incident commander tells them it's okay. Sometimes, firefighters think they have the fire out but it rekindles and actually does more damage the second time. I've seen that happen many times in my career. Worst of all, letting your guard down can kill you! Chief John Salka explains why:

> Being aware of the conditions around you while operating inside a building that is being attacked and consumed by fire is vital to a firefighter's survival. This awareness of surrounding conditions is not simply taking note of the obvious happenings but it is the deliberate monitoring of every possible condition that could suddenly increase such as heat, or decrease such as visibility that may signal a dangerous change in the fire's development, direction or travel or intensity.[1]

Many times, if Christians had just monitored the conditions around them, they could have avoided trouble. The trouble I'm talking about is sin. There will be times when we trip and stumble through the door of temptation, only to sprint to sin and ultimately suffer the consequences that might be irreversible. Accordingly, we must choose our steps to eternity wisely so we can say with Job: "My feet have closely followed his steps; I have kept to his way without turning aside" (Job 23:11). Stay out of trouble!

That's why it's so critical that we pay close attention when we're in a dangerous spiritual situation–which we've learned is pretty much all the time! We have to monitor conditions and pay heed to all those evil desires that open the trapdoor to sin. Not paying attention to evil circumstances and letting down our guards may cause us to trip and fall. Too often, when we don't monitor conditions, we quickly get entangled in the world's snares.

> So watch your step, friends. Make sure there's no evil unbelief lying around that will trip you up and throw you off course, diverting you from the living God.
>
> Hebrews 3:12 (MSG)

Think about how many godly relationships and ministries have been destroyed by ignored troubles. If these Christians had just monitored conditions in the first place, they could have avoided the resulting pain and sorrow from tripping and falling. We've all been there! As a matter of fact, we spend most of our time there. And, just as firefighters die by not paying attention during basic day-to-day fire operations, Christians get killed or injured spiritually in their simple daily battles.

How in the world do we get into so much trouble so quickly? A minor incident can quickly soar into disaster and escalate into a catastrophe because our own evil desires produce a temptation so strong that we fall into an inescapable hole we would never have intentionally jumped in. Just because we weren't paying attention! Too many times, we finally become aware of the dangerous conditions after we've fallen in and it's way too late to escape. The survival strategy of monitoring conditions will teach us that proactively paying attention to certain critical indicators will usually keep us out of trouble.

Judas' tragic life shows us that sin can develop over a period of time when we don't monitor the conditions around us. It pulls us in deeper and deeper until we are attempting things that we would never have thought ourselves capable of doing. And just as firefighters sometimes mistakenly consider this strategy as their secondary nature, Christians often fall into the same false belief that they will discover the attack when it becomes obvious. But when the dangerous condition finally grows evident, it may be too late to do anything about it just as the betrayer of Christ tragically found out. Judas' act was the inevitable result of the destruction of his own character, just the same as happens to Christians who continually fail to recognize the evil desires deceivingly towing them down the road to disobedience and perhaps death.

SIN BURNS LIKE A FIRE IN ALL OF US

Its Products Can Be Killers!

Fire and sin are a lot alike. Both can burn with unrelenting fury and destroy everything in their paths. Left unchecked, they completely consume their victims. Direct contact with either will burn you or even kill you. If you survive, severe burns will cause unbelievable pain over a long period of time and leave terrible scars–psychologically as well as physically. Like fire, sin is not just an event, it's usually a predictable process. Sin doesn't just happen! It starts with an ignition point and grows larger–sometimes exploding rapidly into what the fire service calls "flashover," while at other times it burns very slowly, unnoticed for a long period of time until it becomes deadly.

Combustion produces many indirect consequences like smoke, carbon monoxide, and other deadly toxins that you often can't even see. Although the dangerous heat energy and flames of a fire burn or kill anyone directly exposed to them, smoke actually causes the most deaths in structure fires. The deadly materials that make up smoke vary from fuel to fuel, but generally all smoke can be considered potentially lethal. Just as combustion produces physical products that jeopardize survival to firefighters, sin produces ugly and poisonous byproducts that endanger Christians' spiritual survival.

Smoke generated in a fire contains narcotic (asphyxiant) gases and irritants. Similarly, the consequences of sin choke the life right out of you! Products of incomplete combustion gases like carbon monoxide, hydrogen cyanide, and carbon dioxide depress the central nervous system. The depressing byproducts of sin often result in reduced awareness, intoxication, and lead to the loss of spiritual consciousness and even death. Irritants in smoke are those substances that cause breathing discomfort (pulmonary irritants) and inflammation of the eyes, respiratory tract, and skin (sensory irritants). Think about the irritating effects of sin that produce discomfort and drastically interfere with all your senses and emotions.

Monitoring spiritual conditions around us in our daily lives is just as critical to Christians as firefighters monitoring the rapidly changing situation in raging fires. The following quote from the bible of firefighters, *The Essentials of Fire Fighting*, describes the physical nature of fire.

> Fire is a rapid chemical reaction that gives off energy and products of combustion that are very different in composition from the fuel and oxygen that combined to pro-

> duce them. To understand the reaction we call fire, how it grows, and its products (products of combustion), we need to look at some basic concepts from physical science. Physical science is the study of the physical world around us and includes the sciences of chemistry and physics and the laws related to matter and energy.[2]

Remembering back to the survival strategy of "Knowing and Understanding Our Enemy," we already have a pretty good idea of where sin came from, why it directly impacts us, and what it is. But now let's look carefully at how sin affects us. Let's rephrase the above definition about the physical nature of fire from the *Essentials* book, only this time using sin and its spiritual nature to set the stage for the essential survival strategy of monitoring conditions.

> Sin is a human reaction, at times rapid and other times leisurely, which gives off energy and products resulting in consequences that are very different in composition from the desires and atmosphere of temptation that combined to produce the sin. To understand this evil reaction we call disobedience to God, how it grows, and its products (the consequences to us and others), we must look at some basic concepts of desires and temptation from a spiritual perspective. Spiritual knowledge involves the understanding of the unseen (supernatural) world around us and includes the natural human reaction we call sin to desires and temptation in conflict with the spiritual laws given by the holy and sovereign Creator.

DON'T IGNORE THE ADAM VIRUS–INSTALL PROTECTION!

The Flesh, the World, and the Devil are All Out to Infect Us

Scripture clearly declares that "by one man sin entered into the world…" (Romans 5:12). Let's review what we learned from Moses in Genesis 3. Sin is a very real and terrible fact of all human life. It came through the sin of one man, Adam, and thereby became inherited by all humans. Both the Old and New Testaments teach us that Adam's fall brought disastrous consequences upon himself and all his descendants. "Behold, I was shapen in iniquity, and in sin did my mother conceive me" (Psalm 51:5). In essence David admits the same thing that Paul says in Romans 5, namely, the natural depravity of all humans somehow gets transmitted to all their offspring because of the Fall. "The wicked are estranged from the womb; they go astray as soon as they are born, speaking lies" (Psalm 58:3).

Starting with the account given in Genesis 3, all the scriptures inspired by the Holy Spirit agree that sin entered the human race through the disobedience of Adam and thereby infected all humans throughout history with the Adam virus. We all commit sins because our hearts are infected with the depravity of sin. No one is exempt! "If we say that we have no sin, we deceive ourselves, and the truth is not in us" (1 John 1:8). "That which is born of the flesh is flesh" (John 3:6). "What is man, that he should be clean? And he which is born of a woman, that he should be righteous?" (Job 15:14).

The virus of original sin directly attacks the hearts of all people. Jesus tells us, "For out of the heart proceed evil thoughts, murders, adulteries, fornications, thefts, false witness, blasphemies" (Matthew 15:19). The heart gives birth to all thoughts, words, and actions. "Above all else, guard your heart, for it is the wellspring of life" (Proverbs 4:23). And since sin attacks every one of us, no one can expect immunity from this evil, age-old, heart-killing virus. "The heart is deceitful above all things, and desperately wicked: who can know it?" (Jeremiah 17:9).

People often compare the human mind to a computer. What do we fear the most with our computers? Vicious virus attacks that somehow enter our computers from outside sources and crash and destroy everything valuable on them! Consider the analogy between a deadly computer virus attack and the mind being plagued by virus-like sinful thoughts. Just as a virus can cause a computer to behave in an abnormal fashion, imagine how Adam's virus severely impacts the health of our spiritual lives. Spiritual viruses disrupt our lives, fog the truth, introduce evil thoughts, devastate our own capacity to think clearly, crash our lives, and program us to pass the virus on to others–even those we love.

Our natural inclination to original sin opens the door for other harmful spiritual viruses to enter and then thrive inside of us if we don't install the proper protection to keep them out in the first place. A firewall restricts access to your computer from unwanted outside elements. Monitoring sin and its destructive effects provides firewalls designed to protect our hearts and minds. It thwarts virus attacks and provides the security for our spiritual survival. The key to successful computer virus protection is to constantly update and monitor your virus shield software and run it regularly.

Hackers, spammers, bombers, and crackers will keep changing their attacks to get past our computers' protection. The same holds true for spiritual virus protection. As we learned about our deceitful enemy, sinful hackers, evil spammers, wicked bombers, and immoral crackers will keep changing their evil attacks just to get past our spiritual protection. We have the perfect spiritual virus protection–the Word of God! However, for it to work, we must have it installed properly, keep it turned on and operating all the time, and do daily virus scans–both incoming and outgoing.

A major strategy in the Christian's life and survival is to monitor the continuous and ever-changing virus attacks of sin that come from three distinct sources: the *flesh,* the *world,* and the *devil.* The *flesh* is our old nature, or Adam's original virus, that we all inherited from the first man—the unholy tendencies that come from within us. The *world* refers to the system all around us that is opposed to God and continually offering its alluring beauty and personal gain and deceitfully trying to gain access to our operating systems. The world actively spreads the Adam virus. And, we've already been introduced to the lies and deeds of evil personified by the leader of the fallen angels we call the *devil.* The enemy constantly updates the Adam virus to the latest version, while actively maintaining all the old versions.

MONITOR THE ATTACK FROM YOUR FLESH

Something Inside Us Really Opposes God!

Scripture calls it many things: the old man, the sinful nature, the natural man, the old nature, and the flesh. We've simply called it the Adam virus. But essentially it is that part of us that is in opposition to God. One of my favorite Bible teachers, the late Pastor Ray Stedman, taught that the flesh "is that inward urge within us toward total independence, toward being our own little gods and running our worlds to suit ourselves. It is that continual drift within us toward self-centeredness and selfishness."[3] The term *flesh* thus refers to the sinful tendencies that rise from within us–lust, pride, self-centeredness, which lead us into sin.

Peter writes, "Dear friends, I urge you, as aliens and strangers in the world, to abstain from sinful desires, which war against your soul" (1 Peter 2:11). And later, he adds that we are not to live for or chase after "evil human desires, but rather for the will of God" (1 Peter 4:2). We carry the damaging effects of the virus of sin within us and it accompanies us everywhere we go. This infiltration of the flesh virus remains with us until we die, as an ongoing battle in which we are all engaged, every moment of our lives. It's a war to infiltrate, capture, and crash our very souls!

The byproducts of fire create a toxic environment that seeks to destroy life and property. Sin's byproducts generate a lethal atmosphere, making it difficult for Christians to survive. The Apostle Paul lists many of the ugly byproducts of sin that develop from our fleshly and sinful nature:

> ...repetitive, loveless, cheap sex; a stinking accumulation of mental and emotional garbage; frenzied and joyless grabs for happiness; trinket gods; magic-show religion; paranoid loneliness; cutthroat competition; all-consuming-yet-never-satisfied wants; a brutal temper; an impotence to love or be loved; divided homes and divided lives; small-minded and lopsided pursuits; the vicious habit of depersonalizing everyone into a rival; uncontrolled and

uncontrollable addictions; ugly parodies of community. I could go on.

Galatians 5:19–20 (MSG)

Is it any wonder that God hates sin and its evil byproducts so much? The obvious survival question here is why don't we hate it as much as our Creator?

PAY ATTENTION TO THE ATTACK FROM THE WORLD

Beware An Affair With the World!

The "*world*" refers to the fallen system of human life on this planet that entices us away from holy living. It is the world order—all the ideas and purposes humans engage in—that has been severely distorted by sin. Have you noticed that the world violently opposes what is good and holy? Just like non-believers, Christians face the constant and enthralling struggle against loving what the world offers and getting completely caught up in earthly things. We're inundated by the world's marketing schemes for Adam's virus!

So here we are, surrounded by the world with its cultures, "in crowd" groups, and social networks. The world offers its shining goods and dazzling role models, and we like them. As a matter of fact, we'd like to own them and be just like them. The world offers us its belief system and thinking patterns, and we like them because they make us "feel" good and they ease our minds about doing what we know is wrong because they tell us it's normal.

Sin is such an ugly little word, but it comforts us to know that others sin just like we do and it's okay. And it's not really sin, it's just human nature. Don't worry about it, just enjoy it like everyone else. I remember the little book, *I'm O.K. - You're O.K.* Today it would be called, *I Sin, You Sin, Don't Worry About It, We All Sin!* And even though we Christians criticize and righteously attack that thinking and belief system, we still secretly like the worldly philosophy because it somehow justifies and condones our actions and reduces our convictions and ultimately pushes us to compromise.

The world continually reminds us that our Christian ways are really out of step. We begin to think that one way or another we can balance our daily spiritual walk with God with the world. So, just like the Israelites, we slowly begin to abandon the ways of the Lord and walk in the ways of the world as we feel the pressure and attraction around us. And every day we're handing our gold to the world to melt down into idols! Can you hear Moses smashing the stone tablets on the rocks? Since the Fall, there's been a worldliness growing in our own hearts that's constantly tugging us in the direction of hell.

Monitoring and curtailing our relationship with the world keeps us out of spiritual trouble. Think about this. Our relationship with the world is directly proportional to our relationship with our Heavenly Father.

> Don't love the world's ways. Don't love the world's goods. Love of the world squeezes out love for the Father. Practically everything that goes on in the world–wanting your own way, wanting everything for yourself, wanting to appear important–has nothing to do with the Father. It just isolates you from him. The world and all its wanting, wanting, wanting is on the way out–but whoever does what God wants is set for eternity.
>
> 1 John 2:15–17 (MSG)

Now, let's reword 1 John 2:16 in a more positive manner: "Love the Father's ways! Love the Father's laws and everything he gives you because everything good that goes on with the Father has nothing to do with this evil world! Love of the Father squeezes out love for the world." Loving the world destroys your relationship with God. Loving God reduces your need for the world.

What does God think about his followers loving what the world offers? Most Christians miss the tremendous significance of how God feels when we become involved with the world. James explains our natural but misguided tendencies to love the world in a very simple evil term. He calls it adultery—an affair with the world! "You adulterers! Don't you realize that friendship with this world makes you an enemy of God! I say it again, and if your aim is to enjoy this world, you can't be a friend of God" (James 4:4, NLT). An affair is sneaking away from your very closest, deepest, and most intimate relationship and going to someone else to get your needs and wants met. Imagine how God, the Creator of all things who loves us in a way we can never fully understand, feels when we go somewhere else to get our needs and desires met! He tells us he will meet all our needs, yet we still love those golden idols just as much as God's first chosen people and it still breaks our Father's heart.

Adultery is a terrible and ugly thing in human terms because it destroys intimacy and forever hurts not only the participants, but also all the closest people around them. It's the ultimate betrayal! Adultery more often than not kills your relationship with your mate and the collateral damage severely wounds those you love the most and who love you the most. Multiply that by a billion times a billion! God considers a loving relationship with the world as committing adultery against him and seeking an intimate friendship someplace else. And when the divorce happens, and you walk into court with all your worldly possessions and affections, who will represent you when you stand before the Judge, the very One you abandoned and cheated on?

BE AWARE OF THE ATTACK FROM THE DEVIL

Deception to Disobedience to Death is His Game!

We earlier identified the enemy all Christians battle–that old serpent Satan. Just as Satan deceived Eve in the Garden, he continues to spread his lies of deception today. Remember, he is a liar by his very nature and prowls about like a roaring lion seeking to devour Christians as his prey. While God loves us to life, Satan hates us to death! Paul calls him the "ruler of the kingdom of the air, the spirit who is now at work in those who are disobedient" in the world (Ephesians 2:2). The devil desires to lead people astray and strives to hinder the work of God, using all the evil resources at his disposal. Nothing makes the enemy happier than seeing God's people disobey him.

Peter encourages his readers, "Resist him, standing firm in the faith" (1 Peter 5:9). By staying oriented, knowing and understanding our enemy, by constantly monitoring the conditions around us, and by relying on the Holy Spirit within, we can avoid Satan's traps and keep the enemy from gaining a foothold in our lives. Lest we never forget how much this evil being hates God and his followers, Ray Stedman sums up exactly why the devil attacks Christians.

> The devil is especially interested in defeating Christians. After all, the unredeemed worldling is no problem to the devil. As Jesus put it, "When a strong man, fully armed, guards his own palace, his goods are in peace" (Luke 11:21, RSV). All the quite sincere but rather pathetic efforts of worldlings to solve the problems of their lives through legislation, education and a change of environment do not bother the devil in the least. He is quite content to let them go on rearranging the pieces of the puzzle without ever solving it. But the presence of every Christian in this world bothers the devil greatly. Why? Well, because each Christian is a potential threat to the solidarity of the devil's kingdom, to his rule over the rest of mankind.[4]

WHY DO I DO THE THINGS I DO?
Give Me Some Virus Protection to Save Me From Myself!

Following Christ is frequently such an intense struggle. In my Christian walk, there have been so many times when I've complained that it was so much easier before I became a committed follower. Sin didn't bother me nearly as much because I resisted the Lord more than sin. But after giving my life to the Lord, it seems that the harder I try to do what I absolutely know to be right, I often discover that I just can't (or won't!). Why? What's wrong with me? Is my Adam virus out of control and terminal? Is the ultimate crash coming?

The Holy Scriptures are loud and clear on how I should live

my life, yet so many times I just can't seem to live up to them. As a growing Christian, I understand the commandments of God and the requirements of his Word. Am I the only one who struggles to keep those commandments in spite of loving the Lord so much? Paul's words in Romans 7 give me some sense of hope! "What I don't understand about myself is that I decide one way, but then I act another, doing things I absolutely despise" (Romans 7:15, MSG). The words indicate that even the great Apostle Paul felt frustration and struggle with sin and that we Christians have the utter inability to live righteously in our own strength.

> We know that the law is spiritual; but I am unspiritual, sold as a slave to sin. I do not understand what I do. For what I want to do I do not do, but what I hate I do. And if I do what I do not want to do, I agree that the law is good. As it is, it is no longer I myself who do it, but it is sin living in me. I know that nothing good lives in me, that is, in my sinful nature. For I have the desire to do what is good, but I cannot carry it out. For what I do is not the good I want to do; no, the evil I do not want to do–this I keep on doing. Now if I do what I do not want to do, it is no longer I who do it, but it is sin living in me that does it. So I find this law at work: When I do good, evil is right there with me. For in my inner being I delight in God's laws; but I see another law at work in the members of my body, waging war against the law of my mind and making me a prisoner of the law of sin at work within my members.
>
> Romans 7:14–23

Romans 7 illustrates that Paul despaired in agony over his sin condition. He understood that his battle was not with God, but as a follower of Christ, he struggled with sin living within him. He understood the virus and hated it. I think that I understand it, but I just feel a little better knowing others have a sin problem too. Too often, after asking myself why do I do what I don't want to do, I have failed to agonize over my sin. As a matter of fact, I have lacked intense remorse for the most part. Instead, like Adam and

Eve, although I feel bad, I claim many lame excuses because it's usually just someone else's fault anyway and I keep trying to fix the problem in my own righteousness.

Paying close attention provides virus protection with the knowledge of the only antidote and fix available. Remember our Christian personal protective equipment? Our breastplate of righteousness? God has provided a righteousness impossible for us to accomplish on our own. We cannot struggle victoriously in our own strength, and we quickly discover how futile it is to even try. We should monitor everything around us because the person sinning is not the real you. "But if I am doing what I don't want to do, I am not really the one doing it; the sin within me is doing it" (Romans 7:20, NLT). But I can only use these words as an explanation, never an excuse!

As Christians, we have been liberated and set free from sin. By his death on the cross and resurrection, Christ overcame the *flesh*, the *world*, and the *devil*. And just like all Christians should do when we sin, Paul finally calls out "mayday" in total frustration, "What a wretched man I am! Who will rescue me from this body of death?" (Romans 7:24). Mayday, Someone help me! The great and glorious Rescuer responds to Paul's distress call for help.

> I've tried everything and nothing helps. I'm at the end of my rope. Is there no one who can do anything for me? Isn't that the real question? The answer, thank God, is that Jesus Christ can and does. He acted to set things right in this life of contradictions where I want to serve God with all my heart and mind, but am pulled by the influence of sin to do something totally different.
>
> Romans 7:24–25 (MSG).

SIN SMOLDERS IN ALL OF US

"The Flesh Burns and is in Flames" - Danger Deceitfully Lurks in Our Burning Desires!

One of the most famous descriptions of temptation came from a pastor and theologian whose life was taken from him at an early age by the Nazis in 1945. Dietrich Bonhoeffer personally understood the meaning of temptation because he faced it everyday, yet he did not yield to the easy way out and instead died standing up against Hitler. In his classic booklet, *Temptation*, Bonhoeffer described the seriousness of the human condition we all battle every single day.

> In our members there is a slumbering inclination towards desire which is both sudden and fierce. With irresistible power desire seizes mastery over the flesh. All at once a secret, smoldering power is kindled. The flesh burns and is in flames. It makes no difference whether it is sexual desire, or ambition, or vanity, or desire for revenge, or love of fame and power, or greed for money, or, finally, that strange desire for the beauty of the world, of nature. Joy in God is in course of being extinguished in us and we seek all of our joy in the creature. At this moment God is quite unreal to us, he loses all reality, and only desire for the creature is real; the only reality is the devil. Satan does not here fill us with hatred of God, but with forgetfulness of God.... The lust thus aroused envelops the mind and the will of persons in deepest darkness. The powers of clear discrimination and decision are taken from us.[5]

Temptation seduces, persuades, and allures Christians into something we know to be wrong. It constantly solicits us to do evil. Temptation is inevitable in our daily lives, and no one is exempt! The word itself means to entice to do wrong with great promises of pleasure or gain. James, the brother of Jesus, sums up the whole concept of the four-step process of temptation very well in the first chapter of his epistle. Notice in the following passage, however, James doesn't say "if" you're tempted, he says "when" you are tempted.

> When tempted, no one should say, "God is tempting me." For God cannot be tempted by evil, nor does he tempt

> anyone; but each one is tempted when, by his own evil desire, he is dragged away and enticed. Then, after desire has conceived, it gives birth to sin, and sin, when it is full-grown, gives birth to death.
>
> James 1:13–15

After dealing with the positive aspects of suffering and trials earlier in his letter's first chapter, James turns his attention to the evils of temptation. Temptations are not trials. Then, what's the difference? Knowing the distinction is extremely important because trials and temptations command different responses. We discern from reading verse 2 of James 1 that we should: "Consider it pure joy, my brothers, whenever you face trials of many kinds, because you know that the testing of your faith develops perseverance." Trials are thereby obviously intended for good and to benefit us, that is, to make us "mature and complete" (James 1:4).

An important difference between a test and a temptation is that the test will reward you but the temptation may kill you. "Blessed is the man who perseveres under trial, because when he has stood the test, he will receive the crown of life that God has promised to those who love him" (James 1:12). Trials serve to make us grow and temptations drag us down. God tests us to strengthen our relationship with him and to build in us a deeper understanding and faith in him.

James makes it very clear that temptation comes from evil desires inside us and not from God. God is never the source of our temptations. Nonetheless, how often are we just like Adam and blame God for our temptations? James emphatically denies that God is the author of evil because, by his very nature, God cannot tempt or deceive anyone to do evil. James tells his readers not to be deceived because, "Every good and perfect gift is from above, coming down from the Father of the heavenly lights, who does not change like shifting shadows" (James 1:17). God bestows only good and perfect gifts in our lives to cause us to grow in Christ. Calvin realized the absurdity of the idea of God seducing man, "It hence follows that he tempts or seduces no man to what is sinful. Being himself unassailable by evils, he cannot seduce others to what is evil. As God cannot be tempted to do what is sinful, he cannot possibly tempt others to sin."[6]

How many times have we said, "The devil made me do it!"? The devil cannot make Christians do anything. But, he will certainly tempt us and he will take advantage of our own evil desires. He will put something in our paths to deceive us or trip us up, encouraging us to do something wrong, but he can never make us do the wrong thing. Let me repeat, the devil cannot make us sin! He will attack our weaknesses, but he cannot force us do anything. Eve reached up and took the fruit and then ate it, no one put it in her mouth. Sin is always our choice. No one can take the blame for us, nor should we fault anyone else!

"EACH ONE IS TEMPTED WHEN, BY HIS OWN EVIL DESIRES..."

We're Drawn Away by Our Own Lusts and We Pitch Our Tents Toward Sodom!

All of our troubles begin with desire. Sin always starts with lust! Our lust! Notice that James says it's by our desires not someone else's: "…but each one is tempted when, by his own evil desire." He tells us that our own evil desires initiate the process of the downward spiral of sin. We are not tempted by God into sin but by our own inward lusts. The word "lust" (*epithumia*) means a strong desire, and the New Testament nearly always uses it in a bad sense. Since the Fall, our desire to sin always lurks somewhere within us so we tend to desire things to satisfy our own gratifications rather than God's pleasure. And since our desires grow extremely strong, we must be particularly careful when certain desires overwhelm us and fill our hearts, minds, and souls.

Desire in and of itself is not necessarily bad. Not all longings are wrong. As a matter of fact, many desires keep us alive and cause us to be healthy, well-adjusted people. But even good desires, taken to excess, can cause us great harm. Any good craving may go bad if it spins out of control. If we seek to satisfy these desires in ways outside of God's will, that's when we get into trouble. Dr.

Tony Evans explains that the process of temptation usually starts when we try to meet a good desire in a bad way.

> The desire for food is good, but gluttony is sin. The desire for sex is legitimate, but immorality is sin. The desire for sleep is good, but lying in bed all day is laziness and sin. Satan knows you can't just skip the desire, because our desires are God-driven. So the enemy wants to control how your desires are met. This is the issue in temptation. Satan wants your desires to master you, rather than you mastering your desires. He wants the desire to take control. It's call addiction.[7]

At the beginning, sin often appears beautiful and desirable with its promises of satisfaction, pleasure, and freedom. As we get more intimate with our desire, we spend more and more time with it. It feels good for a while and it's pleasurable to think about its rewards. The slippery path from temptation to sin begins with our intense lust and continues until we make love with that desire. The promises of sin entice and allure us, presenting such an evil craving that it blinds our eyes to the real facts—sin is always filthy and poisonous and deceitful in all of its promises. The desire to have those eagerly anticipated promises, at whatever cost, stands out as the essential element of temptation. Author David Wilkerson in his wonderful book, *Two Of Me, The Struggle with Sin*, describes the mirage of sin's promise.

> This war between good and evil is raging in all mankind. A minister, exposed for adultery, confessed: "My evil nature held a strange charm over me. It made me chase false dreams that I knew would fade away. It kept me chained to a lust that finally destroyed me. It forced me into compromises that weakened me. Its promises of true love ended up only as a mirage. And, even though I knew I would keep on getting hurt, I followed the dictates of my evil mind like an obedient slave."[8]

In a fire, firefighters know that there are certain atmospheres and circumstances that put them at so much risk that they have to monitor conditions even more closely to stay out of trouble. Here's the firefighting survival point. It's much better to stay out of trouble in the first place rather than suddenly find yourself in such a bad situation you must yell mayday to get out.

Monitoring conditions to stay out of trouble applies to Christians too. We also get caught in high-risk environments with strong desires that promote sin and cater to our carnal natures. If we don't pay close attention to these environments, our chances for spiritual survival rapidly deteriorate. Each of us knows what environments are especially toxic to us. Some people can't go online without being drawn to a pornographic website. Some people who struggle with their weight can't even walk by a donut shop without indulging in sugar and empty calories. Alcoholics can't walk by a bar without being drawn to the addiction of alcohol. When we let ourselves get into personal circumstances that tempt us, our risks for failure dramatically increase.

When we don't monitor conditions, we become just like Lot. His Uncle Abraham let him decide which part of the land he wanted, and the Bible tells us in Genesis 13:12 that Lot "pitched his tent toward Sodom." If you remember the tragic story, Sodom turned out to be the ancient Las Vegas, with all its alluring attractions and bright lights and extreme sin. Isn't that what most of us do every day? Our strong desire is to go where the action is. But that's also where sin thrives and prospers. In Lot's case, he barely made it out alive. Unfortunately, his wife didn't.

When we don't pay attention to the evil conditions around us, we constantly put ourselves in hostile environments. We just keep getting closer and closer to the fire until we get burned! When we pitch our tents toward Sodom, why are we so surprised when we plummet into sin? Paul warns Timothy, "Run from anything that stimulates youthful lust. Follow anything that makes you want to do right. Pursue faith, love, and peace and enjoy the companionship of those who call upon the Lord with pure hearts" (2 Timothy 2:22, NLT). Unfortunately, we still naturally think we can pitch our tents toward Sodom and survive.

"HE IS DRAGGED AWAY AND ENTICED"

There's Always a Hook in the Bait!

Temptation is, by its very nature, deception, a lie! The dictionary defines deception as the act of deceiving or misleading or the state of being deceived or misled. It's an act that deceives or is intended to deceive by false representation, cheating, or fraud. In this next progression of the sin process, James explains that the illicit development of desire within us leads to deception that puts us on the wrong path and pushes us off the cliff into sin. "...but each one is tempted when, by his own evil desire, he is dragged away and enticed."

We are *dragged away* by our sinful passions, which is a hunter's word meaning to trap or catch with bait. It literally means to be snared like an unsuspecting animal. James also compares us to a fish swimming in a straight course and being drawn away to something that appears to be attractive by using the word *enticed*. Proverbs uses the same word to tell us, "...if sinners entice you do not give in to them" (1:10). The hunter and the fisherman use bait to attract and catch their prey because no wild animal is deliberately going to walk into a trap and no fish will knowingly bite a hook. James tells us temptation is a deadly trap in which an attractive bait has been placed. And Satan always packages temptation in such a way that it carries with it just the right enticement that appeals most to our natural desires.

The fisherman lures a fish out of its safe hiding place with bait, convincing it to come out from its security under the rocks or protective vegetation. The idea is to camouflage the trap or hook with temptation. We get attracted out of our safe retreats by some shining allurement, and we go after the bait. The bait persuades and ultimately deceives our inner desires to go for the inducement. It's what we want and we have to get it now! James describes being dragged away and enticed as a violent action with a very bad ending. The purpose of the bait is deception, resulting in death. Fishermen bait their hooks with worms with two purposes in mind: lure the fish, then firmly hook it so it can't escape!

Not only does temptation always include bait that appeals to an evil desire, but it also attempts to conceal the destructive consequences of yielding. This enticement hides the fact that yielding to the desire will eventually bring us painful results or costs. The devil's attraction deceives us from seeing the consequences of sin. The fish does not see the hook. And neither do we! But the hook is always there. We are simply fooled into believing that it is not. If we saw the consequences of sin clearly, we might make better choices!

The strength of our lusts blinds us to the real consequences of sin. If we would just focus on the consequences of temptation, we might make different choices. Monitoring conditions before the sin prevents predictable trouble after the sin. This is really the key strategy to the deception! Anticipate that every bait has a hook! If David had seen the terrible consequences of his lusts when he stared down from his balcony at his neighbor's beautiful wife, do you think he would have still pursued his evil desires?

The media continually hypes and glamorizes adultery with its short-term excitement and fulfillment (the bait), but they never reveal the long-term consequences (the hook) of the broken relationships: children who will seldom if ever recover, broken hearts and lives, and bankruptcy. Beer commercials make alcohol so attractive with good-looking men and women in exciting action-filled situations, but the ads never show the broken lives and homes of alcoholics or the mangled victims of the people who foolishly drank the beer and got behind the wheels of their vehicles. Credit card companies advertise, "Buy now, pay later!" Don't worry about the consequences of spending money you don't have, just keep spending yourself into poverty and despair! The bait always looks so good, and we get so hooked!

Satan is an expert human fisherman. He just keeps on trying different baits until he finds the one that really entices us. Serious experienced fishermen constantly change their baits and tactics to meet the conditions and situations. Satan looks at humans in the very same way. He tries flies, floating cheese, marshmallows, powerbait, corn, spinners, worms, grasshoppers–anything that will get our attention away from swimming our course to eternity. The bait is usually some human need glittered up with some shining stuff, smelly stuff, or colorful stuff to get our attention. But the bait is always hooked! And Satan never uses catch and release. He gleefully adds us to his stringer. Have you ever put a fish on your stringer and thrown it into the water and watched this once free fish try to swim away, only to be held by a chain and violently struggle to escape until it eventually slows down, gives up, and dies gulping for life attached with the other dead victims of the bait? This is what Satan does to us.

"AFTER DESIRE HAS CONCEIVED IT GIVES BIRTH TO SIN"

Conception, Pregnancy, and an Ugly Baby!

James changes his figure of speech from the sporting world to an illegitimate birth in verse 15. "Then, after desire has conceived, it gives birth to sin…" He uses this image to picture an evil seduction enticing a person and then conceiving a terrible offspring. Desires conceive a way to get the bait, and then the will approves and acts in disobedience, resulting in sin. And once the offspring has been conceived, its birth is sure to follow. When lust gives birth, it's an ugly baby named sin. The torrid picture James gives us of this particular stage of temptation is one of conception, pregnancy, and birth. In other words, committing disobedience could be compared to the reproductive process after an illicit sexual affair.

Whether we feel it immediately or not, we're hooked or trapped and sin is born. The seed of an aroused desire has been planted in the heart, and then grows and develops. James infers it is like childbirth because the child is really alive before its actual birth and the result will always show up after a period of time. The child of disobedience is sin, and like any other child, sin will continue to grow and mature once it has been born.

"AND SIN, WHEN FULL GROWN GIVES BIRTH TO DEATH"

The Wages of Sin–There's Always a Payday!

When it reaches maturity, the sinful lifestyle brings forth death according to James, "...and sin, when it is full-grown, gives birth to death." This is the ultimate consequence of yielding to temptation. Sin or disobedience results in spiritual and perhaps eternal separation from God. That is one of the fundamental truths we learned from the sin of Adam and Eve. And just as in the Garden of Eden, this result is not immediately apparent. We disobey, but God does not strike us dead on the spot. To be out of fellowship with God is, for a Christian, a form of living death–*dying we shall die*. And if we continue to sin and do not respond to God mercifully forsaking our sins, death will follow. This represents the opposite of the "crown of life" James described earlier.

When sin reaches full growth, it produces a monstrous offspring: death. James has set forth the terrible temptation process: desire (lust), deception, disobedience (sin), and then death. So whenever we're faced with temptation, we need to get our eyes off the bait and look ahead to see sin's terminal aftermath. There's *always* a hook! Just visualize the consequence to see where you will end up! Paul writes, "The wages of sin is death" (Romans 6:23). The payday of sin is death, and with sin there is always a payday.

I recently saw a news story on television that painted a vivid picture for me of the result of sin. It was a video of a six-year-old little boy who had just caught his first fish in a local fishing derby. He proudly held up a flopping twelve-inch rainbow trout to the camera with both hands in a death grip around the fish's brightly colored middle, with the remains of a worm still dangling out of its quivering mouth. In the lethal environment of air, the poor squished fish was struggling to take its last breath through gills that only desired the freedom of fresh water again, and its little eyeballs were popping out of its speckled head. It burned an ugly image of sin's slow, tortuous death into my mind for future recall whenever I'm tempted to take the worm.

GOD IS FAITHFUL

There's Always a Way Out If We Look For It!

So how can we deal with temptation? As Christians, constantly monitoring our surrounding conditions will enable us to rise above the enticement to sin and stay out of trouble. Let me say it again, our strategy must be: Stay out of trouble before we get into trouble! Contrary to Satan's lies and deception, we are not doomed to fall again and again over the same bait. Let's look at one of the most powerful statements in the entire Bible concerning temptation.

> But remember that the temptations that come into your life are no different from what others experience. And God is faithful. He will keep the temptation from becoming so strong that you can't stand up against it. When you are tempted, he will show you a way out so that you will not give in to it.
>
> 1 Corinthians 10:13 (NLT)

Paul encourages the Corinthians who were living in an evil culture, similar to ours today, to resist temptation. He tells them that temptations happen to all of us and no one is exempt. Too often we think that our temptation is somehow unique in the entire world by mistakenly believing that no one has ever faced this specific temptation in a similar way. The same kinds of passions and desires plague all humans. In fact, we are so much alike, the devil doesn't usually have to work too hard or be too creative. The same kinds of temptations that worked thousands of years ago still work today.

If Jesus was not exempt from temptation, we certainly shouldn't expect to be. So don't be surprised when temptation comes. In fact, we must expect it. Jesus came to earth to experience a full range of temptations throughout his life as a human being. We should be comforted knowing that in the mystery of his incarnation, Jesus victoriously faced every temptation so he can sympathize with us in our struggles. "For we do not have a high priest who is unable to sympathize with our weaknesses, but we have one who has been tempted in every way, just as we are–yet was without sin" (Hebrews 4:15).

Additionally, Paul reminds us that God will protect us. He will not let temptation overwhelm us. None of us will be tempted beyond what we can bear. We've learned that even though God may allow temptation to come, he will not allow Satan to bring more than we can handle. There may be times when we are tempted to say, "I just can't take it anymore, God, I'm maxed out." Remember, God will simply not allow anything to come into our lives that is too difficult for us to bear. God promises to protect you! We can resist the temptation because God is always faithful to help us. "All you need to remember is that God will never let you down; he'll never let you be pushed past your limit; he'll always be there to help you come through it" (1 Corinthians 10:13, MSG). God assures his faithfulness! We can rest assured that God is always on our side and will be faithful to support us in our most desperate times of need. It's an absolute promise!

The protection of God extends even further. God says that he will always make a way of escape. But we must take it! Whatever the temptation and no matter how strong, there is always a way out. There may be times when we don't see that way out. If we're not paying attention and monitoring conditions around us, we may miss the way out entirely. You see, if you fail to take the way out that God provides for you, the fault rests with you because you were either not paying attention or did not want to take it. Don't blame God! It is not his fault! So you must monitor conditions to recognize that way out when God provides it! Dr. Doug Rosenau, a licensed psychologist and certified sex therapist in Atlanta, says that we can choose to make positive choices before, during, and after temptation if we take the way the Lord provides.

> Don't you just hate it when you miss your exit on the freeway and you're stuck driving for miles in the wrong direction? Well, the road we all travel between our temptations and the resulting sin isn't a freeway–we can turn around any time we choose to. So why don't we?...Please understand–it's not the desires that are sinful. Desires often happen without any help on our part. Our sexual integrity depends on how we respond to those desires. Integrity requires self-awareness and making immediate positive choices. We must understand when we are vulnerable and choose to head temptation off at the pass. It's often a mat-

> ter of seconds or minutes before we are in the zone. This is when temptation and desire have already given birth to sin and it would take a team of wild horses to stop you.[9]

The teaching of 1 Corinthians 10:13 shows that God intimately involves himself in the lives of his followers, even to the point of providing ways to escape. And yes, it is possible to turn away from temptation, no matter how strong it is. Our responsibility in facing temptation is to resist it with God's help and to stand up against it with God's protection. After giving his vivid illustration of temptation's process, James finishes with a survival statement on how to stay out of trouble.

> So, my dear friends, don't get thrown off course. Every desirable and beneficial gift comes out of heaven. The gifts are rivers of light cascading down from the Father of Light. There is nothing deceitful in God, nothing two-faced, nothing fickle. He brought us to life using the true Word, showing us off as the crown of all his creatures.
>
> James 1:16–18 (MSG)

STAY LOW!

Pride Goes Before Destruction!

Starting in rookie school, new fire recruits learn from experienced fire officers that the most extreme heat and smoke conditions always exist at the highest levels within a burning room. It's really pretty simple—hot air rises. Rookie firefighters receive constant training to stay low when entering a structure fire in order to allow fire, smoke, and heated gases to remain or exit above them. Probies (probationary fire recruits) learn that the natural tendency of gases to form into layers according to temperature defines the important concept of thermal layering. The hottest and most dangerous gases tend to accumulate in the top layer, while the cooler gases form the lower layers. As long as the hottest air and gases can rise, the lower levels stay safest.

For several reasons, understanding thermal layering helps firefighters survive on the fireground. This phenomenon means that they need to always stay as low as possible so they can operate where the heat and smoke conditions will be at their most survivable levels. Hot, toxic smoke rises leaving the lower levels clearer where firefighters can see better if they stay low. Firefighters at floor level have more time to think and escape if suddenly exposed to high heat and flames. And if they run out of air in their self-contained breathing tanks, there may be some breathable air at the lowest level. Staying low simply means survival!

Yet, one of the biggest mistakes still made by firefighters today and the reason for too many injuries and deaths remains not staying low in fires on hands and knees with faces on the floor. Standing tall is where firefighters die! The *Firefighters Handbook* gives a real life testimony of a firefighter caught in an explosive situation:

> My partner made a Mayday call giving our location while I searched for the door. The pain from the heat was like being stung by a thousand bees. At one point I told myself "Stand up and you've really had it. Stay calm, stay together, and they'll get us out."[1]

Many Christians get killed or injured spiritually because they do not stay low. They pridefully try to stand up into the most toxic environments of life. Pride, the act of standing tall and not being humble, severely injures and kills many believers. Just as in the thermal layering in a fire, the worst byproducts of sin hang around at the upper levels. Christians survive these lethal environments, just like firefighters, by staying low on their hands and knees with their faces on the floor!

Even if firefighters stand up in a fire and get away with it, being where the most extreme danger exists still takes a tremendous toll on their physical bodies. In the same sense, even though we may get away with it most times, pride also takes a tremendous toll on a Christian's spirituality. The great theologian Charles H. Spurgeon warned believers to stay low. "Pride, you know is most likely to meet with destruction, because it is too tall to walk upright. It is most likely to tumble down, because it is always looking upward in its ambition, and never looks to its feet."[2]

LOOK AT ME!

Self-Esteem is not so Esteeming After All!

Deep in our hearts, we long to be significant. We want our lives to matter. A popular Christian song asks two great questions. "Have you ever wanted to be someone else? Have you ever wanted just to be someone?" How we feel about ourselves significantly impacts how we live our lives and what we believe to be true. Even though our lives have great worth, self-significance or self-esteem is healthy only if based on an honest and accurate evaluation of our self-worth. Paul T.P. Wong, president of the International Network on Personal Meaning, explains our search for significance.

> Everyone aspires to be somebody, and no one wants to be a no-body. From the depth of our souls, there is a persistent cry for personal significance. This universal search for meaning manifests itself in a variety of ways, from self-seeking to self-sacrifice. It seems that we are prepared to do anything to convince ourselves, if not the rest of the world, that we really matter and that our lives are worthwhile...Significance refers to a sense of one's self-worth and self-esteem.[3]

But our self-image dangerously sets us up for disaster and the Apostle Paul warns, "I say to everyone of you: do not think of yourself more highly than you ought, but rather think of yourself with sober judgment, in accordance with the measure of faith God has given you" (Romans 12:3). This appears contrary to modern culture when the world tells us everyday through the media and our "heroes" that we can be and do anything we want. "Sober judgment" doesn't come naturally to the fallen human spirit. Our tendency is to look for every opportunity to increase ourselves in any way we can! The commercial says to "Be all you can be!" and educational and community leaders highlight and encourage individual self-worth and self-respect to keep kids in school, out of gangs, and off dependencies on drugs and alcohol–all extremely worthwhile. But this also encourages the attitude of "Look at me!" and "Look at what I did!"

In today's society of "me," "myself," and "I," we constantly celebrate our personal achievements–many times at the expense of others. Visualize the 300-pound NFL defensive end who, after previously being run over ten times in a row, finally throws the quarterback for a loss. He runs forward of both teams then dances and carries on, pounding his puffed up chest to bring attention to himself doing a job that pays him millions of dollars and requires ten other players on his team. In the twenty-first century, isn't that the behavior we all admire and mimic? Isn't that what the media teaches and encourages us and especially our children to do? This rampage and thirst for personal recognition screams out, "Look at me!"

Watch some television evangelists in their thousand-dollar suits with their gaudy jewelry and extravagant dazzling accessories flashing in the camera lights. They drive expensive luxury cars and live in multi-million dollar mansions all in the name of Christ, financed on the backs of those poor, humble believers who live much different lifestyles. Isn't their true message essentially the same as the overpaid, pampered sports star? Look at me! Pastor Ed Young of the Fellowship Church in Grapevine, Texas, reacts to this modern "self" aggrandizement in his superb book, *Fatal Distractions*: "Pride. It puts self on a pedestal. Self can do anything. Self deserves things. Self has power. Self makes things happen. Self isn't ever at fault. Self, self, self. That's pride."[4]

This shouldn't surprise us. Since the 1960s we have been bombarded by the "me" generation and continually encouraged by secular humanists who tell us how deserving we all are. Evangelist Billy Graham cautions, "From high school on, young people are indoctrinated with the secular definition of self-esteem, self-image, self-realization, and self-actualization propagated by the prophets of selfism."[5] One of those deceived prophets, Richard Taylor, a noted ethicist and a leading author of the secular humanist movement, extols the virtue of pride in his book, *Restoring Pride: The Lost Virtue of Our Age*:

> Genuine pride is a lost virtue. I say lost, because it was clearly understood by our cultural ancestors, the pagan Greeks of antiquity...Pride was for them the appreciation of one's own special worth and superiority over others. To be proud is to believe that you are in the clearest and truest sense better than other people, and to be correct in so believing.[6]

Nathaniel Branden, Ph.D., a well-known psychotherapist, defines self-esteem as: "The disposition to experience oneself as being competent to cope with the basic challenges of life and of being worthy of happiness."[7] Unfortunately, Dr. Branden doesn't believe God or some supreme being is relevant in any discussion of self-esteem. "With regard to self-esteem, I do not see 'God' as relevant, one way or the other–unless you believe in a malevolent God who wishes human beings to face the challenges of life in a state of terror and paralysis."[8]

Another advocate of self, William Thomas from the Objectivist Center, believes and teaches that pride is the moral principle of valuing one's self-esteem and taking all the steps required to achieve it. When based on this increasingly popular world philosophy, pride regrettably becomes the human compass that points to a "look at me" mentality. Thomas sees self-esteem as a positive self-assessment and states that "we need such a principle because of our profound need for self-esteem, and because a robust self-esteem, grounded in the facts of reality, is not something we can achieve easily or automatically." He warns of groups like Christians who historically have condemned pride as a "deadly sin." Thomas says of Christians, "They have engendered guilt in their adherents by demanding compliance with moral ideals that are incompatible with life and happiness."[9]

In promoting the idea of self-love and self-worth as the driving forces in mankind's existence, Thomas believes that good self-esteem leads to pleasure because pride results in being able to look at one's accomplishments and say both, "I did it," and, "It is good."[10] Does that sound a lot like what Satan said as Lucifer? Remember back in Isaiah 14 when Satan fed the pride of his own heart seeking his own self-esteem? "I will ascend into heaven; I will exalt my throne above the stars of God; I will sit also upon the mount of the congregation, in the sides of the north; I will ascend above the heights of the clouds; I will be like the most High."

Can you imagine telling God to "look at me"? This created being was the first to openly seek his own self-esteem and his resulting rebellion against his Creator shocked and awed the entire cosmos. His need to put himself above God began a celestial war in heaven that became part of the ever-present spiritual warfare on earth. Our pride puts our interests above other people's interests, including God's. Our self-esteem trumps others self-esteem! Look at me!

In contrast, Jesus Christ obviously saw pride differently and he actually declared that it defiled people: "That which proceeds out of the man, that is what defiles the man. For from within, out of the heart of men, proceed the evil thoughts, fornications, thefts, murders, adulteries, deeds of coveting and wickedness, as well as deceit, sensuality, envy, slander, pride and foolishness. All these things proceed from within and defile the man" (Mark 7:20–22, NASB). The Creator of all things placed pride in the same evil category with blasphemy, fornication, adultery, murder, and covetousness. Jesus said that all these evil things that come from within us, including pride, defile us and make us impure. God implicitly does not agree with those who suggest humans need more self-esteem and pride.

Luke recalls a wonderful story that Jesus told about self-esteem. "To some who were confident of their own righteousness and looked down on everybody else, Jesus told this parable" (Luke 18:9). A Pharisee and a tax collector both came to the temple to pray but with completely different attitudes. Jesus described the Pharisee as the one with a very healthy self-esteem and if anyone had "self-love," the Pharisee obviously had it in abundance! He took his position in a very prominent place in the temple so all could see him. Look at me!

Jesus then introduced the humble, lowly tax collector into his parable who obviously desired to remain anonymous in the crowd of worshipers at the temple. The job of tax collecting was not exactly the preferred occupation of Jews in Jesus' day. The Pharisee wanted to be seen and approved by men (Luke 18:11) but the tax collector did not, not even daring to look upward towards heaven (Luke 18:13). As the tax collector stayed low, all he could say was, "God have mercy on me, a sinner."

Jesus' parable of the Pharisee and the tax collector provides valuable insight into self-esteem. I believe that for many, like the Pharisee, a high sense of self-worth is spiritually linked with self-righteousness. This is an important concept in understanding our self-esteem because we've already discovered that self-righteousness belongs in a pile of worthless, dirty rags. As Christians, we must fully realize that a low self-worth is well-founded for all have sinned making us all sinners.

God provides a perfect solution for our poor self-esteem: salvation! Why is it then that we consider poor self-image as a curse and a good self-esteem as a blessing when Jesus clearly presented the opposite point of view? Here's the survival lesson of Jesus' parable: When you stand before God, would you rather be the Pharisee or the tax collector? Will you stand erect with the attitude of "look at me" or will you stay low on your hands and knees with your face to the floor looking up at the Lord God Almighty with the attitude of, "I'm a sinner please have mercy on me"?

However, it is possible and even important to have self-esteem, as long as it is related properly back to the One who made us. Remember our strategy to "Stay Oriented and Know Where We Came From"? We were created in God's image with deep needs for personal security and significance, and God designed a holy way to satisfy those needs but only when we remain rightly related to him. Our true self-worth originates only in God! He personally made us in our mother's womb with an eternal purpose. He created us to be part of his amazing plan. But because of our self-centeredness and exaggerated self-esteem we fell! So, as part of his plan, God sent his Son to pay the price for our imperfections caused by our pride. Now how significant is that?

In spite of the television commercials and media blitz of who and what we should be, God gives us the security of being totally loved and accepted for whom he made, regardless of what we do for a living, what we look like, what we wear, or what kind of car we drive. God sees his followers at their worst and yet he loves us anyway! So our significance comes only as a gift from God, and the only true way to achieve a proper sense of self-esteem is to establish a personal relationship with our Creator, the Living God. In this unique relationship, Christians humbly attain the highest possible self-esteem in the entire universe!

Howard E. Butt, Jr., President of the H.E. Butt Foundation, is a highly successful Texas business leader, spiritual reformer, bridge-builder, communicator, innovator, and author. In those roles, he became one of the earliest and most consistent advocates of servant leadership. Even as a highly regarded and influential leader, Butt still fully understands that the true source of his success and significance is his personal relationship with God, and he realizes how dangerous self-esteem can be when it pridefully turns into self-delusion. In 1963 he talked about the "Art of Being a Big Shot."

> It is my pride that makes me independent of God. It's appealing to me to feel that I am the master of my fate, that I run my own life, call my own shots, go it alone. But that feeling is my basic dishonesty. I can't go it alone. I have to get help from other people, and I can't ultimately rely on my self. I'm dependent on God for my next breath. It is dishonest of me to pretend that I am anything but a man–small, weak, and limited. So, living independent of God is self-delusion. It is not just a matter of pride being an unfortunate little trait and humility being an attractive little virtue; it's my inner psychological integrity that's at stake. When I'm conceited, I am lying to myself about what I am, I am pretending to be God, and not man. My pride is the idolatrous worship of myself. And that is the national religion of Hell![11]

> This is what the Lord says: "Let not the wise man boast of his wisdom or the strong man boast of his strength or the rich man boast of his riches, but let him who boasts boast about this: that he understands and knows me, that I am the Lord, who exercises kindness, justice and righteousness on earth, for in these I delight," declares the Lord.
>
> Jeremiah 9:23–24

PRIDE BURNS AS A SIN IN ALL OF US

Standing Tall Has Never Been More Destructive!

Pride is at the heart of all sin. It's often been said that pride is the first sin to enter a person's heart and the last to leave. Pride is sin's approach to dealing with the human condition of a nagging sense of inadequacy. Dictionaries define pride as an unduly high opinion of one's self, exaggerated self-esteem, conceit, haughty behavior resulting from this, and arrogance. Synonymous words reveal even more disturbing characteristics: vanity, vainglory, arrogance, egotism, self-glorification, self-love, self-congratulation, pomposity, immodesty, hubris, haughty, big-headedness. All characteristics most of us would rather avoid.

The Holman Bible Dictionary calls pride the "undue confidence in and attention to one's own skills, accomplishments, state, possessions, or position. Pride is easier to recognize than to define, easier to recognize in others than oneself. It is the opposite of humility, the proper attitude one should have in relation to God."[12] Proud people preoccupy themselves with self and perpetually exalt themselves over others in hopes that this will provide them a better sense of worth and self-esteem.

Great theologians and wise teachers for hundreds of years have recognized the ugliness and sinfulness of pride. As we've already seen, pride was the first sin and it cast Lucifer from heaven, and it was pride that cost Adam and Eve their place in Paradise and caused the human race to fall. Notice what topped King Solomon's list of things that God hates: "These six things the Lord hates, yes, seven are an abomination to Him: a proud look, a lying tongue, hands that shed innocent blood, a heart that devises wicked plans, feet that are swift in running to evil, a false witness who speaks lies and one who sows discord among brethren" (Proverbs 6:16–19). In the Old Testament, no sin was more offensive to God than the sin of pride.

In the sixth century, Gregory the Great named pride as being one of the seven deadly sins. Interesting that someone with the title of "Great" in his name listed pride as a sin. In the thirteenth century, Thomas Aquinas noted that pride was deadly not merely because it was a serious moral offense, but because it gave rise to other sins. In the nineteenth century, the great theologian Charles Spurgeon articulately added his strong feelings about pride: "I might paint it as being the worst malformation of all the monstrous things in creation; it hath nothing lovely in it, nothing in proportion, but everything in disorder."[13] In the twentieth century, C. S. Lewis claimed that pride leads to every other vice. "Unchastity, anger, greed, drunkenness and all that, are mere flea-bites in comparison: it was through Pride that the devil became the devil…Pride has been the chief cause of misery in every nation and every family since the world began."[14]

Today, in the twenty-first century, the problem has not changed. As a matter of fact, it seems to have intensified. Everyday, we see the devastation and destructiveness of pride in every area of life: marriage and the family, religion, politics, business, sports, and entertainment. We live in a proud and defiant age! The sin of pride is responsible for much of the confusion, sorrow, heartache, and tragedy in the world today. Humans continue to wage war against each other because of pride. How many hundreds of innocent people die every day because of someone else's pride?

Since the very nature of pride moves people to exalt themselves above others, is it any wonder that pride breaks up more marriages, destroys more families, ruins more ministries, and damages more relationships than any other sin? It alienates husbands from wives, parents from children, bosses from employees, and friends from each other. Pride places obstacles between people and those they love most, especially their Heavenly Father! No wonder God hates pride so much!

Many even believe the world's increasingly prideful condition indicates that we are living in the last days as described by Paul in 2 Timothy 3:1–2: "But mark this: There will be terrible times in the last days. People will be lovers of themselves, lovers of money, boastful, proud, abusive, disobedient to their parents, ungrateful, unholy." Paul's descriptive list certainly depicts our culture and society. Just watch the evening news! Everyone wants to be a big shot! What does Paul tell us to do with people who exhibit those behaviors? "…Have nothing to do with them" (2 Timothy 3:5).

Pride destroys leaders. So many chief executives bankrupt their corporations and business organizations by their selfish management and treatment of people, funds, and stockholders that it seems like everyday news. Politicians place themselves above the laws they legislate and exempt themselves from the same responsibilities they expect from their subjects. Prominent politicians and CEOs find themselves in prison because they have succumbed to greed or to temptation in one form or another. Clergymen who were prominent and active in their churches are publicly exposed after being gripped by some terrible condition originating with pride. Read between the lines of every story of leadership failure and it's painfully obvious pride lies at the root of these dreadful breakdowns. In addition to breathing polluted air, standing tall exposes an unbalanced and top-heavy foundational weakness that makes it easy to trip and fall but very difficult to get back up.

In July 2002, the BBC News reported on a speech given by a disgraced and fallen former British cabinet minister. The talk's backdrop was a prominent and high-class London restaurant–the scene of many of his past political press conferences. Jonathan Aitken, who was jailed for eighteen months in June of 1999 for perjury and perverting the course of justice, had humbly returned to speak to a group of Christian broadcasters. He honestly, but regretfully, admitted pride was his chief downfall along with its terrible consequences of defeat, disgrace, divorce, bankruptcy, and imprisonment. Recalling his fall from grace with great sadness, Aitken told the crowd, "I was puffed up with pride. I had been in the wrong relationship with God. I rather condescended to God... I was a very important politician."[15] Spurgeon sums it up very well: "God hates high looks, and never fails to bring them down. All the arrows of God are aimed at proud hearts."[16] Solomon's words still ring true today! "Pride goes before destruction, a haughty spirit before a fall" (Proverbs 16:18).

In addition to all the current reports of fallen people, the Bible tells story after story of high-minded and self-centered humans who became too impressed with themselves. The severity in which God deals with pride is without equal in the scriptures. Nothing provokes the wrath of God like pride. All these stories of the downfalls of great kings and those in high positions of authority illustrate the powerful truth that pride will bring destruction, humiliation, shame, iniquity, and condemnation. When we stand tall, God will get our attention in various ways and at any time.

Therefore, we must constantly stay low and examine ourselves in the light of the clear standard operating procedures in the Word of God.

KING NEBUCHADNEZZAR

Look at Me and My Power! Grazing on the Grass of Pride!

Why did King Nebuchadnezzar, the mighty builder of Babylon, creep on the earth, devouring grass like an animal until his nails had grown like bird's claws and his hair like eagle's feathers? The book of Daniel tells us that King Nebuchadnezzar became puffed up with pride saying, "Is not this the great Babylon that I have built as the royal residence, by my mighty power and for the glory of my majesty?" (Daniel 4:30). "Look at me and my power!" The king's proud heart was hardened so much that God humiliated him and took away his glory by deposing him from his throne. "Your royal authority has been taken away from you. You will be driven away from people and will live with the wild animals; you will eat grass like cattle. Seven times will pass by for you until you acknowledge that the Most high is sovereign over the kingdoms of men and gives them to anyone he wishes" (Daniel 4:31–32).

What an extremely painful lesson God used to bring this mighty man down, to break his arrogant spirit and to make him cry unto God for mercy! Daniel tells us that Nebuchadnezzar remained in this state for seven years until he finally recognized exactly what we all must come to settle in our hearts: "Now I, Nebuchadnezzar, praise and exalt and glorify the King of heaven, because everything he does is right and all his ways are just. And those who walk in pride he is able to humble" (Daniel 4:37). If we exalt ourselves, God will most certainly humble us. If we humble ourselves, God, by his grace, will exalt us.

KING UZZIAH

Look at Me and My Success!

After King Amaziah fell from grace and was murdered, the people of Judah had enough confidence in his sixteen-year-old son, Uzziah, that they unanimously acclaimed him as their king. So, God made Uzziah the king of Judah. "As long as he sought the Lord, God gave him success" (2 Chronicles 26:5). As he grew up in the fear of the Lord, Uzziah sought after the Lord. Look at what God did for him. "His fame spread far and wide, for he was greatly helped until he became powerful" (2 Chronicles 26:15). History shows that Uzziah became a great and famous military conqueror and renowned city builder.

But according to the Bible, toward the end of his life, Uzziah stood tall in his achievements, and foolishly forgot the God who had made it all possible. "But after Uzziah became powerful, his pride led to his downfall..." (2 Chronicles 26:16). "Look at me and what I did!" "Look at my accomplishments!" When he had grown very great and considerable in wealth and power, instead of lifting up the name of God in thanksgiving and praise, Uzziah pridefully overestimated his own importance and lifted himself up to a high position.

With his heart puffed up, Uzziah forgot about the Word of the Lord and decided to do things his own way. "He was unfaithful to the Lord his God, and entered the temple of the Lord to burn incense on the altar of incense" (2 Chronicles 26:16). Even the great king had no authority or right to enter the temple because God's law clearly restricted this privilege only to the priests. And in spite of the warnings from the high priest and eighty of his priestly staff in the temple at the time, Uzziah still angrily violated God's law and entered the Lord's temple. Uzziah quickly discovered that even the most powerful kings are still subject to God's rules. "While he was raging at the priests in their presence before the incense altar in the Lord's temple, leprosy broke out on his forehead...because the Lord had afflicted him" (2 Chronicles 26:19–20). The God that blesses also reigns as the Sovereign who can quickly reverse those blessings.

Uzziah had to live the rest of his life in a place apart from the kingdom and thereby experienced isolation and shame in death. "King Uzziah had leprosy until the day he died. He lived in a separate house–leprous, and excluded from the temple of the Lord"

(2 Chronicles 26:21). And he effectively lost all his power, since Jotham, his son, was put in charge of the palace and began to govern the people. All the things Uzziah had built and worked for were taken from him in a life changing instant. He had to leave them all behind and live in isolation in a separate house, apart from his wife and children, his friends, and his advisors. And most sadly, he was also forever excluded from the very temple of the Lord he had violated.

At the age of sixty-eight, Uzziah died a shameful and painful death from leprosy, and the Bible forever records this sad event: "Uzziah rested with his fathers and was buried near them in a field for burial that belonged to the kings, for people said, 'He had leprosy'" (2 Chronicles 26:23). Look closely where they buried the king. They wouldn't even bury him in the royal burial plot, but only in a field near it because they wouldn't contaminate the royal cemetery with a leper. And even though much of his life Uzziah did "what was right in the eyes of the Lord," in death he was disgraced and remembered for his arrogance and pride, rather than the great success God gave him.

The story of Uzziah teaches us some strong survival lessons about pride. Pride deceives us into believing we don't always need God, thereby hurting our relationship with him. Pride also destroys our relationships with others and alienates us from our loved ones. Pride will even cause us to do things that violate God's laws. When your heart's full of pride and you're struck down, people will remember you more for your arrogance than the good accomplished in your life. Pride destroys our legacies.

MIRIAM AND AARON

Look at Us - Not Moses!

Even though Miriam was a prophetess and Aaron was the priest, the brother and sister of Moses desired even more importance and recognition. "Miriam and Aaron began to talk against Moses because of his Cushite wife, for he had married a Cushite. 'Has the Lord spoken only through Moses?' they asked. 'Hasn't he also spoken through us?' And the Lord heard this" (Numbers 12:1–2).

Their complaints about Moses' wife didn't fool anyone, especially God who was listening to their complaints. Miriam and Aaron were really jealous of Moses' leadership and intimate relationship with God. "Look at us, not Moses!"

Pride often manifests itself as jealousy! Can you detect the devious hissing of the enemy of all souls slithering through the Hebrew camp? This is his ever favorite device to make one servant of the Lord envy the greater success enjoyed by another. Miriam and Aaron swallowed the bait - hook, line, and sinker! Desiring equality with their younger brother, Miriam and Aaron truly believed in their hearts that Moses' close relationship with the Lord unfairly denied them the same intimacy and significance. Criticism of others indicates unchecked and uncontrolled pride and always occurs while standing tall.

Miriam and Aaron had been given extremely important roles to play in arguably the most important forty years in the history of the Israelites. During the confrontation with Pharaoh in Egypt, Aaron filled the significant role as the spokesman for Moses. Now, however, older brother Aaron had been assigned to what he probably considered a second-string position. Miriam's role as prophetess probably gave rise to her desire to be more in the spotlight. In her mind she thought, *If I'm important enough for God to speak through my prophecies, shouldn't I have more of a leadership role?* Their pride caused them to envy Moses and his "higher" position. But their pride and criticism were about to get them in serious trouble because "the Lord heard this." We can learn a very valuable lesson immediately! The God who hates pride hears all our prideful thoughts and jealous criticisms of others.

It's interesting that the writer of this story inserts a parenthetical statement in verse 3 about Moses' meekness. "(Now Moses was a very humble man, more humble than anyone else on the face of the earth.)" The statement clearly contrasts Moses' character with that of his brother and sister. But I am surprised by this description of Moses. Moses doesn't appear to be the poster child of humility as I view it. A Chief Rabbi also thinks this is an unusual statement considering what Moses has done.

> The sentence is strange, both in the sentiment it expresses, and in its place in the narrative. Moses humble? The man who spoke words of fire, who was undaunted in the presence of Pharaoh, who led an entire people out of slavery, who was unafraid to argue with himself, the man who smashed the tablets after seeing the golden calf. Was this a humble man? Why is Moses so calm in the face of this seeming betrayal by those closest to him, when in the previous chapter he had been so agitated by the people's request for meat–a challenge of a type he had faced and overcome before? The questions answer one another. The people's challenge was directed against God–or fate or circumstance–not against him. That is why he cared. Miriam and Aaron's challenge was directed against him. It was personal. That is why he was serene. Moses did not care about himself. If he had, he would not have been able to survive a single day as leader of this fractious, unstable people. He cared about the cause, about God and freedom and responsibility. That was what made him humble.[17]

"At once the Lord said to Moses, Aaron and Miriam, 'Come out to the Tent of Meeting, all three of you'" (Numbers 12:4). So, all three went with no arguments. Obviously, God thought this was a really big deal because he came personally to discuss it with them. "Then the Lord came down in a pillar of cloud; he stood at the entrance to the Tent and summoned Aaron and Miriam" (Numbers 12:5). While all three were commanded to come out to the tabernacle, God spoke only to Miriam and Aaron. They were about to get the close, personal attention they desired, but it probably wasn't quite what they had in mind.

God told them to listen carefully to his words and explained that Moses was not like them. God then reminded Miriam and Aaron why Moses was the leader he had personally called to deliver his people to the Promised Land. "'...he is faithful in all my house. With him I speak face to face, clearly and not in riddles; he sees the form of the Lord'" (Numbers 12:7–8). Why do you suppose this was true? I see a direct connection to Moses being recognized as the most humble person on the face of the earth and being the one God chose to use instead of Miriam and Aaron, or anyone else for that matter.

The writer of this passage in Numbers 12 tells us in verse 9 that, "The anger of the Lord burned against them, and he left them." God hates pride so much he strikes Miriam with leprosy! "When the cloud lifted from above the Tent, there stood Miriam–leprous, like snow" (Numbers 12:10). As we've already seen, it's pretty difficult to remain proud as a leper! But why doesn't Aaron get leprosy too? The text seems to indicate that Miriam probably initiated and led in most of the criticism. Also, Aaron served as the High Priest, and God may not have desired to dishonor the position of High Priest with something like leprosy. Aaron also responded to Moses in great remorse when he saw his sister, "Please my lord, do not hold against us the sin we have so foolishly committed" (Numbers 12:11).

At this point, if I were in Moses' sandals, I might have been tempted to say, "Well, now I guess you really know who's chief around here! I hope you've learned your lesson." But note how Moses responded to their painful situation. He didn't take any delight in the drastic consequences of his siblings' foolish pride and criticism against him. Instead, the most humble person in the entire world immediately prayed for Miriam's healing and God responded with mercy.

This passage teaches us two extremely crucial survival lessons about pride and humility. One lesson by Aaron and Miriam on pride: God takes great exception to it no matter who you are, especially when you jealously stand tall pointing your finger towards another believer who's faithfully doing God's will. God's leader and follower choices and assignments are always right and perfect, so we must embrace them whether we like them or not! And one valuable lesson by Moses on humility: Even though he had every right to react to their criticism, Moses did not retaliate against Aaron or Miriam because spiritual meekness is the ability to let your own honor come behind the honor of other people or the Lord's. In other words, stay low and leave the rest to the One who rightfully stands high above all his creation!

HUMILITY IS THE ONLY ANTIDOTE FOR PRIDE

It's the Choice of True Discipleship!

We struggle with the word humility. It seems to describe weakness. As a matter of fact, most people don't consider meekness as a strength at all. The world, for the most part, still views humility as foolishness. Today, humble people get taken advantage of, abused, scorned, and run over in a hostile world that exalts pride and arrogance. Humility, by definition, excludes all pride, boasting, arrogance, self-confidence, and independence. I really like this Jewish definition of humility: "True humility is mindlessness of self."[18]

Humbleness is staying low or as the dictionary defines it: low in condition, rank, or position; lowly; unpretentious. Biblically speaking, personal humility also carries the notion of lowering or abasing oneself in such a manner as to attain a place of lowliness. The survival strategy for Christians to "Stay Low" translates simply into "Stay Humble!"

Perhaps the best way to understand humility is attempting to see ourselves through God's eyes rather than our own. Spurgeon preached these wise words to his congregation in 1856, "It is not humility to underrate yourself; Humility is to think of yourself, if you can, as God thinks of you."[19] Making a proper estimate of ourselves allows us to accept ourselves as we really are before God. It gives us freedom from a sense of our own importance, with total dependence on God and honest concern for others and a willingness to serve them. Pastor Rick Warren in his *The Purpose Driven Life* writes, "Humility is not thinking less of yourself; it is thinking of yourself less."[20]

Humility, then, is an absolute dependence on God for everything in life–physical, emotional, and spiritual. Every moment of every day is to be lived in total dependence upon the resources of the Living God. Over and over again, Scripture insists that we either walk humbly with God, or not at all. Micah declares that humility is one of three main virtues that ought to govern our lives and define our relationship to God: "He has showed you, O man, what is good. And what does the Lord require of you? To act justly, and to love mercy and to walk humbly with your God"

(Micah 6:8). C.S. Lewis explains why a proper relationship with God results in true humility.

> And He and you are two things of such a kind that if you really get into any kind of touch with Him you will, in fact, be humble–delightedly humble, feeling the finite relief of having for once got rid of all the silly nonsense about your own dignity which has made you restless and unhappy all your life. He is trying to make you humble in order to make this moment possible.[21]

Being humble essentially means denying yourself. The Lord Jesus often spoke of self-denial and mentions it several times as the measure of a true disciple. Look what Jesus says determines whether you will be counted as a disciple or not. "Then Jesus said to them all: 'If anyone would come after me, he must deny himself and take up his cross and follow me'" (Luke 9:23). He connects it directly with cross-bearing and life loss. To deny yourself means to reject your own desires, self-interests, and priorities. Discipleship is denying yourself, picking up your cross, and following Christ at all costs. It's a choice only you can make!

God expects three distinct actions from his disciples: deny, carry, and follow! Notice the order of discipleship! Staying low and denying our ways are the essential acts of following Christ. Denying yourself is the first step in discipleship and the other steps depend on it. You can talk all you want about *taking up your cross* and *following Jesus*, but if you fail to deny yourself first, they are only wasted words and efforts! Jesus makes it absolutely clear that humility is not an option for his disciples because only a humble person can truly follow Christ.

Deny yourself and you reject pride! Pick up your cross and you die to yourself! If we are to be his disciples, we must first stay low and then we are to die to ourselves. But the poison of pride runs through our veins and it will kill us unless we take the only known cure. Pride constantly lurks as a discipleship killer so we must willingly and continuously seek its only antidote–humility.

How important is denying yourself and giving up everything?

Listen to what Jesus tells the large crowd traveling with him: "If anyone comes to me and does not hate his father and mother, his wife and children, his brothers and sisters–yes, even his own life–he cannot be my disciple. And anyone who does not carry his cross and follow me cannot be my disciple'" (Luke 14:25–27). I suppose the people hearing Christ's piercing words had as much trouble with their meaning as we do today! What does Jesus imply by telling us that we must hate our closest family members? He's contrasting our allegiance to him in the strongest possible terms. No earthly relationship, however intimate, loving, and legitimate, can take precedence over our humble obedience to Jesus.

Jesus tells the multitude traveling with him: "Unless I am your first priority over every other person, place, and thing in your lives, you can't be my followers." In Matthew's gospel, Jesus shares the same message in different words, "Anyone who loves his father or mother more than me is not worthy of me; anyone who loves his son or daughter more than me is not worthy of me; and anyone who does not take his cross and follow me is not worthy of me" (Matthew 10:37–38). Jesus seemed aware that most of his listeners were only fair-weather fans or "groupies," and that this was just a traveling circus or a "happening" attended by curiosity seekers. Jesus used an extreme statement in order to make a point with maximum impact to measure their true commitment and allegiance. We must be willing to put Christ ahead of every other relationship. "In the same way, any of you who does not give up everything he has cannot be my disciple" (Luke 14:33).

Jesus made another shocking statement while teaching in the synagogue in Capernaum. "I tell you the truth, unless you eat the flesh of the Son of Man and drink his blood, you have no life in you. Whoever eats my flesh and drinks my blood has eternal life, and I will raise him up at the last day" (John 6:53–54). Jesus was not recruiting cannibalistic disciples to actually eat his flesh and drink his blood, but he was saying his life had to become their own. How did this crowd react? "On hearing it, many of his disciples said, 'This is a hard teaching. Who can accept it?'" (John 6:60). And in one of the turning points of his earthly ministry, Jesus seriously began to separate the curiosity seekers from his true followers:

"From this time many of his disciples turned back and no longer followed him" (John 6:66).

Those disciples who stuck around faced a tough question from their Leader. "'You do not want to leave too, do you?' Jesus asked the Twelve. Simon Peter answered him, 'Lord, to whom shall we go? You have the words of eternal life. We believe and know that you are the Holy One of God'" (John 6:67–69). However, after responding favorably to Jesus' question, Peter, along with the other disciples, failed miserably up to and through the death and resurrection of the Savior. But after Jesus rose from the grave, the disciples finally grasped what he had told them to do–deny, pick up, and follow.

Radically transformed from the time he first followed the Lord Jesus, Peter demonstrated a new view of leadership and discipleship. In wholehearted allegiance to Christ, the disciple who had such a tough time staying low during Jesus' earthly ministry calls for humility toward God and others: "All of you, clothe yourselves with humility toward one another, because, 'God opposes the proud but gives grace to the humble.' Humble yourselves, therefore, under God's mighty hand, that he may lift you up in due time" (1 Peter 5:5–6). Commanding us to be humble, Peter takes on the same leadership perspective as that of his Lord: Deny yourself! The disciple who would be greatest now passionately preaches lowliness. Compared to his previous power seeking personality, what changed Peter? The great classic hymn by Isaac Watts captures the spirit of why all Christians should stay low.

> When I survey the wondrous cross,
> On which the Prince of glory died;
> My richest gain I count but loss,
> And pour contempt on all my pride.[22]

JOHN THE BAPTIST

He Must Become Greater–I Must Become Less!

When I think of humble people in the Bible, I immediately picture John the Baptist. He stands out as one of the most remarkable men in the entire book, yet the spirit of humility paved the road of his entire life. His life was filled with greatness and fame that most of us would covet and let go straight to our heads. Isaiah prophesized in the Old Testament that John the Baptist would prepare the way for the Messiah. The same angel that announced the birth of the Savior of the world first proclaimed the coming birth of John the Baptist. John had such a popular ministry that people from Jerusalem and all Judea were flocking to see and hear him. The ministry became so popular that many even wondered if John the Baptist might be the long awaited Messiah.

The Gospel writers record John's life with greatness and a direct connection to God. Jesus told the crowds, "I tell you the truth: Among those born of women there has not risen anyone greater than John the Baptist" (Matthew 11:11). Luke verifies that John's birth was due to the direct and miraculous intervention of God (Luke 1:7, 13) and that he was "filled with the Holy Spirit even from his mother's womb" (Luke 1:15). Matthew states that John was specifically sent by God to prepare the way of the Lord (3:3). The Apostle John tells us that he was a man "sent from God" (John 1:6).

This mere mortal humbly baptized the true Messiah. Can you imagine any greater honor? But what did John the Baptist say? "'I baptize with water,' John replied, 'but among you stands one you do not know. He is the one who comes after me, the thongs of whose sandals I am not worthy to untie'" (John 1:26–27). Loosing the sandal was the task of the lowest slave. John the Baptist says he was not even worthy to be this man's slave. A note about John the Baptist in my study Bible says, "If such a great person felt inadequate even to be Christ's slave, how much more should we lay aside our pride to serve Christ! When we truly understand who Christ is, our pride and self-importance melt away."[23] Even a disciple would not be expected to perform this menial task. In his excellent and comprehensive commentary on John, Leon Morris emphasizes the lowliness of the act of loosing the sandal thong in Jesus' time.

> There is a Rabbinic saying (in its present form, dating from c. A.D. 250, but probably much older): "Every service which a slave performs for his master shall a disciple do for his teacher except the loosing of his sandal-thong." John selects this task which the Rabbinic saying stresses as too menial for any disciple, and declares himself unworthy to perform it.[24]

In spite of his God-given greatness, John the Baptist modeled the humility and true servanthood God desires from all of us. But in contrast to John, we see the jealousy and frustration of John's disciples. "Rabbi, that man who was with you on the other side of the Jordan–the one you testified about–well, he is baptizing, and everyone is going to him" (John 3:26). They were frustrated that Jesus and his disciples were attaining more success than they were. His disciples stood ready to pronounce John as the Messiah, not "that man." They looked upon Jesus with jealousy because of his growing popularity. Ray Stedman in one of my favorite commentaries on the Gospel of John, *God's Loving Word*, suggests that the motives of John's disciples are not that much different than some of Christ's disciples today.

> Now they complain, "everyone is going to him!" Note the similarity of these words to the words of the Pharisees; "Look, the world has gone after him!" (John 12:17–19). How can this be explained? What went wrong here? How quickly and easily we lose sight of Christ's preeminence, and start to think of our position and our pleasure. Is this not what characterizes the disciples of our Lord? Are they not interested in promoting Christ so that they can prosper with Him?[25]

But John the Baptist continued to stay low below the smoky atmosphere contaminated with selfishness and ambition and power. In their worldly aspirations, his disciples got caught up in this upper thermal layer of pride and its dangerous byproducts of criticism and dissatisfaction. Standing tall, they were ready to falsely announce to the world that their leader was the savior who would raise a revolt against Rome. But now, much to their amazement and frustration, John makes a statement in extreme humility that should be echoed by every disciple of Christ.

> To this John replied, "A man can receive only what is given him from heaven. You yourselves can testify that I said, 'I am not the Christ but am sent ahead of him.' The bride belongs to the bridegroom. The friend who attends the bridegroom waits and listens for him, and is full of joy when he hears the bridegroom's voice. That joy is mine, and it is now complete. He must become greater; I must become less."
>
> John 3:27–30

The best man at a wedding receives great honor, but the best man never gets the bride, except maybe in the movies. After the bridegroom takes his bride, the mission of the friend has been fulfilled and he quietly exits the scene, all the while rejoicing in the happiness of those whose union he has promoted and blessed. John now tells his disciples that his joy is fulfilled and completed just like the best man at a friend's wedding. "I've done what I was called to do, now he must become greater and I must become less!"

John the Baptist's life provides many valuable lessons in humility. Those who are true in their discipleship to Christ will not seek honor for themselves. They will be eager to be emptied of self and totally swallowed up with the person of Christ Jesus. They will deny themselves! When God calls a disciple to do a certain work, the Lord may eventually enlist others to carry it further still. But just like John's disciples, many Christians feel that the success of the work depends totally on the first called. Too often, we pridefully fix our attention on the human instead of the divine, resulting in jealousy that actually interferes with God's work. Remember Miriam and Aaron? John knew he had an important supporting role as the best man and he accomplished his mission with great authority and enthusiasm and commitment.

True humility has nothing to do with weakness but everything to do with the confidence to stay low and focus clearly on the environment where the mission can be safely and successfully accomplished for the One who sent us! True disciples of God recognize that it is their responsibility to stay low and daily proclaim just as John did, "Behold the Lamb of God, which taketh away the sin of the world" (John 1:29). Only when we stay low, can we rejoice and say with John the Baptist, "Our joy is now full and complete. Jesus must increase and we must decrease!" It's always and only about Jesus, never ourselves.

What was John the Baptist's great reward for being the greatest man on earth? A television show on his own cable network? A book deal and numerous talk show opportunities and book signings? An interview with Larry King or Oprah? No, but he did get to spend some time in a palace and become the "head" attraction at a royal banquet! What's the key survival lesson? God loves humility and the world hates it. So don't expect a reward on earth—our prize will be in heaven! If this scares or discourages you at all, jump forward a few pages and take a peek at the last survival strategy: "Stay Oriented - Know Where You're Going!"

CHRIST JESUS: THE VERY NATURE OF GOD

He Made Himself Nothing and Humbled Himself as the Lowest Servant!

The perfect One who had the ability and right to stand at the very highest level of existence did just the opposite. Christ's humility modeled God's preferred way of living and Jesus told his disciples: "Take my yoke and learn from me, for I am gentle and humble in heart: and you shall find rest for your souls" (Matthew 11:29). He continuously submitted to his Father's will and fully devoted himself to God's calling. Even as the King of the universe, Jesus put aside his self-interests in order to serve God and others wholeheartedly. Jesus stayed low his entire human life. Ed Young beautifully describes how impossible it should be for anyone to stand tall when we consider the life of Jesus.

> You can't stand beside the cradle of Jesus and be proud. You

> can't stand beside the carpenter bench of Jesus and pump out your chest. You can't stand beside the One who was a friend of prostitutes, tax collectors, and sinners and still be stuck-up. You can't stand beside the cross on Golgotha and remain proud. The Bible tells you that Jesus was rich, but He became poor for your sake. He laid aside all kinds of stuff to put on the garment of a servant. And that is what you must do.[26]

So when we consider this strategy for survival, Jesus sets the perfect example. He existed as Elohim before his human birth. He existed in the beginning with God the Father who made all things through him. Jesus was God! Yet, he humbled himself and became a servant to all. He emptied and abased himself. He did not exalt himself. Paul describes Christ's attitude of humility to the Philippians and tells us that as his disciples we are to possess this very same spirit and attitude of staying low.

> Do nothing out of selfish ambition or vain conceit, but in humility consider others better than yourselves. Each of you should look not only to your own interests but also to the interests of others. Your attitude should be the same as that of Christ Jesus: Who, being in very nature God, did not consider equality with God something to be grasped, but made himself nothing, taking the very nature of a servant, being made in human likeness. And being found in appearance as a man, he humbled himself and became obedient to death–even death on a cross!
>
> Philippians 2:3–8

During the last night he was to spend with the apostles, Jesus chose a lesson of extreme service that he would leave with them as one of his last object lessons: a final lesson in humility that would burn in the disciples' hearts and minds forever. What was this important lesson Jesus taught them on that last night? Jesus went even further than John the Baptist's illustration about the lowliness of loosening the straps of the sandals. Not only did he do that, the Savior of the world removed those dirty and worn out sandals and washed his disciples' grimy and smelly feet! The very same hands that created all the galaxies of the universe now took each filthy foot and tenderly washed away all traces of dirt and road grime. Fingers that formed the foundations of the world now dried ugly, disgusting toes. What could be lower? No doubt the disciples looked with shock into eyes that simply looked humbly back in love at each amazed follower.

Jesus performed a service for the disciples that was the duty of the lowest servant of the household–an act of service that was despised by all others. The lowest slave was subject to everyone else because to be the lowest servant was to be looked upon with disdain from all others, even other slaves. Jesus taught a clear message. The next time we are asked to do something we feel to be beneath us, something that makes us feel small, we need to do it. We must come to see that only the servant who stays low will be lifted up. After washing their feet, Jesus asked his disciples, "Do you know what I have done for you?" (John 13:12). Apparently they had no clue, so he explained: "I have set you an example that you should wash one another's feet" (John 13:15). Peter eventually remembered his Master's example as echoed in his words and forever recorded in God's Word.

To Jesus, greatness came from serving–giving of himself to help God and others. Jesus came as a servant and did exactly what he told his disciples to do: He denied himself, he picked up and carried his cross, and he followed exactly where his Father led him! In his darkest hour with the sins and pains of the entire world waiting for him on the cross, Jesus prayed, "Father if you are willing, take this cup from me; yet not my will, but yours be done." So in obedience to the One who sent him, the crowning moment of his human life occurred when the world, led by its prideful evil master, lifted him up on a wooden cross in order to defeat him with the ultimate humiliation; yet in the final act of staying low, Jesus forever won the victory!

It really is my choice to be humble or proud. Christ makes the statement several times: "Be humble or be made humble!" If we humble ourselves, God will exalt us as his disciples; if we exalt ourselves, God will eventually bring us back to reality. But we can avoid a lot of pain if we do it before God does. Why do you suppose Jesus chose humility as one of his final lessons to his disciples? Because humility would be absolutely crucial for their survival.

> The greatest among you will be your servant. For whoever exalts himself will be humbled and whoever humbles himself will be exalted.
>
> Matthew 23:11–12

Humility's role in every believer's life cannot be overemphasized. It's the foundational attitude that every act of service in the Christian life must rest on since it's the true cost of discipleship! We can stay low or we can foolishly stand up into the toxic environment of sin and the world. Our better choice remains the same as the firefighters who instinctively stay low to survive and successfully accomplish their mission. As Christians, staying low is the only place where we effectively serve and survive!

STRATEGY 7

STAY ON THE LINE!

It's All About Being Connected

Firefighters pull a hoseline off the fire engine and then carefully and courageously extend it into a burning building to attack the growing fire. The line stays securely attached to the fire engine because that's the source of water being pumped to them at a high pressure through the strong and durable hose to extinguish the fire. Training and experience teach the firefighters to stay low on their hands and knees and stay together, especially when pulling their hoseline into the fire. Veteran firefighters stress how important it is to not only keep contact with team members but also with the hoseline. As long as crews stay on that hoseline with the nozzle open, they have water for protection from the heat of the enemy and it usually keeps them out of trouble. Working as a team, firefighters use the hoseline as a powerful offensive weapon to extinguish the fire and accomplish their mission.

But if something goes terribly wrong and the firefighters get in trouble, the hoseline provides an effective defensive weapon as long as they keep holding on to it. Their hoseline always provides a way out–back to the source of the water and safety. Now it really serves as a lifeline! Firefighters just have to follow their hoseline and it will lead them out of danger. In bad conditions, if firefighters get off the hoseline, they've lost their lifeline and put themselves at great risk! If they lay their line down in a hostile and dark environment and let go, they may never find it again. And they may never find their way out of the inferno. Chances are they may not survive!

Yet time after time, when conditions in a burning structure deteriorate, firefighters leave their lifelines and perish. After investigations into the loss of firefighters' lives at structure fires, NIOSH consistently makes three recommendations as part of their Firefighter Fatality Investigation Reports: (1) fire departments should always ensure that a hoseline is in place; (2) firefighters should follow a hoseline when entering or exiting a smoke-filled structure; and (3) refresher training must be provided to reinforce these survival procedures. Klaene and Sanders stress in their highly regarded book on structural fire fighting: "The hoseline is used as the lifeline to safety. Members should stay within range of this protective line, not only for fire suppression purposes but also as a means of finding the stairway in heavy smoke conditions."[1] Then the simple question is: why would firefighters ever leave the security of their hoseline if it puts their lives in jeopardy?

As Christians, maybe we should ask ourselves that same question. We have an eternal lifeline in the person of the Lord Jesus Christ. And yet, when we wander away from that Lifeline, we place our spiritual lives in great jeopardy and reduce our chances of spiritual survival. If that happens, then how can we ever expect to accomplish our mission of knowing God and making him known on the road to eternity? We expose ourselves and sometimes others to the ever-dangerous environment we live in and become fruitless and lost. Our Living Water can and will extinguish all the fires of the enemy, but he instructs his firefighters to stay on the line! "Apart from me," says the Lifeline, "you can do nothing and you will fail miserably on your own, so stay on the Line!"

Defensively, we are doomed to be lost forever without Christ's lifeline providing eternal security on the path to life. If we separate from him when we get into trouble, we can't survive for long! But if we stay in him and abide in him, which essentially means staying connected, we have the refuge of our eternal Savior. How do we maintain our connection and follow him to safety? Ray Stedman answers this question about staying on the Line:

> Our responsibility is to remain in Jesus. That means following Him, staying close to Him, talking with Him daily, reading His Word, doing His word, obeying His commands, and worshiping Him. These are the disciplines of the Christian life. As Christians, we are called to discipline our lives. That means building habits that bring us closer to Jesus, while doing away with those habits and sins that hinder our relationship with Him. The more we practice these disciplines, the closer we grow to Jesus, and the more consistently we remain in Him.[2]

THE LAST WALK IN THE VINEYARD
It's all About Being Connected!

Picture the Savior of the world as he faces the final few hours of his human life and prepares for the pain and suffering of the cross awaiting him at Calvary the next day. High drama and intrigue abound that night in an upper room in Jerusalem among all those who sit with him around the table at what has become known as the Last Supper. As he looks around the room, Jesus studies all the characters involved in this scene on the cosmic stage of his final night: the eleven believing disciples who love him; Judas, swayed by evil desires and deceived and consumed by an unseen dark force; and the powerful invisible enemy who loves only himself.

Only Jesus fully understands what's going on and he knows this final act was lovingly and sovereignly scripted long ago in eternity. Jesus identifies his betrayer and removes the non-believer Judas from their midst. "What you're going to do, do quickly!" It's the last divine command Judas will ever obey and Satan leaves with him to make sure his pawn succeeds! The Apostle John retrospectively reminds us of the unsuspecting attitudes of Jesus' eleven friends still reclining at the table, "but no one at the meal understood."

The actions and words of their loving leader in the upper room confuse and puzzle his closest friends who have followed him for three years. Jesus has washed their feet and talked about going home to his Father without them. "My Father is calling me home so I'm only going to be with you a little longer. Where I'm going you can't come." How can that be? What's Jesus saying? "I'm leaving you and where I am going, you cannot follow now, but you will follow later."

Jesus knows he is going to be briefly separated from his Holy Lifeline when he dies the next day. In his heart, Jesus wonders if the broken connection can possibly be avoided. It's not the brutal physical abuse he will have to endure or even the humiliating death itself, it's the first and last silent absence of his Father and the face-to-face encounter with all the horrible, vile, and despicable sins of the entire world that greatly trouble him. "Father take this cup from me?...Father?...Is there another way?...Father?...Not My will but yours My Father!"

Now he's down to his eleven most intimate and loving disciples who have no earthly idea that they will soon carry on the greatest ministry in the history of the entire universe with the help of Jesus' promise. "I will not leave you as orphans; I will come to you. Before long, the world will not see me anymore, but you will see me. Because I live, you also will live. On that day you will realize that I am in my Father, and you are in me, and I am in you" (John 14:18–20). They have no idea at all of the connection he's talking about. Unfortunately, too many Christians today don't get that survival message either!

Throughout the fourteenth chapter of his gospel, John faithfully records that Christ comforts his perplexed disciples with some final teachings of hope before his imminent arrest and crucifixion. "But the Counselor, the Holy Spirit, whom the Father will send in my name, will teach you all things and will remind you of everything I have said to you" (John 14:26). David Harsha captures the classic beauty and importance of those last loving words spoken to best friends in the intimacy of the upper room.

> And while the last words of the great and good are carefully treasured in the mind by surviving friends, should not the dying words of the Lord Jesus be much more deeply engraved in the hearts of His followers?...Let

> us listen with heartfelt joy to those tones of more than human tenderness and love, which fall from His lips in that upper room at Jerusalem, while the eleven disciples are gathered around Him. In that outpouring of His heart He there speaks of the deep mysteries of the glorious gospel–tells His sorrowing friends that He is now glorified, and that God is glorified in Him–reminds them of His sudden departure–commands them to love one another–gives them of His peace–promises them His Holy Spirit–assures them He is going to prepare a place for them in those "many mansions" in His Father's house; and that He will come again to receive them home to glory.[3]

As we come to the end of John chapter 14, Jesus tells his disciples, "Come now; let us leave" (John 14:31). Many commentators believe that the Lord and his followers then leave the upper room in the southwest corner of the old city of Jerusalem and begin a stroll up to Gethsemane's garden on the Mount of Olives as Jesus continues to teach. On their way out of the city, they probably pass his Father's house one last time. Some scholars even speculate that before leaving the city that fateful night, Jesus may have even stopped at the temple one last time to teach and pray.

We do know that this is Passover season, which means the small band of friends walked under a full moon on a familiar route that most likely took them across the Tyropoeon Valley, which separated the Temple from the rest of the city, around the walls of Jerusalem, into the Kidron Valley, up over a brook and then eventually into the garden sanctuary at the foot of the Mount of Olives. They've taken this walk to one of Jesus' favorite spots many times before but this special night will forever shine in the memories of his disciples.

With time running out and eternal destiny bearing down on him, the Lord gives some final everlasting instructions to his disciples on how they can maintain fellowship and fruitfulness in the difficult days that they unknowingly face. In the days to come, the nature of the relationship between Christ and his followers will change from physical to spiritual so Jesus paints a picture of unity–the closest kind of connection anyone can possibly imagine. Jesus says that even though he's physically stepping off the world's stage for a while, it's possible—yes, even necessary for survival—to experience an intimate relationship with him and through him with the God of all eternity. Jesus speaks these survival words to his disciples during their last hours together, underlining their extreme importance.

> I am the Real Vine and my Father is the Farmer. He cuts off every branch of me that doesn't bear grapes. And every branch that is grape-bearing he prunes back so it will bear even more. You are already pruned back by the message I have spoken. Live in me. Make your home in me just as I do in you. In the same way that a branch can't bear grapes by itself but only by being joined to the vine, you can't bear fruit unless you are joined with me. I am the Vine, you are the branches. When you're joined with me and I with you, the relation intimate and organic, the harvest is sure to be abundant. Separated, you can't produce a thing. Anyone who separates from me is deadwood, gathered up and thrown on the bonfire.
>
> John 15:1–6 (MSG)

Even though he is leaving these disciples, Jesus knows they will remain connected to him through an amazing and mysterious link. But how can Jesus explain this spiritual relationship that has yet to occur in such a way these mere men might possibly grasp? In all likelihood, on the way to Gethsemane, they pass through one of the numerous vineyards that grew around Jerusalem. So, the Lord gives them an illustration they can completely understand and never forget. Can you visualize Jesus stopping and squatting down to pick up a grapevine to illustrate the importance of staying connected to him as their eternal lifeline?

What would a dying man tell his best friends? Time is so short that every word must count and each has immense significance. Jesus tells them he is the true vine, believers are his branches, and his Father is the vine-keeper. The Savior uses a figure of speech that the apostles must have been quite familiar with because the grapevine grew extensively throughout Palestine. Living in the first century agricultural society of Israel, they quickly understand the viticulture imagery but slowly grasp the spiritually significant application that God incarnate is making.

The illustration of a grapevine depicts an intimate divine union with its branches. The disciples will be personally intertwined and organically connected to Jesus Christ, just like a branch to a vine. To stay alive and productive, branches can obtain their nutrients and water only through the vine. It's the branch's only source of life! When a green, vibrant branch gets separated from the vine, it stops growing, slowly begins to die, turns brown, and eventually becomes deadwood that will absolutely never produce fruit of any kind.

The chief value of the vine lies in its fruit-bearing branches and as Jesus will explain, if a branch is cut-off it can do nothing in the same way that none of us can accomplish any spiritual good on our own, because life in the vine is a life of utter dependence and obedience to God. Absolute, unalterable dependence upon God alone stands as the essence of Christianity. Andrew Murray, a prolific Christian author in the late 1800s and early 1900s, wrote about the "Absolute Surrender" the branches must make to the Vine by paraphrasing John 15:5.

> I am the Vine; I will receive you. I will draw you to Myself; I will bless you. I will strengthen you; I will fill you with My Spirit. I, the vine, have taken you to be My branches. I have given Myself utterly to you; children, give yourselves utterly to Me. I have surrendered Myself as God absolutely to you. I became man and died for you that I might be entirely yours. Come and surrender yourselves entirely to be Mine.[4]

To Christ's disciples and all the Israelites, the vine was an essential part of their history, their identity, and in particular, their unique relation with the living God. In the more historical and religious sense, Israel had been likened to a "vine" again and again in the

Old Testament. The people of Israel saw themselves as the special vine chosen by God and rooted in him. As a matter of fact, the vine had actually become the symbol of the nation of Israel. As Jews, the disciples undoubtedly recognized the immense significance of the comparison.

One of the glories of the Temple in Jerusalem was the great golden vine representing Israel with its branches trailing down from a great height and growing above the curtain at the entrance of the Holy Place. This gigantic gold grapevine had grapes that Jewish historian Josephus wrote were the height of a man. Wealthy citizens reportedly brought gold to be crafted and added to the vine by metal workers to the ever-growing vine (m. Middoth 3:8).[5] During the revolt against Rome (AD 68–70) the Jews even minted coins that bore the vine symbol.

In fact, throughout the Hebrew Scriptures we see the imagery of the vine portrayed several times. In Psalm 80:8 the Psalmist sings, "You brought a vine out of Egypt; you drove out the nations and planted it." Israel had been taken as a vine out of Egypt and planted in a foreign place in order to bear fruit for God. The prophet Isaiah likens the nation Israel to a vineyard: "The vineyard of the Lord Almighty is the house of Israel, and the men of Judah are the garden of his delight" (Isaiah 5:7). "I had planted you like a choice vine of sound and reliable stocks," says God's prophet, Jeremiah (Jeremiah 2:21), as a message to Israel. According to Hosea, "Israel was a spreading vine" (Hosea 10:1). Later in Psalm 80, the psalmist continues, "Return to us, O God Almighty! Look down from heaven and see! Watch over this vine, the root your right hand has planted, the son you have raised up for yourself. Your vine is cut down, it is burned with fire; at your rebuke your people perish. Let your hand rest on the man at your right hand, the son of man you have raised up for yourself" (Psalm 80:14–17). When Jesus comes along in John 15 saying, "I am the true vine," he is making the ultimate proclamation that "I am truly the Messiah!"

Even though Israel was indeed the vine of God's own planting and he had done everything to cultivate the fruit and ensure a rich and bountiful harvest, the vineyard of Israel proved to be a terrible disappointment to God. The covenant people more often than not failed to bear good fruit, and story after story tells of the severe pruning of its branches. Isaiah's "Song of the Vineyard" sings of the Father's dedicated love for his people and his careful attention, detail, and devotion to his vineyard. But instead of good fruit, all he got was sour grapes!

> I will sing for the one I love a song about his vineyard: My loved one had a vineyard on a fertile hillside. He dug it up and cleared it of stones and planted it with the choicest vines. He built a watchtower in it and cut out a winepress as well. Then he looked for a crop of good grapes, but it yielded only bad fruit. Now you dwellers in Jerusalem and men of Judah, judge between me and my vineyard. What more could have been done for my vineyard than I have done for it? When I looked for good grapes, why did it yield only bad?
>
> Isaiah 5:1–4

"MY FATHER IS THE GARDNER!"
It's His Vineyard!

Just as firefighters on the fireground, believers need to understand and accept the lines of authority and communication to survive on their battlegrounds. And now Jesus clarifies the divine chain of command: He is the vine, his Father is the vinedresser, and you and I as believers are the branches. We receive our commands from the Father who owns the vineyard and personally tends the farm. He sustains us in everything we do in and through him. The vinedresser is the one who cares for the vines and all the branches in a vineyard. Jesus identifies his Father as the vinedresser–the "Husbandman." The Old Testament represents the Father as the Proprietor of the vine called Israel, but here Jesus describes him as the Husbandman, the One who lovingly cares for the True Vine and its branches.

God the Father was caring for the Son while he walked the face of the earth. In the Old Testament, Isaiah prophesied that the

Messiah would grow up before the Father as a tender plant and as a root out of the dry ground. "A shoot will come from the stump of Jesse; from his roots a Branch will bear fruit. The Spirit of the Lord will rest on him - the Spirit of wisdom and understanding, the Spirit of counsel and of power, the Spirit of knowledge and of the fear of the Lord" (Isaiah 11:1). Think how often the Father intervened to protect Jesus from the enemy who slithered around trying to rip the vine apart and destroy those believers connected to the vine. How jealously and closely did the Father watch over him who "grew up before him like a tender shoot, and like a root out of dry ground"? (Isaiah 53:2).

In the same way, Jesus says that the Father also personally takes care of all believers–the branches of the Living Vine! The Father must care a great deal about his vineyard since he paid such an extreme price for his branches—nothing less than the precious blood of his only Son. Keeping that in mind, remember that only believers can grow in this beautiful vineyard!

As the watchful Husbandman, God lets nothing escape his relentless attention. Just as a good gardener daily observes the condition of each branch of the vine, nourishing, watering, and pruning as the circumstances arise, the divine Farmer constantly monitors the needs and welfare of those believers who are joined to Christ. Contrary to the general view held by the Jews of that time that God was some far off deity not involved with the day to day lives of his people, Jesus says that his Father gives intimate care and personal attention to his vineyard.

Notice also that the Caretaker does not assign to others the task of caring for the vine and its branches because they are so very precious to him. Since he has such a vital interest in his vineyard, he takes care of the branches himself through the Vine. He faithfully and personally tends to his vineyard! Constantly occupied with the needs and welfare of those who are joined to his Son, the Father jealously keeps his vineyard and nothing escapes his protective attention.

As the vineyard owner, God is interested in only one thing–fruit. God the Father is the vinedresser and he wants more than just a little fruit, he desires abundant fruit. If a branch is bearing limited fruit, he cleanses it and lifts it up so it will bear even more fruit. He will not accept cheap substitutes or bad fruit and especially no fruit!

"I AM THE REAL THING!"
Accept no Substitutes!

Over the previous three years of his public ministry, Jesus made six emphatic and divine "I am" statements attached to certain illustrations, highlighting very important aspects of his person and ministry: "I am the Bread of Life," "I am the Light of the world," "I am the Door," "I am the Good Shepherd," "I am the Resurrection and the Life," and, "I am the Way, the Truth, and the Life." The Jewish hearers of these "I am" statements immediately recognized their significance and recalled God's personal words to Moses, "I AM WHO I AM. This is what you are to say to the Israelites: 'I AM has sent me to you'" (Exodus 3:14).

Now Jesus makes his last and final "I am" statement regarding who he is. "I am the true vine...I am the vine; you are the branches..." (John 15:1, 5). On the last night of his earthly life and in the serene setting of a vineyard under a full moon, he addresses only the eleven apostles - his most loyal followers. Judas has already departed from their midst with his evil leader. Now Christ speaks this message not to unsaved people, not to a mixed audience, not to mere professors of faith, but to confirmed and committed believers only–his true disciples.

With his believers filled with grief and bewildered at the terrible thought of losing their beloved leader, Jesus takes them to the next level of their relationship–true discipleship! He has slowly weeded out those who would not deny themselves, pick up their crosses, and follow him. Now he gives them the final secret of how to be disciples. They must connect to him and then stay connected. Jesus tells the disciples, "I am the true vine that you must be joined to." Jesus says that he is the real thing. He is the authentic and genuine vine! The people of Israel saw themselves as the vine chosen and rooted in God, but now Christ claims to be the true vine, the perfect fruit of Israel.

All these "I am" sayings by Christ recorded in John's Gospel loudly echo God's personal name, just as he first disclosed it to Moses at the burning bush. But this time "I AM" personally comes in the flesh to make God the Father known.

> The Word became flesh and made his dwelling among us. We have seen his glory, the glory of the One and Only, who came from the Father, full of grace and truth...For the law was given through Moses; grace and truth came through Jesus Christ. No one has ever seen God, but God the One and Only, who is at the Father's side, has made him known.
>
> John 1:14, 17–18

As the one true vine, Jesus physically represents the one true God.

If we look at the wider context of the "I am" sayings in John, we will find that Jesus' "I am" statements quickly landed him in serious trouble because this "ordinary" man was actually proclaiming to be God–"I AM WHO I AM!" His followers were most likely thrilled hearing the inspired words with the infinitely divine complexity they inferred, but detractors, especially the Jewish leaders, were highly offended and irate at the extreme blasphemy of Jesus! The Jews knew exactly what he was saying! To any serious Israelite, these words rang out as highly provocative and inflammatory but to the Jewish leaders, his words demanded death! "'Believe me,' said Jesus, 'I am who I am before Abraham was anything.' That did it–pushed them over the edge. They picked up rocks to throw at him" (John 8:57–58, MSG).

For three years, Jesus had illustrated the absolute necessity of holding on to his Lifeline–his Father in heaven. If the secret to the daily life of the Son of God was his constant fellowship and divine connection with his Father, how much more should we cling to the Son? While he walked as a human on this planet, the Creator of the universe totally and continually submitted to the will of his Father.

> So Jesus said, "when you have lifted up the Son of Man, then you will know that I am the one I claim to be and that I can do nothing on my own but speak just what the Father has taught me. The one who sent me is with me; he has not left me alone, for I always do what pleases him."
>
> John 8:28–29

The branches are to surrender themselves completely to the vine just as the Son of God absolutely surrendered himself to his Father's will.

ABIDING!

Never Leave Your Line!

> Abide in Me, and I in you. As the branch cannot bear fruit of itself unless it abides in the vine, so neither can you unless you abide in Me. I am the vine, you are the branches; he who abides in Me and I in him, he bears much fruit, for apart from Me you can do nothing.
>
> John 15:4–5 (NASB)

The word "abide" (or "remain" depending on which translation you read) is found eleven times in this short passage of only seventeen verses in John 15. It means to stay connected or using fire service terminology–to stay on the line! This is a key word in John's theology and the vital term in our survival strategy. Not only is it used eleven times in these verses but John, through the Holy Spirit, also uses it forty times throughout his gospel and twenty-seven times in his epistles. Can it be any clearer that God desires Christians to grow in an ever-deepening relationship or intimate connection with him?

Abiding in Christ means being true disciples–true followers and representatives. Phillip asks Jesus in the upper room at the Last Supper, "Lord show us the Father and that will be enough." And the Savior of the world replies to his disciple: "Anyone who has seen me has seen the Father" (John 14:8–9). When we stay securely and spiritually connected to our Lifeline, we can confidently say as true disciples of the One and Only, "Anyone who has seen us has seen the Son!" But apart from him, the only life that can be seen is our own.

To "abide," "dwell," "remain," or "stay" in Christ always refers to the perseverance of close fellowship with our heavenly Lifeline. To abide in Christ signifies the constant connection of our hearts, souls, and spirits with him as branches who must absolutely depend on our one true Vine. We abide in Christ only when we merge our will into his will and we allow God's will to prevail over our own will in every aspect of our life. Our spiritual survival requires his will to be our wills, his thoughts to be our thoughts, his ways to be our ways. That's staying on the line! Abiding equals discipleship, which results in survival. We must remain inseparably linked to Christ as the unbroken source and sustainer of our lives. J. C Ryle wonderfully paraphrases Jesus' life-changing message. "Cling to Me. Stick fast to me. Get nearer and nearer to Me. Roll every burden on Me. Cast your weight on Me. Never let go your hold on Me for a moment."[6]

Abiding means growing "much" fruit–being fruitful as a true disciple. The only way we can do this is by staying on the line because abiding in Christ is absolutely essential for bearing "much fruit." But, as we'll see, not being fruitful results in some fiery consequences for believers. Jesus says the purpose of abiding in Christ and producing a large amount of fruit is to bring great glory to the Father, thereby demonstrating our discipleship. "My true disciples produce much fruit. This brings great glory to my Father" (John 15:8, NLT). Ultimately, our faith in Christ should lead us into a place of discipleship, into a place where we completely deny ourselves and are willing to pick up our crosses and follow him whenever and wherever he leads at whatever cost. That's staying on the line!

Abiding in Christ as disciples requires absolute obedience to the Word of God. "Then Jesus said to those Jews who believed Him, 'If you abide in My word, you are My disciples indeed'" (John 8:31, NKJV). Notice that these particular Jews are already believers and Jesus gives them the key to being disciples. The difference between a believer and a disciple is simple: a true follower abides in God's Word! How important is this? Listen carefully to what Jesus tells those believers who become his true disciples: "Then you will know the truth, and the truth will set you free" (John 8:32).

A Christian who does not know and abide in God's Word remains just a believer. But as disciples, we daily stay on the Line by studying, learning, and obeying the life sustaining Word of God. It strengthens our grip to help us hold on to the Line when trouble strikes! This is a primary requirement for his disciples! "The words that I have spoken to you are spirit and they are life" (John 6:63). And how powerful and secure are his words? "The Message is as true among you today as when you first heard it. It doesn't diminish or weaken over time. It's the same all over the world. The Message bears fruit and gets larger and stronger, just as it has in you" (Colossians 1:6, MSG).

YOU ARE THE BRANCHES!

Real Disciples are Branches that Bear Fruit!

The Lord Jesus twice makes the statement "I am the vine." First he links himself with the Father–the Husbandman. Then he connects himself with his true believers–the branches! When the Lord says, "You are the branches," in John 15, he directly addresses the eleven true disciples and thereby all true believers from that moment on. "Every branch in Me..." There is probably no other form of expression that indicates a believer more emphatically and explicitly than, "in Me," "in Him," or "in Christ." These terms don't apply to any but the children of God. "Therefore, if anyone is in Christ, he is a new creation; the old has gone, the new has come!" (2 Corinthians 5:17). Keeping this in mind, it seems very evident that Christ is not here addressing a mixed audience with some combination of true believers and those who were merely professors, like Judas. He's not speaking to the original twelve–Judas has left to serve his real master and do his evil deeds!

Christ's relationship to the branches and ours to him is such that he is the vine, the source of our life, our strength, and our salvation. Therefore, we depend on him as our total spiritual support for everything, just as the branch depends on its vine for everything. Since every Christian is a branch of the Living Vine with the divine purpose of bearing fruit, more fruit, and much fruit, Christ makes it very clear that every branch in him is accountable and expected to bear quality fruit in great quantity.

But, Jesus says that his followers are like two kinds of branches: fruit bearing and non-fruit bearing. Some of his followers are vibrant fruit-bearing branches, while others are totally useless because they bear little or no fruit. Those who stay on the line and bear fruit are pruned, enabling them to become even more fruitful. Those believers who let go of their lifeline do not produce any fruit at all and risk not surviving in a hostile spiritual environment.

YOU'RE FRUITFUL ONLY WHEN YOU STAY ON THE LINE!

Producing a Fruitful Harvest!

At this point, when Jesus declares, "I appointed you to go and bear fruit–fruit that will last" (John 15:16), all branches of the true Vine must ask a couple of questions in response. "What exactly is this fruit that God is expecting from us?" and "What kind of fruit will last for eternity?" I used to believe that Christ was primarily speaking about winning souls as the fruit of his branches. Even though that's certainly a spiritually tasteful element of fruit, it's so much more than that. It goes to the very heart of discipleship.

A great place to start is in Galatians 5:22 where the Apostle Paul says, "The fruit of the Spirit is love, joy, peace, patience, kindness, goodness, faithfulness, gentleness, and self-control." As branches of the one true Vine, do we continually see clusters of these nine eternal fruit being produced in our lives? Notice especially during the last few hours of his life, Jesus emphasizes three significant life fruit that he abundantly produced in his own human life. Christ exhorts his disciples to bear the fruit of a godly character, mirroring his very life's image–love, joy, and peace! "My command is this: Love each other as I have loved you" (John 15:12). He says it again! "This is my command: Love each other" (John 15:17). "I have told you this so that my joy may be in you and that your joy may be complete" (John 15:11). "Peace I leave you; my peace I give you..." (John 14:27). "I have told you these things that you may have peace..." (John 16:33).

But it's not simply witnessing or just the fruit of the Spirit emphasizing love, joy, and peace. If you really think about it, the fruit that Jesus is referring to here is essentially Christlikeness–his divine character reproduced in us every day as his children. The fruit that Jesus speaks of relates back to our survival strategy of staying oriented to where we are. It's the fruit or evidence of daily discipleship—a real, visible, living, working faith! As children of light, it is the fruit produced in our holy walk to eternity that pleases God when we confess the name of Christ personally, publicly, boldly, and unashamedly before the entire world, every step of the way. "For you were once darkness, but now you are light in the Lord. Live as children of light (for the fruit of the light consists in all goodness, righteousness and truth) and find out what pleases the Lord" (Ephesians 5:8–10).

Since branches on a grapevine grow rapidly, they must be tended to continually and carefully, which requires pruning on a regular basis. The farmer of the vineyard bears the responsibility to cut off the branches that bear no fruit because they rob energy and life from the fruit-bearing branches. Jesus clearly teaches that this is what the Father will do in our lives to make us more fruitful. Pruning can be simple or it can be a drastic process. And in the same way that the fruit-producing branch is pruned so that it will produce even more fruit, disciples are often put through the "pruning" of testing, hardship, and suffering in order to make them even more mature, faithful, and productive. I think Bruce Wilkinson in his definitive book on John 15, *Secrets of the Vine*, describes pruning's value extremely well.

> That's why the vinedresser cuts away unnecessary shoots, no matter how vigorous, because a vineyard's only purpose is...grapes. In fact, pruning is a grower's single most important technique for ensuring a plentiful harvest. For the Christian, rampant growth represents all those preoccupations and priorities in our lives that, while not wrong,

are keeping us from more significant ministry for God. Without pruning, growing Christians will only be able to live up to a fraction of their potential.[7]

The heavenly Vinedresser will lovingly and tenderly pick the branches up, wash them off, and draw them to himself so he can prune them as necessary. Remember, his purpose for his vineyard is the spiritual fruit of good works that bring him glory! The vinedresser carefully snips away all the shoots and other things that gather on the fruit-bearing branches and tend to sap the strength of the vine and reduce the fruit-bearing capability of the other branches. Any fruit in our lives that does not bring God glory is basically useless. God will drastically cut back our lives in a holy cleansing process because pruning removes dirt, spider webs, decayed and damaged leaves, and any fungus that may have collected. Staying on the line in terrible and stressing conditions with spiritual fires raging around us is not always easy or comfortable, but "Blessed is the man who perseveres under trial, because when he has stood the test, he will receive the crown of life that God has promised to those who love him" (James 1:12).

Why would a loving God prune or allow suffering? Considering the eternal Husbandman forever sees the big picture of the entire vineyard and every branch connected to the vine, he at all times has our best interests in mind, just as Paul tells the Romans, "And we know that in all things God works for the good of those who love him, who have been called according to his purpose" (Romans 8:28). "All things" represents the painful as well as the pleasant. Pruning makes the whole plant healthy so God's ultimate purpose may be accomplished. "Not only so, but we also rejoice in our sufferings, because we know that suffering produces perseverance; perseverance, character; and character, hope. And hope does not disappoint us, because God has poured out his love into our hearts by the Holy Spirit, whom he has given us" (Romans 5:3–5). Comparing our pruning in this world to the joy of God's "Afterward," Charles Spurgeon described our fruit.

See, then, the happy estate of a Christian! He has his best

> things last, and he therefore in this world receives his worst things first. But even his worst things are "afterward" good things, harsh ploughings yielding joyful harvest. Even now he grows rich by his losses, he rises by his falls, he lives by his dying, and becomes full by being emptied; if, then, his grievous afflictions yield him so much peaceable fruit in this life, what shall be the full vintage of joy "afterwards" in heaven?[8]

Staying on the line is easy in good times but much more difficult with conflagrations raging all around you. Our survival requires us to hang on tightly to the lifeline in the most difficult of times because that's our connection to life when we need it most! Every Christian experiences the pruning process at one time or another, but our loving Father's discipline in our lives produces more fruit, even though the cutting process is not usually pleasant. As a matter of fact, it can be downright painful! "All discipline for the moment seems not to be joyful, but sorrowful; yet to those who have been trained by it, afterwards it yields the peaceful fruit of righteousness" (Hebrews 12:11, NASB).

YOU'RE A FRUITLESS BRANCH WHEN YOU LET GO OF YOUR LIFELINE

No Connection, No Fruit!

There exists significant disagreement among Bible teachers concerning fruitless branches here in John 15. Are these good branches gone bad, bad branches disguised as good branches, or just good branches not staying on the line? A common practice of viticulture then and now is the pruning and burning of unproductive branches. As we've seen, this passage's application of fruitless branches to unproductive believers can be easily seen. But the key questions remain. Who is Jesus talking about and what happens to them? Keeping in mind the context and audience of Jesus' last remarks here in John 15, let's look carefully at his life changing warning of what happens when we don't stay on the line.

Jesus paints a picture of the worthless branches being "cast out," "withered," "gathered," "thrown into a fire," and "burned." None of these actions represents good news for the fruitless branches. Some commentators suggest that since Jesus is actually comparing branches to believers, then unfruitful believers must lose their salvation and get cast into the lake of fire and spend eternity in hell and burn in judgment with unbelievers. Is it possible the Savior is telling his closest followers and most intimate disciples that if they don't produce fruit, they will be condemned to hell?

This view certainly contradicts Jesus' earlier words. "My sheep listen to my voice; I know them, and they follow me. I give them eternal life, and they shall never perish; no one can snatch them out of my hand. My Father, who has given them to me, is greater than all; no one can snatch them out of my Father's hand. I and the Father are one" (John 10:27–30). It also seems to be an impossible view in Paul's mind. "For I am convinced that neither death nor life, neither angels nor demons, neither the present nor the future, nor any powers, neither height nor depth, nor anything else in all creation, will be able to separate us from the love of God that is in Christ Jesus our Lord" (Romans 8:38–39). Scripture does indicate there are serious consequences for what believers do with their lives but absolutely never the loss of salvation or hell!

A significant number of conservative commentators and Bible scholars believe that in this passage Jesus addresses unfruitful believers who prove that they are merely professors only and not truly believers. This view seems to be the most prevalent among scholars. The Father removes these useless branches, and they ultimately spend eternity in hell with all the other non-believers. These scholars nominate Judas to serve as the poster boy of the ones who profess to believe, yet by their actions, prove otherwise. In fact, these experts get no argument from me that Judas was strictly a non-believing professor, even though for a time he closely followed Christ. I have no doubt of his final judgment or, for that matter, anyone who does not truly accept Jesus Christ as Lord and Savior.

However, in the setting of John 15, Judas has already left the scene and is not present when Jesus declares the consequences of fruitless branches to his real disciples. So keeping that in mind and understanding there are no false professors present to hear Jesus give the warning, to whom is he talking? Some commentators express the belief that these unfruitful branches are just believers who experience temporal judgment and that here in John 15:5–6, Jesus is still talking to and about his branches–his believers. He has not switched to another subject. He's addressing only his closest friends—those disciples whom he has just proclaimed to be clean. "You are already clean because of the word I have spoken to you" (John 15:3). So the Lord again compares branches to real believers, only this time they are producing bad fruit or no fruit at all, just like Christians whose faith consists of profession without daily practice and empty words without heavenly deeds.

Christ describes Christians who are useless branches—all leaves and no fruit! The NIV's translation of verse 6 of John 15 may help: "If anyone does not remain in me, he is *like* a branch that is thrown away and withers; such branches are picked up, thrown into the fire and burned." The pivotal word is "like." Jesus compares the unfruitful believer to the unfruitful branches that are cut off and burned. It implies that they are about as useful as the branches that are burned because they don't bear any fruit. But it clearly does not say that the believers will be burned in hell. The value of an unfruitful believer's life is as worthless as those branches that are cut off and burned. The fruitless child of God is temporarily cast out of fellowship with God, but not into the Lake of Fire.

This presents a solemn warning for every Christian. As difficult as it is to comprehend, we who are commanded to abide as disciples often fail miserably to do so. When we allow ongoing sin into our lives, we break our personal fellowship with Christ. When we don't stay on the Line, we are in immense danger of being set aside as his witnesses on earth, to bear only that which has no value and absolutely does not bring glory to God. That makes us as useless as branches that do not produce fruit and are cut off the vine and disposed of. Fruitless branches are fruitless believers! Without fruit, Christians produce nothing of worth! Bruce Wilkinson agrees.

> Therefore, I believe we can safely conclude that it's possible to be "in Christ," yet be like that branch that produces

> no fruit for a time. Experience bears this out. If you're like me, you've gone a week or a year living in such a way that you know you didn't bear fruit. I believe that's what Jesus is talking about.[9]

Spiritually, there have been times in my life that I chose to put my hose line down and charge forward or usually just retreat on my own. There was never any doubt in my mind or heart that Jesus Christ was my Lord and Savior and I never directly denied him, but my living was fruitless and barren, rejecting the very nature of God. I was a believer but far from being a disciple. As a boy at summer camp, I had answered his call and happily come to him and because of his grace and mercy, accepted the free gift of salvation with its guarantee of eternal life. For many years I kept the free gift but never denied myself, picked up my cross, and certainly never followed Christ. I knew where my Bible was, but I didn't know God's Word! As an unabiding Christian disconnected from my Lifeline, is it any wonder I never told anyone about him, that I struggled understanding his words, and always wondered why he wasn't listening to me? Worship was usually just a boring requirement but seldom a joyful celebration.

Just as the fruitless branch gets cut off from the vine, the believer who chooses his own path over God's way quickly loses fellowship with Jesus Christ. I was the poster boy of a fruitless branch–not Judas! My eternal destination was known and I loved God, but I was as fruitless and useless as a branch could be! Once we are off our line, we cannot produce fruit at all. My spiritual life was withered and dead. When that happens, God chastens those believers who persist in this willful disobedience. Through discipline and pruning, I discovered real life is so much more than doing my own thing and waiting for heaven, and true discipleship means much more than just believing!

WE WILL BE JUDGED ON HOW WELL WE STAY ON THE LINE!

Good Works, Bad Works, or No Works?

While attending my daughter Melanie's freshmen orientation at Dallas Baptist University (DBU), I heard a challenging talk by one of the school's professors, Jamie Lash. He said that every believer would one day stand before the Judgment Seat of Christ and give account of his or her entire life. He told us that understanding this concept had radically changed his life but unfortunately many Christians remain ignorant of this biblical truth. And just like many believers, I realized I tended to steer clear of any discussion or thought about the judgment of Christians.

To address this significant issue, Jamie Lash coauthored a wonderful book with Rick Howard called *This Was Your Life*. The book's powerful subtitle *"Preparing to Meet God Face to Face"* should bring chills (of either excitement! or concern?) to every believer's heart and soul:

> Our purpose is to bring attention to a truth of incredible power. Nothing in our travels has been so strange as the absence of knowledge and discussion among Christians concerning the Judgment Seat of Christ. Hugh portions of the Church seem almost completely ignorant of one of the most wonderful truths in the Word of God. Understanding the Judgment Seat of Christ has catapulted many great Christians forward in their spiritual growth. George Miller, Amy Carmichael, Charles Finney, Hudson Taylor, General William Booth and Martin Luther are among those who testified to the incredible impact this truth had on their lives.[10]

"For we must all appear before the judgment seat of Christ, that each one may receive what is due him for the things done while in the body, whether good or bad" (2 Corinthians 5:10). This passage should be heart searching for every believer struggling like beat up firefighters in the heat of the battle to stay on the line. Keep in mind that the Judgment Seat of Christ is not a place of punishment, for Christ Jesus took all our punishment for sin. However, it is a place of evaluation where all believers will be assigned a position of service for all eternity. Thus, the eternal stakes are very high, as Lash and Howard fervently point out.

> Although we will live in heaven forever, the Scripture makes no mention of earning rewards after we arrive there. The rewards are for the deeds done "in the body." How we will serve God in heaven forever is being determined by how we live this life! The importance of how we live here and now cannot be overstated.[11]

The Judgment Seat of Christ clarifies the words of Jesus about the branches who either produce fruit or become fruitless "while in the body." The words of the Apostle Paul to the Corinthians will greatly help us put John 15:6 into proper perspective. But how do the words in this verse reflect the consequences of fruit or no fruit? Consider a longer passage from Paul's first letter to the Corinthians that refers to that "Day" of judgment.

> For no one can lay any foundation other than the one already laid, which is Jesus Christ. If any man builds on this foundation using gold, silver, costly stones, wood, hay or straw, his work will be shown for what it is, because the Day will bring it to light. It will be revealed with fire, and the fire will test the quality of each man's work. If what he has built survives, he will receive his reward. If it is burned up, he will suffer loss; he himself will be saved, but only as one escaping through flames.
>
> 1 Corinthians 3:11–15

The only secure foundation is the one that is already laid–Christ Jesus! When we become saved, we begin to build upon this rock solid foundation. Paul says that all believers are building on this foundation either bearing worthwhile, Christ-centered fruit (gold, silver, precious stones) as disciples who abide in him or bearing worthless, human-centered unfruitful behavior, reflecting a life not abiding in Christ (wood, hay, straw). A disciple will build with eternally valuable, divine, and fruitful good works: gold, silver, and precious stones. Or unfortunately, on the other hand, a believer may choose to build on the foundation already laid with a sinful and fruitless lifestyle with valueless works of a human nature that will not endure in heaven: wood, hay, and straw.

The fire that will "test the quality of each man's work" does not refer to the judgment of unbelievers to the eternal damnation fire known as the "Great White Thrown of Judgment" described by John in Revelation 20. It's a different judgment fire that will judge the works of only Christians (good and bad fruit or no fruit at all!), but it will not determine the eternal destination of believers. The unacceptable works of believers are "burned up" but clearly not the believers themselves, because they have already been eternally judged as a result of faith in Christ alone as the foundation built by God.

The fire burns the works of the believers–the assessment of what they did while physically alive on the earth. Compare this with Jesus' words to his disciples in John 15, "Men gather them, and cast them into the fire, and they are burned." Jesus does not say "men gather him and cast him into the fire, and he is burned," as if he would most certainly have said had he been referring to the judgment of an unbeliever. Rather, notice Jesus' use of plural pronouns in relation to what gets burned. The change from singular to plural here is very conspicuous and critical in the determination of the consequences of unfruitfulness. The singular is the believer (unfruitful branch) and the plural are the "things" burned! The "them" and the "they" are the dead works from the one who has been cast forth "as a branch."

Paul, in 1 Corinthians 3, identifies the dead works as being as worthless as "wood, hay, and stubble," and they will not withstand the fire that tests everything built on the foundation of Christ. In his statement, "If any man's work is burned up," Paul uses the very same word Jesus used in John 15:6 for burned up! If believers do not abide in Christ and do not produce works that are divinely fruitful, their earthly works will be consumed in the fire, destroying all the bad works, leaving nothing of value on which to receive eternal rewards in heaven. Fruitless believers' lives in heaven will be limited for all eternity!

However, if the believer's work survives the fire test (gold, silver, and precious stones are typically refined by fire and not destroyed), then a reward will be received in heaven for eternity. The believer's divine fruit did not provide eternal life–that foundation was already built by faith alone in Jesus Christ. Disciples who stay on the line connected to the Living God receive rewards for doing the good works that God has appointed them to do through his Word.

ALWAYS COMMUNICATE!

God Hears His Disciples Who Stay On The Line!

> But if you make yourselves at home with me and my words are at home in you, you can be sure that whatever you ask will be listened to and acted upon. This is how my Father shows who he is–when you produce grapes, when you mature as my disciples.
>
> John 15:7–8 (MSG)

The best evidence of staying on the line and the resulting fruitful life is the impact of answered prayer and direct communications with the Supreme Commander. The more we abide in Christ, the more we want to commune with him in prayer. We cherish those precious moments when we are in his presence, and we linger there because we do not want to leave. Staying on the line makes our communications more effective and productive. Abiding in Christ and his Word results in the confidence of receiving the answers to prayers because abiding connects our hearts, minds, and strengths to the will of God. It is clear that when we stay on the line, our thoughts and desires conform to his and we learn the will of God.

Like the branches of a vine, Christians were designed to bear fruit. But always remember, the branch does not grow the vine.

"No branch can bear fruit by itself." Too many times, Christians try to produce fruit of their own. Even with the best of intentions this will absolutely never work. As foolish sinful branches, we think we can accomplish good works on our own. We try to do it by our own strength, through our own will and on our own terms. Jesus says clearly we can only produce fruit if we abide in him. "Apart from me, you can do nothing," *so stay on the Line!*

Cut off the branch and it withers and dies, but the vine keeps going. But as anyone familiar with horticulture will confirm, if you cut off the vine then the whole plant dies–including all the branches! At Calvary, Satan's plan was to cut off and destroy the True Vine. For the first and last time, the Savior of the world became briefly separated from his Father to take care of the ancient serpent, as God promised back in Genesis 3. Even though the enemy wounded the descendent of Eve, he failed miserably because the Vine ultimately stayed on his eternal Lifeline and securely connected with his Father's will and survived the definitive cosmic battle of all time.

So now in his desperation, the mortally wounded enemy pursues the Vine's branches–us Christians. His goal is to ruin our good fruit, using deception, before the crop ever matures, leaving us barren and useless. Using the world and its evil darkness, he encourages, waters, and fertilizes our own worthless fruit! The serpent is not into pruning because he loves useless and fruitless weeds; then he stands back and hisses that a good god would never prune his followers if he really loves them!

But the loving and living God lifts up fruitless branches and takes away and burns the worthless wood, hay, and stubble–all the valueless crops that are not his. The Vinedresser takes care of all his precious branches but demands quality fruit in great quantity for his everlasting glory. Christians can only accomplish that by staying on the Line!

> And we pray this in order that you may live a life worthy of the Lord and may please him in every way; bearing fruit in every good work, growing in the knowledge of God, being strengthened with all power according to his

glorious might so that you may have great endurance and patience, and joyfully giving thanks to the Father, who has qualified you to share in the inheritance of the saints in the kingdom of light.

Colossians 1:10–12

STRATEGY 8

STAY TOGETHER!

There's Strength in Numbers

You're weighted down with survival gear and wearing your full protective ensemble–boots, turnout pants, coats, gloves, and helmet–and heavy self-contained breathing equipment. Outside your facemask, the atmosphere deteriorates to a dark cloud of choking poisonous gases mixed with super heated particles of soot. As you pull your hoseline to attack a yet unseen enemy, you quickly realize that the room is becoming unbelievably hot with the air temperature just above your head climbing to over 1,000 degrees. You crouch low, hugging the floor where it's somewhat cooler. The powerfully bright beam shining from your specialized heavy-duty flashlight barely penetrates a couple of feet into the pitch-black smoke, revealing what you already know–you can't see! Tightly clutching the hoseline, you sense close contact with your company officer in front of you leading you onward, and you feel a reassuring hand on your shoulder from your partner firefighter right behind you pushing you forward.

In these rapidly deteriorating and increasingly dangerous conditions, there's no better survival strategy and secure feeling than staying together. You enter together and you stay together and when you accomplish your mission, you leave together! Company integrity–keeping the firefighting crew together - stands out as one of the most important keys to firefighter survival. A recent study of all the firefighter deaths during the past twenty years caused by disorientation states that in 100 percent of those fatalities, company integrity was lost and played a significant factor in those firefighters getting lost and not surviving.[1] In their reports on firefighter fatalities, NIOSH consistently recommends that fire departments must ensure constant team continuity during firefighting operations.

> Team continuity relies on some very important key factors: knowing who is on your team and the team leader, staying within visual contact at all times (if visibility is obscured then teams should remain within touch or voice distance of each other), communicating your needs and observations to the team leader, and watching your team members (practice a strong "buddy-care" approach). These key factors help to reduce serious injury or even death resulting from the risks involved in firefighting operations by providing personnel with the added safety net of fellow team members. Company or crew members should enter and exit the environment together.[2]

The larger the emergency, the greater the need for more and more firefighters staying and working together in increasing numbers until the fire is out. More so than all other professions, fire service crews that fail to perform as coordinated teams are eventually doomed to fail. Failure results in excessive damage, poor crew performance, injury, and even death to firefighters and civilians. Sadly, the NIOSH reports can never really measure the actual human side of fatal fires and the resulting tragic feelings of hopelessness and failure on the part of those members who survive while their comrades die. In the fire service, it is in fact all about staying together when you get in trouble because that's how you survive!

Retired New York City firefighter and now famous author and publisher Dennis Smith spoke at a National Fallen Firefighters Memorial service about the significance of firefighters staying together. "We are truly a group, and togetherness is our byword. We are communal in our living, and we are communal in our shared risks."[3] And Dr. Harry R. Carter, the preeminent philosopher of the American fire service believes that this survival strategy of staying together has formed the "brotherhood" or an exclusive membership bond that strongly exists today in the fire service.

> I believe that it was the aura of coming together in times of danger that made the fire service great in the first place. That was what formed the basis for the sense of brotherhood we share to this day. It was the bond of brave men placing their lives on the line in pursuit of a common goal…A brotherhood is, I believe, more than a mere association. It involves deep feelings of trust, honor, loyalty and dedication![4]

And, just like firefighters, Christians must consider membership as a key factor in surviving. At any one time, we may rely on some or all but we conquer our enemy together in the power of Christ. Never by ourselves! Christianity and firefighting are not for do-it-yourselfers. It's all about relationships and being members of a community in pursuit of a common goal. A Christian alone completely contradicts Christian membership. Jesus even said, "For where two or three come together in my name, there am I with them" (Matthew 18:20). You can't be a Christian by yourself and expect to survive! Someone once said, "It takes two to gospel." Pastor Rick Warren emphasizes this scriptural requirement for spiritual membership and the importance of staying together in the Christian's *Purpose Driven Life*:

> We are commanded to love each other, pray for each other, encourage each other, admonish each other, greet each other, serve each other, teach each other, accept each other, honor each other, bear each other's burdens, forgive each other, submit to each other, be devoted to each other, and man other mutual tasks. This is biblical membership![5]

Much of the joy and success in Christ results from our connections with other Christians. Christians, just like firefighters, never do well in isolation nor are we very successful. Community is essential for Christians. When Dr. Carter talks about the sacred bond between firefighters, he could just as easily be describing the sacred connection between Christians: "I believe that we need to create a sacred bond that will serve as the basis for our service. We need to drink from the cup of common dedication to a cause greater than any one of us. All it takes to begin growing a brotherhood is another person with whom you can share the joys, danger, and sorrows of our common efforts."[6] Christianity is, first and foremost, a relationship based on a divine bond of love as the Apostle John describes.

> This is how we know what love is: Jesus Christ laid down his life for us. And we ought to lay down our lives for our brothers. If anyone has material possessions and sees his brother in need but has no pity on him, how can the love of God be in him? Dear children, let us not love with words or tongue but with actions and in truth.
>
> 1 John 3:16–18

How we relate to God directly influences how we relate to others. This unique relationship or connection describes who we are. We are a community of people bound together by our connected lives, sharing our divine blessings jointly through our mutual relationship and love with Christ. This connection results in an enterprise and passion in which we work together with a common purpose of daily living the gospel of Jesus Christ for the glory of God.

Life together stands as the very essence of Christianity along with the required call to live in unity with our fellow believers. God continually emphasizes the strength of togetherness in scripture. He created us to work together, whether in marriage, the family, the fire service, or other teams, and especially the church. Because it's a basic internal human need, we all need each other. Author and psychologist Dr. Henry Cloud discusses this individual desire to be connected with others.

> God created us with a hunger for relationship–for relationship with him and with our fellow people. At our very core we are relational beings. Without a solid, bonded relation-

> ship, the human soul will become mired in psychological and emotional problems. The soul cannot prosper without being connected to others.[7]

One of the first decrees of God following the creation of the human race was that "it is not good for man to be alone" (Genesis 2:18). As a matter of fact, it was the only aspect of his creation that he said was not good. God created Adam and Eve and instructed them not to leave the other's side. In grace and mercy, God assembled an imperfect new people out of the wreckage of Adam and Eve's tragic choice and the result was a fallen and rebellious human race. Peter makes it clear: Christians have been chosen by God as his community. "But you are a chosen people, a royal priesthood, a holy nation, a people belonging to God, that you may declare the praises of him who called you out of darkness into his wonderful light. Once you were not a people, but now you are the people of God..." (1 Peter 2:9–10).

Being connected to other Christians develops close and intimate relationships that continually unite us back to the source of our faith. Henri Nouwen writes, "The basis of the Christian community is not the family tie, or social or economic equality, or shared oppression or complaint, or mutual attraction...but the divine call. The Christian community is not the result of human efforts."[8] This divine and powerful connection not only produces joy, it keeps us faithful to the Lord as the words of T.S. Eliot in his 1934 play, *The Rock,* so beautifully express.

> What life have you if you have not life together?
> There is no life that is not in community,
> And no community not lived in praise of God.[9]

Anyone desiring a productive life together with other Christians will benefit greatly from reading Dietrich Bonhoeffer's *Life Together*. After this young pastor and teacher spent two years in jail and a concentration camp for his involvement in the underground resistance movement, the Gestapo executed Bonhoeffer in 1945 at the age of only thirty-nine. This extremely passionate book emerged from Bonhoeffer's community experiences while leading a clandestine seminary in Germany fighting the Nazi infiltration into the church. "Christian brotherhood is not an ideal which we must realize; it is rather a reality created by God in Christ in which we may participate."[10] In *Life Together* Bonhoeffer describes this special community:

> It is not simply to be taken for granted that the Christian has the privilege of living among other Christians...So between the death of Christ and the Last Day it is only by a gracious anticipation of the last things that Christians are privileged to live in visible fellowship with other Christians.[11]

THE BLESSINGS OF COMMUNITY
How Good and How Pleasant!

> A song of ascents. Of David.
>
> Behold, how good and how pleasant it is for brethren to dwell together in unity! It is like the precious oil upon the head, running down on the beard, the beard of Aaron, running down on the edge of his garments. It is like the dew of Hermon descending upon the mountains of Zion; for there the Lord commanded the blessing - Life forevermore.
>
> Psalm 133 (NKJV)

Because pilgrims most likely sang certain psalms as they ascended to the city of Jerusalem on a hill, Psalms 120 through 134 are usually subtitled songs of "ascents." Some versions use the term "Pilgrim Psalms" because these fifteen songs formed a hymnal for pilgrims to sing and pray as they traveled to their holy city at special times of the year to worship at the temple of God. These pilgrim worshipers usually journeyed in groups for greater safety from thieves, wild animals, and other hazards. As they climbed toward Jerusalem, they sang or recited these psalms together in preparation for their special worship at the holy temple in the holy city. And since we know that Jesus made these pilgrimages with his parents, he probably learned these same songs as a child and sang them on his way to Jerusalem to celebrate the holy Jewish festivals. I wonder if he and his disciples latter sang them in their travels to Jerusalem?

Of the ancient ascent songs, David's Psalm 133 teaches an important lesson to Christians on our pilgrimages to heaven and our attempts to achieve spiritual maturity as we struggle within a faithful community of fellow pilgrims. It's an inspirational song we should sing as we stay together! Unity between members who dwell together is a blessing that comes down from God. David says when God's people live together in unity an anointing gift flows down from God, just like precious oil overflowing completely down over Aaron and just like the refreshing dew of Hermon descending down upon the lower, dryer mountains. And, according to David, there are six heavenly blessings here on earth for Christians who dwell in unity: goodness, pleasure, anointing, refreshing, God's blessing, and eternal life.

David begins his psalm about togetherness with the word "Behold." It's worthy of admiration so pause and gaze upon it! "To dwell" is a word of residence and means more than just coming together. It pertains to staying together in unity. Eugene H. Peterson writes in his marvelous classic book on the ascent psalms, *A Long Obedience in the Same Direction*: "How great to have everyone sharing a common purpose, traveling a common path, striving toward a common goal, that path and purpose and goal being God. How much better than making the long trip alone."[12] Notice that the psalmist uses the word "how" twice. "Behold *how* good! And *how* pleasant!" The condition is just as good as it is pleasant, just as pleasant as it is good.

True happiness (and survival) for Christians comes from first being connected correctly with God (staying on the Line) and then with each other in a special community (staying together). The root of the word "community" means "with unity!" Community is essential for everyone who would know God. Why is it so important for Christians to dwell in unity? Unity is a state of mind connecting shared values, shared vision, and a common destiny. God is an absolute God of order and unity and he will not dwell in disorder or disunity. Demons oppose us by sowing division and discord in the body of Christ. James, the brother of Jesus, tells us in his epistle, "Where you have envy and selfish ambition (the opposite of unity), there you find disorder and every evil practice." And he calls this disorder and lack of unity "earthy, unspiritual, of the devil" (James 3:14–16).

God is triune in his being, making it clear that community is fundamental to the very structure of all reality. Community and relationship were not created but are supernaturally foundational to the entire universe. Working flawlessly in community, the Father, the Son and the Spirit live in perfect fellowship within the Godhead. God does not live in eternal solitude; but, Father, Son, and Holy Spirit live in an eternal relationship, each giving to and receiving from the others from all eternity. They are each different, yet they are one in essence and share the very same nature. No human can fully understand this, but God has always existed in a lifestyle of community. Therefore, being made in God's image, we naturally and supernaturally connect to community; therefore, our relationships as Christians should reflect our God. We relate first to him, and then to one another. There is no greater unity than the tri-unity, and they divinely reign as the supernatural model of staying together!

Paul sings from the same hymnal as David to the congregation in Rome that they live in unity, daily following their Savior, Christ Jesus. Made up of members from all over the world with extremely different backgrounds and cultures, the believers in Rome were anything but homogenous. So you can imagine the difficulty in Paul's prayer calling for a spirit of unity among those very diverse Jews and Gentiles.

> May our dependably steady and warmly personal God develop maturity in you so that you get along with each other as well as Jesus gets along with us all. Then we'll be

> a choir–not our voices only, but our very lives singing in harmony in a stunning anthem to the God and Father of our Master Jesus! So reach out and welcome one another to God's glory. Jesus did it; now you do it!
>
> Romans 15:5–7 (MSG)

In Paul's words to the Roman congregation, living in unity with one another brings God glory and accomplishes his purposes. I love how Paul says unity requires one heart and mouth in a choir. Oh how the Christian community needs that spirit of unity today.

How good and how pleasant applies to the three distinct relational levels of the Christian community. First, it is good and pleasant to God, because he greatly delights in his precious community when they stay connected. Because he is a God of peace and unity, God revels in peaceable and unified Christians. Second, this community unity is also good and pleasant to us when we dwell in the great pleasure of love–both loving others and others loving us. And third, it is also good and pleasant to the other members in our community and makes a lasting impression on the onlookers–good or bad. Non-Christians constantly judge God by the actions (or inactions or disunity or disorder) of his people.

David says unity "is like precious oil poured on the head, running down on the beard, running down on Aaron's beard, down upon the collar of his robes." When God made him the first high priest, Aaron was anointed with oil from above in accordance with a divine recipe.

> Then the Lord said to Moses, "Take the following fine spices: 500 shekels of liquid myrrh, half as much (that is, 250 shekels) of fragrant cinnamon, 250 shekels of fragrant cane, 500 shekels of cassia–all according to the sanctuary shekel–and a hint of olive oil. Make these into a sacred anointing oil...Anoint Aaron and his sons and consecrate them so they may serve me as priests."
>
> Exodus 30:23–30

This anointing oil was so holy that God's people were strictly forbidden to copy it for personal use.

The sanctified anointing symbolized that Aaron was receiving God's blessing on behalf of God's chosen people. All those who came near him could recognize the sweet-smelling oil used for anointing. The diffusive oil was poured upon the head of Aaron so plentifully that it ran down his face and on his beard and then flowed down to the skirts of his garments. Not only was his entire being refreshed in that arid land, but the sweet aroma refreshed those around him.

Why does David use the anointing oil as an example of the pleasure and goodness of community? David paints a picture of an overflow of spiritual blessings because oil often symbolizes God's presence, the Holy Spirit. The oil did not remain confined to the place where it first fell, but it flowed down the High Priest's hair and over his beard, descending down and anointing and perfuming all around. Unity refreshes just like the fragrant, anointing oil running down over everyone who experiences God's community, because it not only refreshes the receiver, it benefits all those around with the aroma of Christian love and fellowship. The divine blessings flowing down from God to the community attract others into good and pleasant fellowship with him. God pours out plentiful blessings just as fragrant holy oil abundantly flowing over us filling us with his presence.

"It is as if the dew of Hermon were falling on Mount Zion." To visualize David's imagery, remember the land and the mountains of Zion are a dry and dusty place. But rising to over 9,000 feet in the Lebanon range several hundred miles north of Israel, Mount Hermon stands as the highest mountain in that area and it is well known for the dew that falls at its highest altitudes. I can remember camping with my son, David, when he was a teenager at the higher elevations of the California Sierras up around 10,000 feet and waking up in the morning, our sleeping bags and tent drenched from the heavy dew. King David sings that this same type of heavy dew falls from the highest mountain, down upon the lower mountains of Zion.

In the same manner, community flows like the dew from above

bringing an abundance of blessings with it. Just as the evening dew cools the arid air and refreshes the dry earth, the Christian community dissipates the scorching heat of disunity and disorder all around them. Imagine how wonderful the cooling and refreshing evening dews of blessing feel after laboring all day in a parched and thirsty land. Similarly, God's Spirit renews his community as symbolized by the living dew that falls down representing God's divine blessings of goodness and grace upon his people.

"For there the Lord bestows his blessing, even life forevermore." Finally, David believes dwelling together in unity is so important that he links it to eternal life. The psalmist proclaims that oil and dew make community an experience of joy and says the Lord bestows his blessing, even life forevermore. David's notion of fellowship is indeed a model of heaven, a glimpse of paradise—heaven on earth. The unity on earth is a foretaste of the divine and eternal community we will have in heaven. Do you ever wonder what heaven will be like? David tells us the best vision we have of heaven can be found in the community God gives us on earth. When we live together in unity and harmony as God's chosen people, we experience a preview of eternal life.

The building of life together–like brethren who dwell together in unity–presents a tremendous challenge for us. The blessings of community so beautifully described by David in Psalm 133 should be understood as the prerequisite for the expected blessings that God pours down on his people. But, Eugene Peterson warns, "Living together in a way that evokes the glad song of Psalm 133 is one of the great and arduous tasks before Christ's people. Nothing requires more attention and energy. It is easier to do almost anything else."[13]

Here's the big challenge. Unity does not mean uniformity! The Christian community exists as a place where we must learn to live with people we did not necessarily choose, all the while remembering the extreme love of a God who is stuck with us all. Doesn't that sound exactly like Nouwen's famous definition of community as "the place where the person you can't stand always is"?

John Courtney Murray, a Jesuit theologian, often described the early church as a "conspiracy." He used this wonderful term in the sense that believers "breathed together" (from the Latin *con*: "with," and *spire*: "breath"). It was their shared sense of breathing together as the chosen people of God that grounded them in the faithful interaction of learning and caring. In such a community, people eternally invest their lives with confidence in one another, pursuing a shared vision and mission. Our survival strategy is that we might breathe together and be a conspiracy of community, dwelling in unity even though we are not exactly alike and may not particularly like every member in our population. Firefighters call this "buddy breathing" when a partner runs out of air during a fire and the other immediately shares his or her air, in essence, they breathe together to both survive.

Because brethren should work together, love, and serve one another, staying together as individuals in community destroys the enemy's schemes! Eugene Peterson points out one of the key points David was making: "When we see the other as God's anointed, our relationships are profoundly affected."[14] It is only when God's community moves strongly as a unified living force to accomplish his glorious purpose that the enemy fears us the most, because he knows the prayerful words of Jesus still sing true. "May they be brought to complete unity to let the world know that you sent me and have loved them even as you have loved me" (John 17:23).

THE TOGETHERNESS OF COMMUNITY

There's Strength in Numbers!

> Two are better than one, because they have a good return for their work: If one falls down, his friend can help him up. But pity the man who falls and has no one to help him up! Also, if two lie down together, they will keep warm. But how can one keep warm alone? Though one may be overpowered, two can defend themselves. A cord of three strands is not quickly broken.
>
> Ecclesiastes 4:9–12

The togetherness of community makes us strong and enables us to accomplish together what we could never do alone. Solomon says that two people working together can get more done than one alone. "Two are better than one." As we live and work together in community, we acquire power we could never achieve individually. Firefighters would never attempt to fight a fire alone. They would call for reinforcements. In the same manner, Christians must never try to fight alone, Satan will easily pick us off. There's definitely strength and survival in numbers!

How many times do you read of the Apostle Paul all by himself? If any one Christian could have succeeded alone, surely it would have been Paul. As you read of Paul's great adventures serving his Lord, notice that just about everything he ever did was in partnership with fellow believers. Look at Paul's epistles and you'll quickly see that most were not from Paul alone, but from "Paul and Timothy," or "Paul, Silvanus, and Timothy," or "Paul and Sosthenes." From Acts 9, it was Paul and Barnabas and Mark, or Paul and Silas and Timothy, or some other combination, from the community of believers. When Paul and Barnabas had a falling out regarding John Mark, these two spiritual leaders did not charge off in isolation, but formed new teams. "Barnabas took Mark with him and sailed away to Cyprus, but Paul chose Silas and departed…" (Acts 13:39).

In the fire service, we have our assigned crew of two to five firefighters working closely together in a company and in whom we daily place our very lives. We have the members of our firefighting shifts who work on other crews or companies and come from other fire stations for support when we call. If we still need help, we can call for mutual aid from all the fire departments from surrounding jurisdictions that will quickly respond to assist. Then we know we can count on the off duty fire department members to come to our aid for the conflagrations (really big fires).

Jesus also had different levels of staying together. As Jesus began his public ministry, he called disciples to share in the greatest adventure in history. As a matter of fact and recorded in his life story in all the gospels, he recruited and gathered around him a small community. Jesus' best friend was apparently John, based on the numerous times in his gospel John referred to himself as "the disciple whom Jesus loved." John sat next to Jesus in a position of honor at the last supper (John 21:20).

Jesus also bonded with an inner circle of close friends and confidants. During the years of his public ministry, he had developed an intimate relationship with Peter, James, and John. He selected these three close companions several times to accompany him on some crucial points of his ministry such as raising Jairus' daughter (Mark 5:37), climbing the mount of transfiguration (Mark 9:2), and praying in the Garden of Gethsemane (Mark 14:33). The fire service would call them Jesus' senior command staff.

Christ chose twelve disciples as his operations team and close partners in life and ministry. "Jesus went up on a mountainside and called to him those he wanted, and they came to him. He appointed twelve–designating them apostles–that they might be with him and that he might send them out to preach..." (Mark 3:13–14). But as the Savior focused his life and energy on the cross and his ultimate goal, he continued to expand his community. So, Jesus picked seventy-two followers for his ministry team whom he sent out to go ahead of him. "After this the Lord appointed seventy-two others and sent them two by two ahead of him to every town and place where he was about to go" (Luke 10:1).

It's very interesting from a firefighting strategy point of view that Jesus sent out his disciples two at a time to minister and to do other things as referred to numerous times in the gospels. "And He called the twelve to Him, and began to send them out two by two, and gave them power over unclean spirits" (Mark 6:7). "Now when they drew near to Jerusalem, and came to Bethphage, at the Mount of Olives, then Jesus sent two disciples" (Matthew 21:1). "So He sent out two of his disciples and said to them, 'Go into the city, and a man will meet you carrying a pitcher of water; follow him'" (Mark 14:13).

A federal standard by OSHA mandates firefighters to always operate in teams of at least two. Because so many firefighters die due to insufficient accountability and poor communications, OSHA requires that all workers engaged in interior structural firefighting operations must use self-contained breathing apparatus (SCBA) and work in teams of two or more. The firefighter survival standard requires that the two firefighters inside the burning building remain in visual or voice contact with each other at all times. In most heavily involved fire situations, visual contact won't be possible, so the two inside must make a concerted effort to stay together. Since their ability to communicate will be severely limited, they will have to remain very close to one another.

OSHA further requires at least one team of two or more properly equipped and trained firefighters to be outside the burning structure before firefighters enter and fight the fire. This requirement assures that the team outside the structure has training, clothing, and equipment to protect the firefighters inside the structure and, if necessary, can safely and effectively rescue them. The outside personnel must at all times account for and be available to assist or rescue members of the interior team. The fire service has dubbed this standard as the "two-in/two-out" rule. With the two-in and two-out regulation, the fire service now routinely accepts and expects that crews on the scene of a fire will always utilize the "buddy system." The buddy system keeps one team member watching out for the other and readily available to affect an immediate rescue or call for help.

With the promulgation of this standard mandating the need for firefighters to work in teams of at least two while in a dangerous life and health environment, the United States fire service has made great strides in reducing the serious problem of "freelancing" on the fireground. Fire service commanders define freelancing as the dangerous situation at an emergency incident where individuals attempt to carry out tasks alone without being assigned or working together as a team. Many firefighters have freelanced themselves to serious injuries or even death causing chaos on the fireground. Freelancing is one of the incident commander's worst fears.

Do you think that the Christian community has a problem with freelancing? Solomon certainly understood this concept thousands of years ago and I'm absolutely positive Jesus drew some of his divine leadership wisdom from the inspired words of Solomon: "Two are better than one" and "a cord of three strands is not quickly broken" (Ecclesiastes 4:9, 12). And "...many advisors make victory sure" (Proverbs 11:14). Just as the fire service succeeds and survives in teams, Solomon explains that the number one rule for God's people should be that we never freelance–we never go into any dangerous situation alone or wander off by ourselves. "But pity the man who falls and has no one to help him up!" This way, if you get into difficulty, there is always a partner to help you immediately. "If one falls down, his friend can lift him up."

Sadly, many Christians live as though they believe that freelancing is a good thing. They act like "independent" Christians or a God-appointed team of one–detached, cut off, solitary—and they probably don't understand the divinely mandated community facet of life in Christ. But just as in firefighting, the consequences of Christian freelancing can be extremely dangerous: idleness, unhappiness, discontent, fear, spiritual stagnation, or even spiritual death. Freelancing is the opposite of staying together!

Even in the worst of situations, firefighters have testified how very important it was to work jointly in teams. Many studies of tragic incidents reveal that firefighters feeling support from crewmembers was absolutely crucial for their survival. Many of them pointed out that help from fellow workers in decision-making was particularly important and that working with a buddy actually facilitated staying on task and remembering life saving training. In addition, togetherness provided reassurance about hard decisions as these pertinent results from a final study on the psychological responses of rescue workers in the crash of an airliner in Sioux City in 1992 indicate. It sounds remarkably like Solomon's instructions of staying together.

> Several fire fighters described how helpful it had been to work in pairs. Together, they felt better able to stay on task and not respond to the cries for help from nearby survivors. They gave each other "moral support" as the work became more difficult, with dead bodies all around. Decision-making became difficult because of the chaos. Many fire fighters thought it was better for two people to make decisions rather than to rely totally on one's own judgment.[15]

Remember our discussion of God's personal protective equipment (PPE) described by Paul in Ephesians 6 and the related strategy of being prepared? The shield of faith as illustrated by Paul was a community piece of survival protection because the shields could be fastened to each other to serve the entire army. The shields Paul visualized in his metaphor of the armor of God were most commonly used when large numbers of troops were deployed in battle. Roman soldiers would line themselves in several rows in a box or rectangular shape with the soldiers in the front and on the sides joining their shields together and forming an impenetrable wall around the entire body. At the same time, the soldiers within this fortification would raise their shields above their heads and join their shields with those who were beside and in front of them. As the Roman army pushed forward into battle, they moved together as one living, armored body. In the same manner, in our Christian community, putting our varying levels of faith together and sharing it corporately tremendously improves our collective faith and gives us an impenetrable wall. I believe this is what Paul had in mind. There's strength in numbers and that's the purpose of the church!

"Also, if two lie down together, they will keep warm. But how can one keep warm alone?" (Ecclesiastes 4:11). Take two coals and heat them up together so both are glowing hot, then try separating them and watch what happens. Their flames quickly extinguish and the heat slowly diminishes. Coals cannot generate heat for very long on their own. Solomon's image explains why it is so important for the Christian community to stay together—physically, emotionally, and spiritually. We stay together to create the heated energy of fellowship that we might warm one another with a burning zeal for serving the Lord. We keep each other warm because very often individual members of our community can run hot and cold in their devotion and commitment so we need glowing, touching embers to help us keep warm toward God and each other. In fact, we all need someone who will as the old expression goes, "hold our feet to the fire!" The bottom line is that Christians rarely survive spiritually apart from their proper heat exchanging relationships with other Christians.

Solomon goes a step further and declares, "Though one may be overpowered, two can defend themselves. A cord of three strands is not quickly broken" (Ecclesiastes 4:12). If two are better than one, then Solomon says that three are superior! Jesus confirms it! "For where two or three come together in my name, there am I with them" (Matthew 18:20). This concept truly defines the Christian community because there is spiritual survival and strength in numbers.

In addition, a cord of three illustrates the important notion of accountability. In firefighting, an accountability system helps prevent a firefighter from becoming lost or trapped during fire operations. It's also part of staying together because teams must stay together for accountability to work. Since firefighters get into trouble when they are by themselves freelancing, no one knows for sure where they are. Accountability reduces freelancing during a fire and fire scene commanders use it to keep track of all the firefighters assigned to the fire.

In the fire service, accountability is essential for survival and Christian accountability is no different. However, one of the biggest ironies connected to Christian survival on the front line is that the proper time to develop personal accountability is when we don't particularly need it. It comes back to being prepared before the emergency! Christian therapist Rob Jackson emphasizes the critical need for Christians to stay together in small groups, holding all the members accountable to each other before attacks, during battles, and then in recovery.

> Accountability occurs in community with other Christians. Having examined ourselves before God we offer what we have learned about ourselves to a few, safe individuals, and they in turn do the same. Here we describe our experiences and invite their feedback. Like everything else in the Christian life, our experience with accountability matures over time.[16]

Why is there strength in numbers? As humans, we find support, comfort, and motivation from others who are struggling with similar life circumstances. Rob Jackson admits, "I can lie to one, I can confess to two, but with a third man the three of them are sure to catch up with me."[17] Solomon was absolutely correct in describing accountability as "safety in a multitude of counselors." Accountability requires an intimate support network of at least two or three safe individuals to be accountable for each other's survival, just like a fire fighting crew. It's especially critical for men since those types of relationships don't usually come naturally to them.

God designed the body of Christ to function best when its members are there for each other in ways that spur them on and hold them responsible to the commitment they have made to follow Christ. "Let us consider how we may spur one another on toward love and good deeds" (Hebrews 10:24). It is important for every believer to have at least one other person in which to confide, pray with, and listen to while encouraging each other to grow in spiritual maturity. 1 Thessalonians 5:11 says to "encourage one another and build each other up…" That's the essence of accountability.

THE DISCIPLESHIP OF COMMUNITY

We Follow Better Together as Members of One Another!

> They devoted themselves to the apostles' teaching and to the fellowship, to the breaking of bread and to prayer.
>
> Acts 2:42

I like the description of the early church as the honeymoon of a brand new community. Luke introduces the origin of Christ's church and its honeymoon period in the first few chapters of Acts. Everything was new and fresh and mysterious. Expectations were high. Just like a new marriage and then the honeymoon–everyone having a wonderful time but with real life and tough times to follow. Even so, the first church in its first years exhibited a level of unity and oneness that should forever be an example and the challenging goal for all Christians.

The honeymoon began on the Day of Pentecost when one hundred and twenty people gathered "all together" in the upper room, awaiting the direction of the Holy Spirit. Sounds like the beginning of a great marriage of many different individuals united with a common bond. When that Spirit drove them out into the streets to preach, they immediately added 3000 more people to their family.

Why was their enthusiasm so high? A deep sense of awe flowed over them, inspired to some degree by the visible evidences of God's power and presence through the many signs and wonders he was performing through the apostles. "Everyone was filled with awe, and many wonders and miraculous signs were done by the apostles" (Acts 2:43). They felt the overwhelming presence of their Lord and fully believed that he was powerfully at work among them, evidenced by the miraculous deeds God was accomplishing through his chosen leaders just as Jesus had promised. "I tell you the truth, anyone who has faith in me will do what I have been doing. He will do even greater things than these, because I am going to the Father" (John 14:12). God still supernaturally moves through a united body with a singleminded purpose and destiny in incredible ways, just as he did in the church during its honeymoon period. Jesus' promise still applies and it's occurring all over the world, but only in those united bodies still filled with a sense of awe of God's amazing love and power.

How does Luke describe the first church? They shared a vision, a common goal, and a singular purpose that they went after with unadulterated zeal. Just like newlyweds, the members obviously did not want to be apart from one another. That was why they were so successful in their unity. During their honeymoon period, the members of the first church unselfishly acted just like brides and grooms in new marriages. Rather than worrying about receiving something, they selflessly devoted themselves to doing something for the other members of the body, anointing their spiritual lives. It was more about giving than receiving!

Unfortunately, some disenchantment eventually surfaces in every marriage–a comedown from the bliss, glamour, and unselfish interest in each other that is common at the beginning of those covenants. A return to reality inevitably occurs and that's when the phrase "the honeymoon is over" puts the relationship to the stress of real life and survival. Those first months or even years are often blissful, give or take the minor adjustments of living together with peculiar people different than yourself. But what happens after the honeymoon is over? Peaked enthusiasm begins a downward spiral. Reality sets in and the warts become visible. The devotion cools off, especially if the gap between the coals widens.

Just like in marriages, disunity kills churches all the time ending in divorces of sorts. Paul implored the Corinthians to regain their unity because the honeymoon was over and division was quickly creeping in. The relationship was on the rocks. He exhorted the church in Corinth to be united because of growing dissension.

> I appeal to you, brothers, in the name of our Lord Jesus Christ, that all of you agree with one another so that there may be no divisions among you and that you may be perfectly united in mind and thought. My brothers, some from Chloe's household have informed me that there are quarrels among you...Is Christ divided?
>
> 1 Corinthians 1:10–11, 13

Just like in a struggling new marriage, the quarrels that emerged were because people were dividing into factions. People were aligning themselves with various influencing personalities. Paul does not suggest that everyone has to agree on everything but they must agree on what truly matters, and that is Jesus Christ is Lord of all no matter who teaches or baptizes. Apparently the discord had grown to the point that Paul had to ask if the quarrels among them had actually divided Christ.

The same source of the Corinthian disunity still causes most church conflict today. It essentially comes down to selfishness. The marriage moves from "us" to "me"—"I" instead of "we." James identifies our own selfish desires as the source of these divisive quarrels and conflicts in the church. "What causes fights and quarrels among you? Don't they come from your desires that battle within you?" (James 4:1). Those who are involved in the quarrels and conflicts consider their own selfish ambitions and personal pleasures above God's will for the common good of the community. They take their eyes off of Christ and stare at themselves instead. Their image in the mirror reigns supreme rather than Christ's! James says the source of these conflicts can be found in their self-centeredness as individuals rather than their unity as a living and loving vibrant community. He says it's "bitter jealously and selfish ambition" in their hearts (James 3:14). Freelancing kills churches!

How many Christian community divisions or breakups do you suppose have occurred since the first church? And how do those continuing divisions impact the world we as Christians are called to change and influence for Christ? The great theologian Francis Schaeffer warned us of the tragic consequences of church divorces happening in the Christian community:

> We cannot expect the world to believe that the Father sent the Son, that Jesus' claims are true, and that Christianity is true, unless the world sees some reality of oneness of true Christians. Now that is frightening. Should we not feel some emotion at this point?[18]

Jesus calls us to a genuine community of discipleship founded on love and mutual support that leads to an eternal honeymoon between the Lord and his Bride–us Christians. As described by Luke, the Holy Spirit introduced four key activities to the early church as absolute priorities of their divine community to maintain fresh and everlasting relationships for the glory of God. Luke names the specific activities required for this united community environment: teaching, fellowship, breaking bread, and prayers.

Notice that Luke says they "devoted" themselves to these corporate actions. These were not options then and they remain the four things to which the saints must constantly devote themselves to now. Staying together shows evidence of the fruit of a community of disciples living fully in Christ and devotedly following him at all costs. In community, we deny ourselves, we pick up our crosses, and as disciples, we follow Christ best together.

DEVOTE OURSELVES TO THE APOSTLES' TEACHING!

Real community can only survive around a common set of ongoing, biblically based teachings. In other words, the early church gave a high priority to understanding the truth being taught by Christ's chosen apostles. Some might question exactly what that teaching is today. The apostles' teaching has been preserved in the New Testament Scriptures, so that we may receive the very same instructions as the members of the first church. This is an extremely important point because we possess the identical teachings as the people hearing the apostles' teaching for the first time in Acts 2. Somebody painstakingly recorded them for us. The Word of God, as originally spoken through Christ's disciples, remains the foundation for every aspect of the Christian life. Today, unfortunately, the teaching has been so watered down is it any wonder the Church does not have the same united outcome?

Firefighters survive in community with a clearly defined set of standard operating procedures or general orders that are constantly trained on. They devote themselves to those teachings because they know their lives depend on them. Christians have eternal standard operating procedures that never change and are clearly written as "the apostles' teachings."

DEVOTE OURSELVES TO FELLOWSHIP!

Luke describes the daily lives of the first Christians as being full of devoted fellowship. What is meant by fellowship in the New Testament? Essentially, it means joint participation or sharing something in common as a type of partnership. Luke uses the word *Koinonia*, usually translated "fellowship," but it can also be translated "sharing, participation, communion." The meaning can be expanded in the context of Acts 2 in the partnership sense of giving to or receiving from others. Sharing what we have with one another is the very essence of the first church's devotion to fellowship. Dietrich Bonhoeffer stressed the importance of Christian fellowship in the community of faith.

God has willed that we should seek and find his living Word in the witness of a brother/sister, in the mouth of a man/woman. Therefore, the Christian needs another Christian who speaks God's Word to him. He needs him again and again when he becomes uncertain and discouraged, for by himself he cannot help himself without belying the truth. He needs his brother as a bearer and proclaimer of the divine word of salvation. He needs his brother solely because of Jesus Christ. The Christ in his own heart is weaker than the Christ in the word of his brother, his own heart is uncertain, his brother's is sure.[19]

Staying together as members of "one another" was an essential aspect of the ongoing instruction of the apostles to the newly created church. "So we, who are many, are one body in Christ, and individually members one of another" (Romans 12:5). "That there should be no division in the body, but that the members should have the same care for one another" (1 Corinthians 12:25). "Therefore, laying aside falsehood, speak truth, each one of you, with his neighbor, for we are members of one another" (Ephesians 4:25). The dictionary defines "one another" as a term used to indicate a reciprocal relationship or reciprocal actions among the members of a community. How should Christ's community live? As believers in Christ, we are to live, think, and stand together as members of one another. By caring for one another, these actions promote harmony and result in greater effectiveness of the church.

The writer to the Hebrews strongly admonishes us to keep meeting together and not to neglect fellowship. "Let us not give up meeting together, as some are in the habit of doing, but let us encourage one another–and all the more as you see the Day approaching" (Hebrews 10:25). We can only experience true fellowship by giving diligent attention to meeting together to encourage all those in fellowship. We do great harm to ourselves and to others when we fail to come together to spend time collectively doing the things of Christ and ministering to one another. Because God has made us in his divine image, he calls us to a life of relationship and mutual giving and receiving. Fellowship is about responsible and accountable sharing as we collectively walk our Christian pilgrimage and stay together on the road to eternal fellowship.

DEVOTE OURSELVES TO THE BREAKING OF BREAD!

Luke refers to the early church's custom of eating meals together. Commentators remain divided in what they believe Luke means by the "breaking of bread." He could mean that the first Christians shared their meals together. In the early church, the sharing of a meal was perhaps the most intimate form of fellowship one could have with fellow believers. Or some scholars believe Luke could mean that they devoted themselves to the ordinance of the Lord's Table. I believe "breaking of bread" may well mean a combination of both since evidence suggests that the early Christians celebrated the Lord's Table as a part of a corporate meal.

The eating of a meal together in the Christian community and the breaking of bread as part of communion are often used as descriptions of our fellowship with each other and with God. Luke points out the necessity of fellowshipping not only with each other, but also with the Creator of fellowship. Bonhoeffer told his readers how important the breaking of bread was in spending their time with others.

> The Scriptures speak of three kinds of table fellowship that Jesus keeps with his own: daily fellowship at table, the table fellowship of the Lord's Supper, and the final table fellowship in the Kingdom of God. But in all three the one thing that counts is that "their eyes were opened, and they knew him." (Luke 24:30–31)…Every mealtime fills Christians with gratitude for the living, present Lord and God, Jesus Christ…and daily table fellowship binds the Christians to their Lord and one another.[20]

Today, unfortunately, corporate prayer seems to be less of a priority among Christians than ever before. Most believe in prayer, but few people really spend much time praying, particularly in community. We may send up a brief individual prayer from time to time, some may even send up several a day in times of trouble. But few spend significant time in prayer, and fewer spend any time intimately bonded together in a prayer group. I can remember the weekly church prayer meeting on either Sunday or Wednesday nights, or even on both. It used to be a really important function of the church, but I don't see those prayer meetings much anymore.

Luke says the first Christians devoted themselves to prayer, which means that they had constant communication with God. In addition to daily personal worship and weekly corporate worship, they constantly devoted themselves to prayer. They focused, as a community, heavenward toward God himself. Without a doubt, they gave themselves to a life of mutual prayer. And here's why the first Christians devoted themselves to prayer. "And when they had prayed, the place where they had gathered together was shaken, and they were all filled with the Holy Spirit, and began to speak the word of God with boldness. And the congregation of those who believed were one heart and soul" (Acts 4:31–32).

Pay close attention to Luke's survival tip on unity and meditate on it daily: Devoted disciples who pray together stay together in boldness with one heart and soul for God and the world not only will notice, it will shake!

STRATEGY 9

STAY CALM!

It Is Well With My Soul

We always tell everyone, including the responders as well as the victims, that in any emergency, especially a fire, the number one thing is not to panic. Easy to say, but the key to all survival is to stay calm! Imagine a firefighter who runs out of air in a completely dark, hot, smoky environment and realizes he's going to die unless he can remember all the training he's ever received and take immediate action. Having mastered all the strategies of survival will do absolutely nothing for the firefighter who panics at that point.

Plus, that firefighter cannot help those victims screaming for the fire department to save them. The *Firefighter's Handbook* teaches: "A team that is lost needs to help each other remain calm and preserve air. Any member that appears to panic can have a negative effect on the others."[1] Fire Captain Jerry Smith of the Los Angeles City Fire Department gives a warning to firefighters about the importance of staying calm.

> Think about this fire ground scenario, you find yourself alone and separated from your firefighting crew inside an enclosed building, and in the next few minutes, it's zero visibility in dense, dark smoke. To make matters worse your anxiety peaks, and for good reason, you're unable to see your hand through your SCBA face piece. You feel your intense emotions being diluted by the growing fear of being disoriented. The environment is heating and you

> know your remaining air supply is being used up with every breath you take. Somehow you sense that panic may be unavoidable as your mental processes are changing to acute desperation. Medical experts could say you're in an acute state of illusion. Yes, false senses of perception or impression as you try to manage a declining air supply while frantically searching for a close by exit door or window.[2]

Even though Americans face more criminal, terrorist, and biological threats than ever before in the history of our planet, Connie Patrick, a thirty-year veteran of law enforcement and the director of the Federal Law Enforcement Training Center, said in an interview with the Methodist Church about fighting crime with her faith, that the worst thing people can do is live in fear because "fear and faith are opposites. You have to stay calm. When you get worried or nervous or upset, your brain shuts down. That doesn't help anything."[3] Simply put, if you lose your calm spirit, you bypass your brain. The inability to remain calm makes decisions difficult, creates depression and produces loud, negative chatter in your head.

Christians face constant and mounting dangers, and we must remain calm in the midst of all our concerns and attacks. Staying calm in the most desperate of circumstances requires putting into practice the eight survival strategies we've already learned. Otherwise, worry creeps into our lives and increases anxiety and then creates panic that maims us spiritually. Solomon wisely tells us, "An anxious heart weighs a man down" (Proverbs 12:25). Excessive worry destroys the soul. When we worry, it reveals a lack of trusting God for our lives and speaks loudly about what we believe about God's character. On the other hand, keeping God at the center of our lives removes the worry and helps us stay calm.

WHAT, ME WORRY?

It's a World-Wide Pandemic That's Killing Us!

As a teenager, I grew up reading *Mad* magazine whose fictional hero was Alfred E. Neuman, a mischievously smiling boy with jug ears, a missing front tooth, and one eye arched slightly higher than his other. His favorite saying, "What, me worry?" became a common household slogan. But, still, we all worry! Worry and stress have infiltrated every culture and religion in the world. No one is exempt! Why? Anxiety, worry, and stress are all afflictions of living in a world gone crazy, impacted by our fallen condition. According to the National Institute of Mental health, approximately ten percent of the American population, or thirty million people, suffer from serious anxiety disorders.[4]

We define worry as something that afflicts us with mental distress, uneasiness, foreboding, and agitation. All people worry when they sense that something went wrong, is going wrong, or could go wrong. Such thoughts always anticipate the very worst and usually become some fearful apprehension of trouble and uncertainty. Worry incessantly goads us inside and drives us to some level of desperation and, if we're not careful, loss of control. Most of us can easily identify with that particular definition of worry, making it very difficult to respond to life with the same philosophy of Alfred E. Neuman.

Amazingly, in spite of all our worries, experts tell us that most of what we worry about never even occurs. Mark Twain once said, "The worst things in my life never happened." If you think about it, worrying never affects the final outcome and no problem has ever been worried away to a positive solution! And someone wisely said, "Worry is wasting today's time cluttering up tomorrow's opportunities with yesterday's troubles."[5] In reality, most things we worry about never live up to the internal fears they caused in the first place.

That reminds me of Earl Nightingale's famous comparison of worry to a dense fog that can obscure our lives. He termed it "the fog of worry" because he discovered that a dense fog covering seven city blocks, to a depth of 100 feet, is composed of only enough water to fill a single drinking glass. Nightingale figured that only eight percent of all our worries are ever worth concerning ourselves about, making the other ninety-two percent pure fog with no substance at all. His memorable point in all this was that people need to condense their worries to a size they truly deserve.[6]

> If we can see into the future and if we could see our problems in their true light, they wouldn't tend to blind us to the world, to living itself, but instead could be relegated to their true size and place. And if all the things most people worry about could be reduced to their true size, you could probably put them all into a drinking glass, too… They often find their lives obscured by the fog of worry. Yet, here's an authoritative estimate of what most people worry about. Things that never happen: 40 percent. That is, 40 percent of the things you worry about will never occur anyway. Things over and past that can't be changed by all the worry in the world: 30 percent. Needless worries about our health: 12 percent. Petty, miscellaneous worries: 10 percent. Real, legitimate worries: 8 percent.[7]

Experts say that the stress worry causes affects every system in our bodies. Even the word "stress" means to draw tight, and we often use it to describe hardship, pain, or affliction. It's no wonder that chronic worriers are so prone to illness. Chemicals released during extended periods of worry wreck havoc on our physical well-being causing migraine headaches, high blood pressure, muscle tension, and ulcers. One anxiety expert warns that stress "is a form of pain that comes to tell you that there is something you need to learn and change…Your body reacts with anger, aggression and hostility or anxiety and nervousness."[8] Healthcare provider Dr. Dorothy McCoy describes the potentially devastating physical impact worry can have on humans.

> In addition to raising blood pressure and increasing blood clotting, worry can prompt your liver to produce more cholesterol, all of which can raise your risk of heart attack and stroke. Muscle tension can give rise to head aches, back pain, and other body aches. Worry can also trigger an increase in stomach acid and either slow or speed up

muscle contractions in your intestines, which can lead to stomach aches, constipation, diarrhea, gas or heartburn. Worry can affect your skin (rash or itch). It can impact your respiratory system aggravating asthma. Growing evidence even suggests that chronic worry can compromise your immune system, making you more vulnerable to bacteria, viruses, perhaps even cancer.[9]

It seems that what we really should be worrying about is worry! Not staying calm is killing us physically, emotionally, and spiritually. Since our bodies and minds generally don't deal well with worry, many medicate themselves with legal, illegal, and "recreational" drugs, especially alcohol, while most others just try to ignore their problems or distract themselves with television, entertainment, working, or spending money. All this, because left unchecked, not staying calm results in great anxiety, which can lead to emotional, physical, and spiritual illness.

THE WORLD GIVES NOTHING TO BE CALM ABOUT

To Stay Calm You Must Have Supernatural Peace!

Fear certainly is something on most people's minds these days. With terrorist attacks, terrible wars, earthquakes and their tsunamis, devastating hurricanes, crashing stock markets, horrifying pandemics such as AIDS, and Hollywood's unending supply of fear-based entertainment, the world doesn't offer much to be calm about. As a matter of fact, Billy Graham says, "Historians will probably call our era 'the age of anxiety.'...Callused hands were the badge of the pioneers, but a furrowed brow is the insignia of modern men and women."[10]

Just watch the evening news and the events of the day will wreak havoc on our anxiety levels–emotionally, physically, and even spiritually. Newscasters actually provoke apprehension by finding the most fear-inspiring possibilities current in our world. Then there are the deep-seated worries and fears about our health or the health of loved ones, about jobs, about money or the lack of it, and about our children being exposed to so many unthinkable dangers never before imagined. Peace in the world appears to be a rapidly disappearing commodity.

I've read many suicide letters from people who had no peace in this world, culminating with them taking their own lives. As a matter of fact, 32,000 people kill themselves in the United States every year, with over a million suicides occurring annually worldwide. That means about every forty seconds a human being gives up on finding any peace of mind in this world! Sadly, our children are taking their own lives at levels higher than ever before. Suicides occur more often than murders.

People, including Christians, just feel life isn't worth living and they want out, often leaving some farewell communication behind to explain. Read the following sentiments taken from actual suicide notes and notice how sorrowfully they express so much hopelessness. Many of us sometime in our lives have heard the same desperate words screaming or whispering in our heads but we haven't followed them through to completion. Pay close attention to the hissing lies of an evil and deadly serpent in every word because suicide represents the victorious deception of the enemy, which takes worry to its ultimate conclusion.

> "I want out of all of it. Please make it stop. Take the confusion away."
> "I'm all alone, nobody cares whether I live or die."
> "I've failed at everything. There is nothing for me here. I don't want to go on."
> "I'm sick of it all. Why should I bother trying anymore?"
> "I just want to leave this world. I'm tired of trying."
> "I can no longer go through this anymore. I keep trying but I can't hold on any longer."
> "I'm all alone, since nobody has ever cared for me."
> "I no longer want to live in this world full of hate and hurt."

Every suicide message tragically inflates how bad things appear and feel at that final moment in the minds and hearts and souls and spirits of those who decide they can no longer deal with life. The unknown appeals much more than the known. All the death bound writers, most suffering from extreme loneliness, in their last words expressed the feeling of being totally on their own with no one to love them or help them or comfort them or understand them. One of the saddest incidents in my fire service career was responding to the suicide of an eleven-year-old boy in a nice family home in a tranquil neighborhood, just down the street from fire station number 3. I still struggle with the question of how one so young had determined he had absolutely nothing to live for. And to top it off, he hung himself from the rafters in the garage so his distorted lifeless body would be the first thing his parents and siblings saw when they came home that day. For too many, peace exists only as a dream in another world, not this one!

Although there are seven suicides mentioned in the Bible, the death of Judas after his betrayal of Jesus probably stands as the definitive example of not staying calm and thereby not surviving—emotionally, physically, and spiritually. I can imagine the suicide note left by Judas.

> Dear John,
>
> Last night at dinner in the upper room you heard Jesus identify me as the evil person I've become. I've always felt like such an outcast since I come from Judea and the rest of you grew up in Galilee. It surprised me at our last meal together that I sat in a place of honor next to Jesus even though he likes you better than all the rest of us, especially me. You were sitting at his breast as usual but he was leaning his head against me. I wondered why I was sitting so close to the Master. Jesus looked straight into my eyes and broke off a piece of bread, dipped it in the juice, and told everyone he would give it to his betrayer. But how could he know I was the one?
>
> I don't think anyone else heard Jesus except you because they all watched with some jealousy as Jesus gave me that

first bite. They're always worrying that someone else will have a higher place in Jesus' coming kingdom. They actually thought he was honoring me in their presence but you know the truth. Something deep inside my heart kept pushing me to take that piece of bread from Jesus and betray this man who has never really done anything wrong or hurt me in any way. When Jesus handed me that piece of bread, I think he was giving me one last chance to change my mind. But I took it with my shaking hand and ate it, and I knew then I was past the point of no return! I was gripped by such a strong, dark force creating so much turmoil within me that I just could not stay calm.

I had this great dream that Jesus would fulfill the prophecies of old concerning the coming Messiah who would deliver Israel from its bondage from the evil Romans. We all did! Jesus even told us he was that person. As a young man, I had memorized the scriptures that spoke of this and I really believed Jesus was the one who would fulfill them. I was ready to make him king at all costs. I saw all the miracles he did and the lives he changed. He had powers like no one else in the world. I was hoping some of his power would spill over on me. I dreamed that Jesus' kingdom would bring us all prosperity! But where is his kingdom now?

When Jesus started offending the very leaders of our people, I wasn't surprised at the growing and great opposition of the Pharisees toward Jesus. They really want to destroy him. I saw their anger when he cleaned out the temple and I hoped then he would once and for all establish himself as king. But, when I saw Jesus do nothing except upset and anger our leaders, I felt my dream fading, and I became resentful and bitter against Jesus. Didn't he see he had such a great opportunity to make our dreams come true? But instead, he chose to associate with lesser people, thieves, whores, and tax collectors and even the Gentiles.

Just a few days ago, he even let that woman friend of his waste three hundred denarii's worth of perfume to clean his dirty feet with her hair in front of other men. The fragrance that filled the whole house made me sick to think what I was losing. She might as well have given it to the poor. I just could not believe she threw away a year's wages for his feet. I began to realize how much I was growing to dislike this man. So much potential and he was just throwing it all away. That finally did it for me! As I walked the mile and a half back to Jerusalem alone, I decided to go to the chief priests to turn Jesus in for a reward. I was so afraid they might end up killing me too. All they gave me was a meager thirty pieces of silver but it was better than nothing. Jesus' days are numbered anyway. He's always talking about dying so it looks like he's going to get his wish - no throne, no power, just death!

There's this evil dark presence all around me now that I've betrayed the only person who brought light to my life. I should have enjoyed that light and stepped out of the darkness that shadowed my heart and now rips it apart. But I fear it's too late for that light to ever bring me peace or joy again. I can't take it anymore. I just want out of all of this.

I have a tree picked out on some rocks overlooking the potter's property so it should be easy just to cut the rope and let my rotting body fall headlong to my burial. After the evil I've caused, no one will want my body anyway. My confusion overwhelms me and I'm sick of life. I've failed at my greatest ambition to overthrow the Romans and reestablish the proper place of our people and now there is nothing for me here. I'm all alone, nobody cares whether I live or die. Even the priests despise me for helping them and they refused to take back the silver. Maybe they will use it to dispose of my body. I just need to find some peace.

Goodbye, Judas.

Judas should have listened more closely because Jesus often spoke about the peace only he could give. The ancient Jewish prophets even called Jesus "the Prince of Peace." At his birth, angels announced he would be a Savior bringing peace to the world. Jesus Christ promised a peaceful life even under the most difficult circumstances. "Peace I leave with you; my peace I give you. I do not give to you as the world gives. Do not let your hearts be troubled and do not be afraid" (John 14:27). On that last night before his death, Jesus comforted the remaining apostles when they became full of worry, turmoil, and anxiety in their hearts at the unacceptable prospect of losing their master and friend. Jesus told them he was leaving them his peace, not the world's. Paul understood Jesus' command to be a key survival strategy. "For he himself is our peace" (Ephesians 2:14). "Therefore being justified by faith, we have peace with God through our Lord Jesus Christ" (Romans 5:1).

Paul outlines God's prescription for staying calm: (1) Don't worry about anything, (2) Pray about everything, (3) Tell God what you need, (4) Thank him for all he has done. "Do not be anxious about anything, but in everything, by prayer and petition, with thanksgiving, present your requests to God" (Philippians 4:6). What happens when we follow those instructions? We stay calm! "Before you know it, a sense of God's wholeness, everything coming together for good, will come and settle you down. It's wonderful what happens when Christ displaces worry at the center of your life" (Philippians 4:7, MSG).

Satan loves chaos and the pain and suffering it causes, and his evil world dishes it out over and over. On the other hand, here is the eternal peace only Jesus can promise his followers: (1) God loves us beyond all measures, (2) God has everything under complete control at all times, (3) God knows us by name and has neither forgotten us nor forsaken us no matter how bad things may seem, (4) God gives us his ultimate comfort and perfect peace, (5) and lest we never forget, God has a divine and absolute purpose for everything. The devil may be the prince of this world, but Jesus reigns as the Prince of Peace just as the late Christian singer and songwriter Rich Mullins sang about.

Sometimes my life just don't make sense at all
When the mountains look so big
And my faith just seems so small.
And I wake up in the night and feel the dark
It's so hot inside my soul
There must be blisters on my heart
So hold me Jesus, I'm shaking like a leaf
You have been King of my glory
Won't You be my Prince of Peace.[11]

Knowing that God remains in control no matter what's happening in our lives brings the peace that is so needed during our most desperate, despairing, and discouraging moments. We've seen that the world doesn't offer any real and lasting peace or answers to our stress. Don't be surprised, Jesus told us it would be this way in John 16:33: "I have told you these things, so that in me you may have peace. In this world you will have trouble. But take heart! I have overcome the world." On the last day of Jesus' human life, Peter crashed into chaos and denial, but after the resurrection he finally got the message and learned how to stay calm in Jesus' peace. "Cast all your anxiety on him because he cares for you" (1 Peter 5:7).

We cast our cares upon the Son of God because he cares for us. Peter tells us to cast "all" our cares on Christ because he is our peace. What does it mean to cast all our cares upon him? It means leaving with him every anxiety, every worry, every grief, and every pain, everything that causes us despair and heartbreak. When we do that, we can proclaim with King David: "When anxiety was great within me, your consolation brought joy to my soul" (Psalm 94:19). Staying calm in Christ brings peaceful joy to your soul in spite of pandemonium around you!

A Methodist preacher born in 1884 by the name of Luther Bridges married Sara Veatch and they had three beautiful sons. In the year 1910, Pastor Bridges accepted an invitation to preach at a conference in Kentucky, and while he was gone, he left his entire family in the care of his father-in-law. After finishing two fruitful and exciting weeks of ministry there, Bridges was looking forward to telling his loving wife all about the trip's many blessings. However, tragically, a deadly fire had burned down the house of his father-in-law and his wife, Sara, and all three of his sons had perished in the inferno. In the very worst moment of his life, Luther Bridges heard the calming whisper of Jesus and cast all his cares on his Savior and wrote these famous words that have blessed so many over the years.

> There's within my heart a melody
> Jesus whispers sweet and low,
> Fear not, I am with thee, peace be still
> In all of life's ebb and flow.
> Though sometimes he leads through waters deep,
> Trials fall across the way,
> Though sometimes the path seems rough and steep,
> See his footprints all the way.
> Soon he's coming back to welcome me,
> Far beyond the starry sky;
> I shall wing my flight to worlds unknown,
> I shall reign with him on high.
> Jesus, Jesus, Jesus,
> Sweetest Name I know,
> Fills my every longing,
> Keeps me singing as I go.[12]

CONTENTMENT

Stay Calm With What You Have Today - Tomorrow Will Take Care of Itself!

According to Jesus, a worrier exercises very little faith. Just as in our survival strategies, faith and worry are matters of orientation. It's the orientation of our hearts and minds as to where we came from, where we are, and where we're going. Where and how we stay oriented eternally affects our priorities. We only live in the present, but far too often our concerns about the past and our questions about the future steal away our contentment with the present.

Yet, recalling the survival strategy to stay oriented, we can only be content in the present. When we stay oriented and know where we came from, no concerns remain about the past, and when we stay oriented and know where we're going every anxious thought should be swept away. When we first seek God's kingdom, he will continuously keep us oriented with a peace that can only come from him in the present.

Even though the first century did not necessarily have terrorists to threaten the Palestinian's lives, they still suffered under the hand of a brutal foreign government as slaves with no hope of freedom, other than the promised eventual delivery by a Messiah. They experienced famine due to crop failure and water shortages and faced the ravages of terrible diseases. And just like all humans since the Fall, they were also dealing with the pressures and fears of everyday living. Anxiety existed everywhere, just as it does today. In one of his most famous sermons, Jesus offered his survival strategy for the worried, anxious hearts of the multitudes of people searching for peace on a mountainside.

> Therefore I tell you, do not worry about your life, what you will eat or drink; or about your body, what you will wear. Is not life more important than food, and the body more important than clothes?...Who of you by worrying can add a single hour to his life?...So do not worry, saying, "What shall we eat?" or "What shall we drink?" or "What shall we wear?" For the pagans run after all these things, and your heavenly Father knows that you need them.
>
> Matthew 6:25, 27, 31–32

The Lord asks the large crowd what good it does to worry anyway. Everyone has to eat, drink, and wear clothes as part of the human existence. But that's not the source of our contentment. And so he reminds the multitude that real contentment is much more than food and clothing. In other words, anxiety is futile because contentment is more than things. It's more than material. It's more than the physical. It extends far beyond the temporary. It has an eternal dimension to it that goes way beyond our mind's capability to fully comprehend. Worry never brings contentment but a lack of contentment will always increase anxiety.

The creature comforts of eating, drinking, and clothing still drive our society. Just watch the television or look at the advertisements in magazines or view the billboards along the freeway. They greatly influence our choices of the products we think we need to eat, drink, and wear. Marketers live off our discontent! When we base our contentment on such things, we become exceedingly unhappy and full of anxiety. So what is it you seek? Jesus says that Pagans and unbelievers seek after temporal things–food, drink, and clothing. They aren't necessarily bad things as Jesus confirms, "your heavenly Father knows that you need them." But they can easily preoccupy us if we don't prioritize our needs, so Jesus issues his eternal priority to every believer.

> But seek first his kingdom and his righteousness, and all these things will be given to you as well. Therefore do not worry about tomorrow, for tomorrow will worry about itself. Each day has enough trouble of its own.
>
> Matthew 6:33–34

Christians should primarily focus on God's kingdom and righteousness, but Jesus says unbelievers consume themselves with creature comforts rather than Creator comforts, seeking to satisfy their desires and build earthly treasures. They seek happiness through temporal things. Both nonbelievers and believers are seeking something. One seeks the temporal for momentary happiness while the other seeks a righteousness that leads to a holier life. One lives for the moment and the other lives with eternity in view. One lives for creature comforts and the other for Creator comforts. Only one finds contentment and Jesus says to seek the Creator comforts!

Earlier in his ministry, Jesus accurately responded to the misguided motives of the people: "'I tell you the truth, you are looking for me, not because you saw miraculous signs but because you ate the loaves and had your fill" (John 6:26). The people were only seeking creature comforts and not Creator comforts. In this case, they were even pursuing creature comforts from the Creator himself. Pastor Ray Stedman insightfully paraphrases Jesus' words:

> You didn't come because you understood the signs I performed–the signs predicted in the Old Testament as the credentials of the Messiah. You didn't come because you want to follow Me as Lord. You came because you wanted to exploit Me. All you want is more free meals.[13]

They completely missed the point of Jesus because he came to give himself. This is the ultimate Creator comfort as Christ promises! "Do not work for food that spoils (creature comfort), but for food that endures to eternal life (Creator comfort), which the Son of Man will give you" (John 6:27). "I am the bread of life. He who comes to me will never go hungry, and he who believes in me will never be thirsty" (John 6:34). Creator comfort lasts forever and that's why Christians should stay calm in this temporary world!

We must remember that Creator comforts and creature comforts both come from God. As we learned in Genesis 3, our desire is always for creature comforts, even though our need is for Creator comforts. But when given the choice between the manna (creature comfort) and the Bread of Life (Creator comfort), which do you think we usually choose? John 6:36 gives the unpleasant answer: "But as I told you, you have seen me and still you do not believe." Creature comforts sustain us (manna); Creator comforts save us (Bread of Life). Creature comforts give us instant gratification; Creator comforts give us eternity. Here's an entry from my journal on January 31, 2003, about my struggles with Creator comforts versus creature comforts:

> ***COMFORT***–As I sit here in Denton, Texas, in my nice, large house with my fireplace burning to keep me warm on this very cold winter morning and in my nice, warm flannel pajamas and as I curl up with a cup of strong, hot coffee on my comfortable leather couch studying John's gospel with my Border Collies, Patches and Loki, snuggled up and snoring next to me, I have all the comforts

> of home. I have five separate translations of your Word and four commentaries on the Gospel of John to help me grasp your precious Word. None of this is bad and I'm so thankful for my abundant blessings, but I think of all the Christians in the world who are freezing right now in this winter of 2003, who are not comfortable in their surroundings. They may not even have a Bible of any translation. Yet, they are comfortable in YOU! No creature comforts, just Creator comfort. They are the ones winning people to you - who are absolutely committed to you and who may well die today in their service to you. In spite of the lack of creature comforts, they are absolutely content with YOU. My prayers are with them. Encourage them and comfort them and may their spirits combined with Your Spirit overwhelm my senses, my heart, and my soul, but mostly my spirit. May I always seek first your comfort and not my own! May your holiness and presence in me bring me total contentment. Now that's true peace and the only way I can ever stay calm and survive on Planet Earth!

Based on his survival advice, Jesus says do not worry about tomorrow for tomorrow will take care of itself because each day has enough trouble of its own. Since we only live in the present, we deal with our problems one day at a time. Real faith looks to a God who is greater than anything we can hear, know, or see and who tells us to stay calm! By the way, he may not work it out the way you want him to. Are you content to remain calm and let him do it his way or would you rather worry about doing it your way?

That's what Jesus meant when he said to seek first God's kingdom and righteousness (Creator comforts) and then everything else (creature comforts) would be given to us as well, but only in his perfect timing. Jesus extends his perfect promise so don't worry about anything; just seek God's kingdom and righteousness and all his Creator comforts will bring us more contentment and peace than we could ever imagine. "Let your conduct be without covetousness; be content with such things as you have. For He Himself has said, 'I will never leave you nor forsake you'" (Hebrews 13:5, NKJV). Now that's comforting!

THE STORMS OF LIFE

Quiet, Be Calm!

> Leaving the crowd behind, they took him along, just as he was, in the boat. There were also other boats with him. A furious squall came up, and the wave broke over the boat, so that it was nearly swamped. Jesus was in the stern, sleeping on a cushion. The disciples woke him and said to him, "Teacher, don't you care if we drown?" He got up, rebuked the wind and said to the waves, "Quiet! Be still!" Then the wind died down and it was completely calm.
>
> Mark 4:36–39

Although the Sea of Galilee (actually a lake) is only about eight miles wide and thirteen miles long, it has a long history of sudden and fierce storms. Situated to the north of the Jordan Valley about 680 feet below the sea level of the Mediterranean, the Sea of Galilee is surrounded by hills–especially on the east where there are high cliffs. Great storms can quickly develop when the cold air from Mount Herman to the north and warm air collide above this natural water basin, causing high waves out on the water capable of swamping boats. All three synoptic gospels describe a strong, dangerous storm that suddenly developed as the disciples set out across the Sea of Galilee.

The whole point of the story applies to our lives because storms happen. Just as the disciples found themselves in the midst of a terrible storm, we all too often have sudden storms come up in our lives and the hardest kinds of storms to weather are those that take us by surprise. Sooner or later the storms of life catch up to all of us and we are met by an overwhelming sense of our boat being swamped, washing us overboard and drowning us. And, if Jesus isn't in the boat with us, we're really sunk!

But, on the other hand, many Christians mistakenly assume

that they will always have smooth sailing with Jesus in the boat with them. We think if Jesus is with us, there will be no storms, no waves, and no fear–only abundant blessings. Some popular preachers have even advocated this "success" philosophy from their pulpits. And sadly, too often we market and sell salvation that way! However, just as the disciples quickly found out on this eventful day, following Jesus may actually put us in the center of the storm! God has never promised us that our lives will be empty of pain, disappointment, or storms. However, his presence is all we need to stay calm in the storms of life. Even though God never guaranteed us smooth sailing, he does assure us that we will always get to the other side with him.

Matthew, Mark, and Luke provide their unique descriptions of the story of Jesus calming the storm and saving the disciples. The chapters leading up to this particular boat ride tell us that Jesus' life had been a blur of activity. This long day of ministry began with confrontations and continued amidst the press of immense crowds. He'd been involved in doing miracles, teaching his disciples, and now preaching to a great crowd on the shoreline from a boat floating just off the beach on the Sea of Galilee. And he says to his disciples. "Let's go to the other side of the Sea of Galilee." Mark tells us they took him just as he was, since he was already in the boat.

Jesus was tired after having been on the go for so long and working so hard with so many demands on his life. As a human, even the Creator of all things could claim no exemption from the fatigue that had worn him out this particular day. So as the ship pushed off on its journey across the big lake with some other boats following, Jesus moved to the stern of his boat, where he wearily collapsed into a deep sleep in his exhausted human body. Then, very unexpectedly and according to Matthew's account "without warning," a terrible storm produced great waves spilling into the boat, making it appear as if everyone on the boat was in imminent danger of drowning. Even the fishermen now turned disciples became extremely frightened. The seasoned boatmen were afraid that all of them, including Jesus, would die.

Matthew, a passenger in the boat, records that they all cried out for help from Jesus: "Lord, save us! We're going to drown!" (8:25). Mark writes that the apostles fearfully questioned Jesus, "Teacher, don't you care if we drown?" (4:38). Luke reports that the disciples feared their impending demise: "Master, Master, we're going to drown!" (8:24). Surely the travelers in the boat made many more panicked pleas for help than those recorded in the gospels, but observe that all the appeals for survival were made directly to Jesus: "Master," "Teacher," and "Lord." Apparently, they all believed he had some powers that they didn't have.

While these veteran sailors were panicking because of the power of the storm, Jesus slept and seemed unaware or unconcerned about their plight. To the travelers on the boat, he appeared indifferent to their deadly dilemma, "don't you care if we drown?" In the storms that we pass through, how often do we think maybe God's taking a long nap and doesn't really care for us? When I'm in the midst of a crisis or some imminent danger or disaster, it often seems that Jesus just doesn't care if I drown! He doesn't appear to be concerned with what I'm going through. He's asleep and not interested in my quandary!

And just like the disciples on the boat in the storm, why do we imagine that our prayers, our requests for favor and intervention, are an imposition to a sleeping Savior? God's enemy continually seeks to portray God as the one who is too preoccupied to help us in trouble, too weak to save us in the face of crisis, or too busy to respond to our maydays. And how often do we believe such lies? This is one of the biggest obstacles to staying calm. The enemy deceives us into thinking that nothing will work–it's too late. We're all going to drown!

Just like those first disciples, I sometimes forget that if Jesus is in the boat I can stay calm. But fear is faith's number one enemy. Fear and anxiety gripped the disciples in the boat because they forgot who was with them. The same fear seizes many believers today because they forget who is in them. Why do we so often forget God's absolute promise? "So do not fear, for I am with you; do not be dismayed, for I am your God. I will strengthen you and help you; I will uphold you with my righteous hand" (Isaiah 41:10).

All three gospels describe a sudden, miraculous, and complete calm. Jesus spoke, "Quiet, be still!" and the fierce storm not only ceased, the Sea of Galilee instantly returned to normal. Notice how simply it was done–"there was a great calm." Generally considerable time is required for high rolling waves buffeted by the wind in a large body of water to subside, but miraculously the winds, along with the waves, immediately diminished. He spoke and it was as if there had never been a storm. Luke says, "all was calm."

The story begins in fear and now it ends in terror and amazement. At the beginning the disciples cry out, "Don't you care that we are about to die?" When the storm came upon them Mark says, "They were afraid"; but after Jesus stilled the wind and the waves just as they asked, Mark adds, "they feared exceedingly." Their fright of the storm was replaced by a new even greater trepidation. After Jesus intervened and calm was restored, you'd think the disciples would be relieved and encouraged. But they were more terrified of Jesus' power than they were of the natural calamity they had just escaped. "He said to his disciples, 'Why are you so afraid? Do you still have no faith?' They were terrified and asked each other, "Who is this? Even the wind and the waves obey him!" (Mark 4:40–41).

This begs the question as to what the disciples expected from Jesus in the first place. They wanted him to do something but even they were shocked by his actions. Why? They were suddenly conscious that the one standing in the boat with them was more than just a mere man. Jesus was greater than all of them, greater than anyone they had ever seen before. And just as his disciples did then, we often underestimate Jesus' power to handle crisis in our lives and help us to stay calm! And just like the disciples, we're often surprised when Jesus intervenes. Mary Ann Baker's classic hymn, "Master the Tempest is Raging," reminds us that our lives are filled with storms like the raging tempest on the sea and the "Master of the ocean and earth and skies" still calms the storm.

Master, the tempest is raging!
The billows are tossing high!
The sky is o'ershadowed with blackness.
No shelter or help is nigh.

Carest thou not that we perish?
How canst Thou lie asleep
When each moment so madly is threatening
a grave in the angry deep?
The winds and the waves shall obey thy will:
Peace be still!
Whether the wrath of the storm-tossed sea or demons,
or men or whatever it be,
No waters can swallow the ship where lies
The Master of ocean and earth and skies.
They all shall sweetly obey thy will:
Peace, be still; peace, be still.
They all shall sweetly obey thy will:
peace, peace, be still.[14]

IT IS WELL WITH MY SOUL
Whatever My Lot!

One of the most famous stories recounted about staying calm under the worst circumstances of life is the account of a Chicago businessman named Horatio Gates Spafford. Some have even compared him to a modern day Job. I've read and heard many versions of his tragic life story, but as I researched this man and his family I discovered there's much more to Spafford's story than one man and a famous hymn. Both Horatio and Anna Spafford stand as true inspirations to the survival strategy of staying calm. So as Paul Harvey says, here's the rest of the story.

At the beginning of the 1870s, Horatio Spafford and his Norwegian-born wife, Anna, were living just north of Chicago in a suburb named Lake View. Horatio had a successful law practice in downtown Chicago as senior partner in the prominent and influential law firm of Spafford, McDaniel, and Wilson. He actively served as a devout elder in a Presbyterian church he helped form and grow. In addition, Horatio had successfully invested heavily in real estate in an expanding and booming Chicago in the spring of 1871.

On October 8, 1871, a fire broke out in a crowded Chicago neighborhood somewhere in or very near the now infamous O'Leary barn. The fire service calls this the Great Chicago Fire and even memorializes it every year with Fire Prevention Week. In spite of blaming the O'Leary cow, no one knows the exact location where the fire began, but hot winds spread the flames straight for the center of the city. The streets, sidewalks, and bridges made of wood quickly burned and engulfed structure after structure, killing an unknown hundreds of men, women, and children.

The Great Chicago Fire burned out of control for twenty-four hours. The flames were so hot that the wheels on streetcars melted and train tracks twisted into steel snakes. At least 17,000 buildings were destroyed and 100,000 people were left homeless. The fire burned more than 1,000 acres and the property loss was a whopping $200 million in 1871 dollars. Here's a vivid description of the terrible fire by Anna Spafford as told years later to her daughter, Bertha Spafford Vester, who recorded her mother's comments in her wonderful book, *Our Jerusalem*.

> The glare lighting lake and sky was terrifying, and adding to the terror were the explosions that continued to shake the burning city for days and that could be heard for many miles...As mile after mile of wooden buildings, homes, stores, and sidewalks caught fire, the glaring illumination showed a city gone mad with terror. Crowds of men, women, and children ran first in one direction, then in another, shouting and screaming, saving objects, no matter how worthless, carrying them, losing them again. Every explosion that shook the city added to their panic.[15]

The fire that destroyed almost the entire city of Chicago stopped just short of the Spafford's home in Lake View, but it plunged the family into a time of immense distress–financial as well as physical and emotional. Spafford's law library and adjoining law office in the city were in ashes. His daughter wrote, "The Great fire was a crushing misfortune to nearly every inhabitant of Chicago. To Father and his associates in the real estate venture it was a calamity."[16] *The Chicago Tribune* newspaper, which was completely destroyed, reported, "It was destruction of the entire business portion of one of the greatest cities in the world. Every bank, insurance office, law office, hotel, theater, railroad, most of the churches and many of the principal residences of the city–a charred mass–property almost beyond estimation gone!"[17]

Despite the large loss of a great deal of their investments and wealth, the Spaffords dedicated themselves to helping those who had been impoverished by the devastation of their city. With such destruction, Chicago suffered great poverty and misery the winter following the fire. Horatio and Anna worked hard in relief efforts for desperate Chicagoans after the fire, serving with all their resourcefulness and strength on relief and aid committees. After two years of dedicated work resulting in the failing health of Anna, the Spafford family felt strongly in need of rest and recuperation so they planned a family vacation in Europe.

The Spaffords and their four young daughters booked passage on the steamship *Ville de Havre* sailing from New York. The great craft was known as the foremost pleasure ship of the seas at that time. Unfortunately, at the last minute, Horatio Spafford was delayed by an offer from a man to purchase part of the land in which he had invested before the disastrous fire. Horatio convinced his wife and daughters to go to Europe without him so he accompanied them to New York where they would sail on the *Ville du Havre,* and he would later join them in France. Several friends and acquaintances from Chicago were also venturing across the North Atlantic with Anna and her daughters.

For some reason that he was never able to explain, just before sailing Horatio changed his family's stateroom from amidships to near the bow of the vessel. "He had chosen them himself, carefully, weeks before. But the feeling was so strong that he could not throw it off, and at almost the last minute he changed the rooms."[18] And as his unfortunate lot in life continued, just before saying goodbye to his family and sending them off to Europe, Horatio received a telegram telling him that the man who had been about to buy the Chicago property had died suddenly of a heart attack and the deal passed away with him.

Anna and the four girls sailed, and halfway to Europe about two o'clock in the morning on November 22, 1873, on a calm black sea, the *Ville de Havre* collided amidships with *The Lochearn*, an English sailing ship. The staterooms originally reserved by Horatio were the first to receive the crushing blow of the iron ship and all their occupants died quickly. As it was, the *Ville de Havre* sank in only twelve minutes claiming the lives of 226 people. The only survivors were six officers, twenty-three crewmembers, and twenty-eight passengers - ten women, seventeen men, and one nine-year old girl - making a total of only fifty-seven saved.

After the terrible crash, Anna Spafford had stood bravely on the deck with her daughters Annie, Maggie, Bessie, and Tanetta clinging desperately to her. Frantically, the dedicated and loving mother fought to save them. Maggie told her mother, "Mama, God will take care of us." And little Annie said, "Don't be afraid. The sea is His and he made it."[19] But Anna and her babies along with all the other people hopelessly clinging to the deck were pulled "into a whirlpool created by suction of bodies, wreckage, and savage water,"[20] into the dark ocean in an instant of lasting horror. Anna Spafford's last memory was baby Tanetta being torn violently from her arms by the force of the waters as she held on to Tanetta's little gown for a fraction of a second before she was wrenched forever out of her mother's hand.

After rolling under and down with bodies and debris, Anna rose unconscious to the surface and a plank miraculously floated under her limp body saving her life. She floated lifelessly in the water for an hour before she was rescued, and her actual first recollection was, "lying in a boat, bruised from head to foot and sick with sea water, her long hair heavy with salt and her thick dressing gown in ribbons. She knew, with no need of being told, that her children were gone."[21]

When the survivors of the wreck had been rescued, Mrs. Spafford's first reaction was one of complete despair. Then she heard a voice speak to her, "You were spared for a purpose." And she immediately recalled the recent words of a friend, "It's easy to be grateful and good when you have so much, but take care that you are not a fair-weather friend to God." A fellow survivor of the collision, a French Pastor named Weiss, recalled Anna saying during the journey to France on the rescue boat, "God gave me four daughters. Now they have been taken from me. Someday I will understand why."[22]

Think about the terrible grief that Anna had to bear alone for those days on the sea after losing her children and sailing completely alone without her husband. She couldn't telephone, email, or text message Horatio. Most of her companions on board the ship, including a good friend and all her children, had also perished. There was no national news on the television describing the terrible disaster letting people at home know what happened. Three days after the shipwreck, still unaware of the disaster at sea, Horatio wrote his wife a letter dated November 25th, which Anna would receive many weeks later in France saying, "When you write, tell me all about the children. How thankful I am to God for them! May He make us faithful parents, having an eye single to His glory. Annie and Maggie and Bessie and Tanetta–it is a sweet consolation even to write their names. May the dear Lord keep and sustain and strengthen you..."[23] When Horatio wrote the names of his daughters, little did he know they were already with God and that his loving wife was sailing by herself on a rescue ship to France. On December 1, 1873, nine days after the shipwreck, Anna landed in Cardiff, Wales, and cabled Horatio, "Saved Alone. What shall I do?"

As a heartsick Horatio Spafford desperately sailed to France to reunite with his grieving wife, the captain of the ship called him to the bridge. Pointing to a nautical chart, the captain told him that they were just passing the spot where the *Ville de Havre* had gone down. Spafford later wrote about this event in a letter to a relative:

> On Thursday last we passed over the spot where she went down, in mid-ocean, the water three miles deep. But I do not think of our dear ones there. They are safe, folded, the dear lambs, and there, before very long, shall we be too. In the meantime, thanks to God, we have an opportunity to serve and praise Him for his love and mercy to us and

> ours. "I will praise Him while I have my being." May we each one arise, leave all, and follow Him.[24]

As Horatio walked the deck in sorrow, he stayed calm sustained only by his faith. As this grieving father watched the waves rolling on the ocean, the Bible teacher and church elder recalled the comforting words of Isaiah 66:12, "For thus says the Lord, I will extend peace to her like a river..." Staying calm, he had the faith to say that whatever his lot, it was well with his soul and then wrote the words of one of the most famous and enduring hymns of strength and staying power during times of peril and hurt. Each verse contains wonderful expressions of faith and truth emphasizing the survival strategy of staying calm.

> When peace like a river attendeth my way,
> When sorrows like sea-billows roll;
> Whatever my lot, thou has taught me to say,
> It is well, it is well with my soul.
>
> Though Satan should buffet, though trials should come,
> Let this blest assurance control,
> That Christ has regarded my helpless estate,
> And hath shed His own blood for my soul.
>
> My sin, oh, the bliss of this glorious thought!
> My sin, not in part but the whole,
> Is nailed to the cross, and I bear it no more,
> Praise the Lord, praise the Lord, O my soul!
>
> For me, be it Christ, be it Christ hence to live:
> If Jordan above me shall roll,
> No pang shall be mine, for in death as in life
> Thou wilt whisper Thy peace to my soul.
>
> But, Lord, 'tis for Thee, for Thy coming we wait,
> The sky, not the grave, is our goal;

Oh trump of the angel! Oh voice of the Lord!
Blessed hope, blessed rest of my soul!

And, Lord, haste the day when the faith shall be sight,
The clouds be rolled back as a scroll,
The trump shall resound, and the Lord shall descend,
Even so, it is well with my soul.[25]

While Horatio gets well-deserved recognition for staying calm under such terrible conditions, Anna deserves equal credit. She wrote from Paris to a friend in Chicago on Christmas Eve following the shipwreck: "We have been so sustained, so comforted, God has sent peace in our hearts. He has answered our prayers. His will be done."[26] When the Spaffords returned to Chicago, Anna went to work for their good friend, the renowned evangelist Dwight Moody. He put her in charge of all women's activities for Chicago. A friend wrote of this period in Anna's life: "She devoted almost her entire time to Christian and philanthropic work. She was the first woman, I believe, who in Chicago encouraged mothers' meetings. They met once a week in the church parlors, and there she taught many a mother to pray."[27] Anna Spafford discovered this survival reality: Only when you stay calm in the midst of heartache can you faithfully serve God!

There's still much more to the Spafford story. After their return to Chicago, Anna gave birth to a son, Horatio, in 1876 and, two years later, a daughter they named Bertha. Sadly, the Spafford's heartbreak continued. After an epidemic of scarlet fever broke out, their only son died in February of 1880 and it seemed that the Spaffords were doomed forever to unhappiness. The Spaffords had suffered one horrible event after another and awful rumors ran rampant through their church because it was universally accepted by many Christians in those days that sickness or sorrow was the result of some dreadful sin. People were asking what terrible thing the Spaffords had done that they should be so afflicted. And their next tragedy occurred as described by their daughter, Bertha: "Father and Mother were asked to leave the Fullerton Avenue Presbyterian Church, the church Father had helped to build, the church of which he was an elder, the church where my sisters and brother had been baptized, the church they loved."[28]

The Spaffords decided to temporarily move their family to the holy city of Jerusalem to get closer to Jesus and to seek solace and God's guidance. In solidarity, several other families from their church accompanied them from Chicago. Delaying only until the birth of their final daughter, named Grace in thanks to God, in August 1881, they set out for Jerusalem with a band of thirteen adults and three children. They moved into a house in the Old Quarter, between Herod's Gate and the Damascus Gate, and tirelessly dedicated themselves to a life of helping the poor of Jerusalem, especially the children. This settlement became known as "the American Colony" and grew over the years as chronicled by their daughter, Bertha, in her book *Our Jerusalem*.

Following Horatio's death in 1888, three generations of Spafford women have sustained the Colony and its humanitarian mission: medical clinics, orphanages, soup kitchens, schools and a pediatric hospital. They ultimately turned their villa into a hostelry, a haven for pilgrims and politicians alike for many years. The Spafford Children's Center, which has saved the lives of hundreds and hundreds of children, still operates in their original Jerusalem home. With the loss of five of their seven own children, Horatio and Anna Spafford could never have dreamed of their ultimate legacy to so many children.

"Whatever my lot, Thou has taught me to say, It is well, It is well with my soul," should be the motto for this survival strategy! What is "my lot"? The world would tell us it's anything that rules or determines our destinies–by whatever serendipitous power available. But to Christians, our "lot" represents our divine mission. Psalm 16:5 says, "Lord you have assigned me my portion and my cup and have made my lot secure." Nothing happens to us by chance or by accident or luck. God divinely allots our destinies. Good or bad luck has no bearing on Christians! The Spaffords, in spite of their anguish, could say along with the apostle Paul, "I have learned to be content whatever the circumstances" (Philippians 4:11).

The words that Horatio Spafford, an experienced Bible teacher with extensive knowledge of God's Word, wrote while sailing on the same sea that had claimed four of his most precious possessions came from 2 Kings 4. They echo the response of an old Shunammite woman to the sudden death of her only child. This faithful and prominent Shunammite woman lived during the time of the prophet Elisha and, just like Horatio Spafford, she continually demonstrated strong spiritual character in the midst of heartache.

Elisha often stayed at her home and enjoyed the hospitality of the old woman and her husband. One day Elisha asked his servant what he might do to repay the old woman for her generosity. The servant responded that she had no child and had no chance of ever having a family because her husband was old. Elisha called the woman and said, "About this season, according to the time of life, thou shalt embrace a son." In due time, she had a son just as Elisha promised.

The child grew up to be a young man. Then one day, when he was out in the harvest field working, he got a bad headache and was taken to his mother where he died on her lap. She carried him up to Elisha's bed and laid him there. The woman got on one of her donkeys and went immediately to get Elisha. When she and her servant reached the foot of Mount Carmel where Elisha and his servant were, Elisha saw her from a distance and sent his servant, Gehazi, to meet her. Elisha said, "Behold, there is the Shunammite. Please run now to meet her and say to her, 'Is it well with you? Is it well with your husband? Is it well with the child?'" In spite of a breaking heart, she simply answered, "It is well" (2 Kings 4:25–26, NASB). She and her husband were old. Her son was dead. The worst possible thing in her life had happened! How could it be well? The miracle that God had given her had been taken away. The only way that it could be well was because she had total faith in God! But, if you remember the story, it has a happy ending. Elisha went to find the dead boy, prayed, and laid down over the body. The boy sneezed seven times and opened his eyes and lived.

How can one say, "It is well," in the face of such hopelessness and anguish? If we look at what the world offers during times of heartbreak and chaos, we will most often find it very difficult to respond, "It is well." But as Christians, no matter what the most difficult circumstances are or how terrible we feel or how hopeless the situation seems, we can faithfully answer, "It is well." The New Testament tells us that this woman was a believer who lived by faith, because in Hebrews 11 the author speaks of the testimonies of Old Testament saints who lived by faith. Among these he speaks of the "women who received back their dead by resurrection" (Hebrews 11:35) and since there were only two mentioned in the Old Testament, the old woman of Shunem was surely one of them.

STAYING CALM IS A SURVIVAL ATTITUDE

Develop Your Endurance to Build Strong Character!

But, here's our dilemma. We don't always get the answer we want. We're not disciples floating in the boat with the Savior of the world or the Shunammite woman expecting a miracle from a living prophet of God. I'm not sure if my family was wiped out that I could write a beautiful song praising God. We've done everything we can and the worst happens–at least in our eyes. Things are not well within ourselves and our lots seem unbearable. We cry out for help in our time of trouble and we patiently wait and wait and nothing seems to happen. Worry about tomorrow begins to creep in when we think God is not listening and our faith begins to wane and we ask God, "Why me?"

Habakkuk asked God a very difficult question that many of us will echo. "How long, O Lord, must I call for help, but you do not listen?" (Habakkuk 1:2). The Lord answered his prophet Habakkuk and simply told him to stay calm and have faith in God's power and love. "…the righteous will live by his faith…" (Habakkuk 2:4). Habakkuk joyfully prayed a prayer of contentment and staying calm: "Though the fig tree does not bud and there are no grapes on the vines, though the olive crop fails and the fields produce no food, though there are no sheep in the pen and no cattle in the stalls (creature comforts), yet I will rejoice in the Lord, I will be joyful in God my Savior. The Sovereign Lord is my strength; he makes my feet like the feet of a deer, he enables me to go on the heights (Creator comforts)" (Habakkuk 3:17–19, author's emphasis). Deer can nimbly run across rough and dangerous terrain with great endurance and leap over obstacles, and God says he will give his followers sure footing through the most difficult of times.

James tells us the purpose of trials is to test and deepen our faith and ultimately develop our endurance to build strong character. He reminds all believers that trials will come and are inevitable: "Dear brothers and sisters, whenever trouble comes your way, let it be an opportunity for joy. For when your faith is tested, your endurance has a chance to grow. So let it grow, for when your endurance is fully developed, you will be strong in character and ready for anything" (James 1:2–3, NLT). However, we still usually take the attitude of resentment and "why me?" Viktor Frankl, the brilliant Viennese psychiatrist, who spent years in Nazi concentration camps, wrote in *Man's Search for Meaning*, "Everything can be taken from a man but one thing: the last of the human freedoms–to choose one's attitude in any given set of circumstances, to choose one's own way."[29]

This generates our essential survival question: What's your survival attitude? Is it, "it is well with my soul whatever my lot"? Or is it, "Why me Lord?" In spite of losing her missionary husband, Jim Elliot, who was speared to death along with four of his friends while trying to reach the Auca Indians in 1955, Elisabeth Elliot continually exemplifies the holy survival attitude of staying calm in the world with joyful endurance because she understands and fully believes that God knows exactly what he's doing.

> "...the unexpected in our lives was expected by God, fully known, anticipated, and it fits somewhere, somehow, mysteriously into a pattern for good...I don't know how the things in my life fit into God's pattern for good. Sometimes He gives us a glimpse. Sometimes we can see the ways in which there were many pieces of a pattern that we didn't know anything about when the thing happened. But God was working on it. It encourages us to know that the pieces do fit together ultimately, but He doesn't often give us clues like that."[30]

STAY ORIENTED!

Know Where You're Going

During the most intense firefight, firefighters must always have an exit plan from the situation where their lives are on the line. Without an orientation strategy to where they're going, firefighters would be just like Alice in Wonderland. "Would you tell me, please, which way I ought to go from here," asked Alice. "That depends a great deal on where you want to get to," said the Cheshire Cat.[1] When fighting a fire, firefighters must stay focused on the orientation of knowing exactly where they're getting so they come out safe and secure and ready to respond again. To that end, the National Fallen Firefighters Foundation has adopted a slogan that sums up the survival strategy of all firefighters in three short words: "Everyone Goes Home!" It's the hope of every firefighter!

After the tragic death of Firefighter Bret Tarver, the Phoenix Fire Department added two words to their mission statement: "to survive." That means at the end of their shift, the same number of firefighters that came to work also go home. No more need for personal protective clothing or emergency tools. The mission has been accomplished and now the time comes to join loved ones outside the danger zone. In the words of Benedictine monk David Steindl-Rast, "Home is where we start from but home is also where we are bound for, the place we always seek." Or, as they always say, "Home is where the heart is!" When firefighters come to work, their orientation is to survive and their hope is to go home.

John Calvin compared us to travelers "who in a momentary

lightning flash see far and wide, but the sight vanishes so swiftly that they are plunged again into the darkness of night before they can even take a step."[2] As pilgrims, we're all trying to get home struggling through the darkness of this world, singing the words of that old 1960's country western hit song, "I wanna go home, I wanna go home, oh Lord I wanna go home!"[3] King Solomon wrote in the book of Ecclesiastes: "I have seen the burden God has laid on men. He has made everything beautiful in its time. He has also set eternity in the hearts of men" (3:10–11). Joseph Stowell in his great book, *Eternity*, says this internal eternal desire to go home "produces courage and strength. It enables us to make choices that dramatically affect all of life."[4] Although we all have that internal desire in our hearts for eternity, the darkness of the world shadows our journey home unless our hope is for something other than what this dark and evil world offers.

Non-Christians walk in the darkness of the world all the time. At times in their lives, the spiritual lightning hits, they see, and then as swiftly as they saw, they become blinded again. Everyone gets a chance to see, however briefly. Even in Jesus' time, the people saw the miracles and signs "flash" before them in the light of his glory and then, just as quickly, they were blinded and right back in the darkness of the world. Why are there so few travelers to an eternal home compared to the non-believers who journey to their eternal death? Remember, Jesus gave the answer: "This is the verdict; Light has come into the world, but men loved darkness instead of light because their deeds were evil. Everyone who does evil hates the light, and will not come into the light for fear that his deeds will be exposed" (John 3:19–20).

Christians also walk in the darkness of the world, but the Holy Spirit flashes the lightning as an eternal beacon and illuminates the signposts to our true home as often as we are willing and ready to walk more in the illumination of his light. All too often, even Christians hide in the darkness because of our evil nature. However, as we mature in the Spirit, the lightning flashes occur more and more until we see clearly the direction home more often than not. The Light marks our path homeward as we travel our road in present time to the future. "When Jesus spoke again to the people, he said, 'I am the light of the world. Whoever follows me will never walk in darkness, but will have the light of life'" (John 8:12–13). Homeward is our holy orientation as we follow that Light to life!

WHAT IS HOPE?

It's Much More Than Wishful Thinking!

Martin Luther once said, "Everything that is done in the world is done by hope." We live our lives saying, "I have hope in something," and "I have hope for something," making "I hope" one of our most optimistic and basic human expressions. A life with nothing to look forward to is a life of emptiness and despair. J.C. Ryle recognized this dilemma in 1877. "'Hoping,' they live on. 'Hoping,' they grow old. 'Hoping,' they die at last–and find too often that they are lost forever in hell! The subject is one of the deepest importance,"[5] Orienting ourselves to where we're going gives us the hope of home because we realize that there's much more to life than just our current existence. Our orientation of where we're going becomes the reason we live and the purpose of our lives.

In its simplest terms, hope can refer to the activity of hoping or to the object hoped for. By its very nature, hope stresses two things: (1) futurity and (2) invisibility. It deals with things we can't see or haven't received or both. The dictionary further defines hope: "a desire of some good, accompanied with an expectation of obtaining it, or a belief that it is obtainable; an expectation of something which is thought to be desirable; a confidence; a pleasing expectancy." The dictionary also describes what hope does: "desires with expectation or believes in the possibility or prospect of obtaining; looks forward to as a thing desirable, with the expectation of obtaining it."[6] In the Bible, the word hope stands for both the act of hoping and the thing hoped for. Our hope moves us toward *something*—toward God or something else.

As you look around at the world today, notice the growing despair of tragic hopelessness and helplessness. Most likely, no one actually hopes for something bad, but some people just unconsciously settle for the hope of nothingness. The German philosopher Friedrich Nietzsche called hope "the most evil of all evils, because it prolongs the torment of man."[7] Consider further these hopeless words by the late atheistic philosopher Bertrand Russell, who had no optimistic orientation of where he was going.

> The life of man is a long march through the night, surrounded by invisible foes, tortured by weariness and pain, toward a goal that few people can hope to reach and where none can tarry long. One by one as they march our comrades vanish from our sight, seized by the silent orders of omnipotent death. Brief and powerless is man's life. On him and all his race the slow, sure doom falls, pitiless and dark. Blind to good and evil, reckless of destruction, tomorrow himself to pass through the gates of darkness, it remains only to cherish, ere yet the blow falls, the lofty thoughts that ennoble his little day.[8]

Yet, everything we humans do includes some aspect of hope. However, the question for non-believers is what sort of hope can they have in the face of death? In our modern worldview, we are only evolving cosmic accidents with no real meaning in our lives. If we have no orientation of where we came from how can we expect to know where we're going? Since our futures make little sense, our lives account for nothing. With a philosophy of "once we're gone, we're gone forever," people can only face death in despair without the faithful comfort of going to an eternal home of everlasting life. Their hopelessness leads to homelessness!

Responding to Bertrand Russell's philosophy of hopeless nonbelief, God's Word identifies the end results of this lifeless hope. "So are the paths of all that forget God; and the hypocrite's hope shall perish: whose hope shall be cut off, and whose trust shall be as a spider's web" (Job 8:13,14). "The hope of the righteous is gladness, but the expectation of the wicked perishes" (Proverbs 10:28). "When a wicked man dies, his expectation will perish, and the hope of strong men perishes. The strong man hopes in his physical strength, his money, or power or position, but ultimately, it must perish" (Proverbs 11:7). Lifeless hopes fade away because they have no roots of an eternal foundation.

Hope anticipates a future reward, which it looks forward to with confident expectancy. "May the God of hope fill you with all joy and peace as you trust in him, so that you may overflow with hope by the power of the Holy Spirit" (Romans 15:13). Pastor and author John Piper preaches that hope is used in three senses: (1) a desire for something good in the future, (2) the thing in the future that we desire, and (3) the basic reason for thinking that our desire may indeed be fulfilled.[9] Since God is called "the God of Hope," only he reigns as the source of all real hope for something good and only he has the power to give it in the future, according to his Word.

> Find rest, O my soul, in God alone; my hope comes from him. He alone is my rock and my salvation; he is my fortress, I will not be shaken. My salvation and my honor depend on God; he is my mighty rock, my refuge. Trust in him at all times, O people; pour out your hearts to him, for God is our refuge.
>
> Psalm 62:5–8

Authentic hope is not wishful thinking, but a firm assurance about things that are unseen and still in the future as the writer to the Hebrews so beautifully describes: "Now faith is being sure of what we hope for and certain of what we do not see" (11:1). Or as the NKJV translates the verse: "Now faith is the substance of things hoped for, the evidence of things not seen." So when faith is directed to the future, we call it hope. As Christians, we place our hope in something or Someone so compelling that it radically changes our lives in the process. Christian hope does not arise from our individual desires or wishes but from God, who is himself the believer's hope just as David declared: "My hope is in You" (Psalm 39:7).

What's the difference between hoping and wishing? When it comes to eternal destinies, it's vitally important to know the difference because too many people confuse the two. Non-Christians can only wish for a good outcome in a possible afterlife because they have no real guarantee. On the other hand, our Christian hope gives us permanence because it is not a mere wish regarding the future, but a strong confidence about the future: "We have this hope as an anchor for the soul, firm and secure..." (Hebrews 6:19). Jeremiah reminds us that God is a God of hope and a future. "'For I know the plans I have for you,' declares the Lord, 'plans to prosper you and not to harm you, plans to give you hope and a future'" (Jeremiah 29:11).

Here's the key survival difference between hoping and wishing: biblical hope not only desires something good for the future, it fervently expects it to happen. And it not only expects it to happen, it confidently knows that it will happen—we bet our lives on it! Believing this, J. C. Ryle explained the change this ultimate hope should make in the believer's life and why the survival strategy to stay oriented and know where you're going is so vital for discipleship.

> It will influence his life, his character, and his daily conduct; it will make him strive to be a holy, godly, conscientious, spiritual man. He will feel under a constant obligation to serve and please Him from whom his hope comes. He will say to himself, "What shall I render to the Lord for all His benefits to me?"[10]

DON'T BE DISCOURAGED BY DECEPTIVE HOPE

Christians Will Prevail no Matter how Difficult our Current Reality!

Many Christians spend significant time thinking and hoping that Christ may return at any minute. Although it's very important to be ready for his certain return, all too often believers get so discouraged or impatient when their lives get full of chaos and intense spiritual warfare. How can these Christians guard against the continual disappointment while waiting for Christ's return when it doesn't happen in their timing?

Some Christians today seem more interested about the precise timing of prophetic events than they are with godly and holy living in God's light. Prophecy remains very important to all believers from an eschatological standpoint, but we should never become so preoccupied that we ignore our divine commission to stay oriented–both where we are and where we're going, to live holy lives and proclaim the gospel of Jesus Christ! The Apostle Peter asks, "...What kind of people ought you to be?" And then tells us the answer. "You ought to live holy and godly lives as you look forward to the day of God and speed its coming" (2 Peter 3:11–13). Focusing solely on the world to come becomes a deceptive hope, which Joseph Stowell believes distorts the true hope of Christians who may turn their backs on this world.

> Earth for these heaven-only types is a naughty, damnable place, waiting for its ultimate destruction...Heaven-only folks become so heavenly minded that they are of little earthly good, and as such they project to a watching world an image that is not only unattractive but unattainable. The extremes cluster in communes waiting for the return of the Lord...The Essenes rejected the validity of this world altogether, cloistering themselves in catacombs to wait for the Messiah, lest they be corrupted and influenced by the world around them. As such they had little interest in or influence on the world around them.[11]

Admiral James Stockdale was shot down in Viet Nam and imprisoned as a prisoner of war for almost eight years. As the highest-ranking officer in the "Hanoi Hilton," the Admiral was tortured over twenty times by an unmerciful enemy. Management researcher and author Jim Collins interviewed Admiral Stockdale for his highly regarded management and leadership book, *Good to Great*, concerning the Admiral's survival from the unthinkable ordeal of being locked away and separated from family and friends and country for so long in the very worst conditions imaginable. Collins specifically asked him who didn't make it out of the prisoner of war camp. Here's Admiral Stockdale's poignant reply:

> The optimists. Oh, they were the ones who said, "We're going to be out by Christmas." And Christmas would come, and Christmas would go. Then they'd say, "We're going to be out by Easter." And then Easter would come, and Easter would go. And then Thanksgiving, and then it would be Christmas again. And they died of a broken heart. This is a very important lesson. You must never confuse faith that you will prevail in the end–which you can never afford to lose - with the discipline to confront the most brutal facts of your current reality, whatever, they might be.[12]

Collins formulated Admiral Stockdale's survival philosophy into what he terms the "Stockdale Paradox": "Retain faith that you will prevail in the end regardless of the difficulties and at the same time confront the most brutal facts of your current reality whatever they might be."[13] The survival strategy to stay oriented and know where you're going makes Collins' Stockdale Paradox particularly relevant to Christians. It's imperative that Christians use this strategy to protect their minds from Satan's constant attacking questions: "Did God really say he's coming back to save you from your horrible life? Do you think it might be today? He doesn't really love you enough to save you from how terrible your life is. What are you waiting for? He's never coming back to save you!"

Our hope should be eternal life with God, not an escape from our worldly problems. Our salvation guarantees a successful ending to our human story and that we will prevail no matter how difficult our current reality becomes during this temporary, earthly battle. Too many Christians die of broken hearts caused by deceptive hope because Jesus fails to come back in time to save them from their earthbound and fleeting difficulties. "Therefore we do not lose heart. Though outwardly we are wasting away, yet inwardly we are renewed day by day. For our light and momentary troubles are achieving in us an eternal glory that far outweighs them all. So we fix our eyes not on what is seen, but what is unseen. For what is seen is temporary, but what is unseen is eternal" (2 Corinthians 4:16–18).

As a human in our earthbound neighborhood, Jesus traveled the same difficult road to eternal life that we all must walk. But he encountered the enormous obstacle of a wooden cross completely blocking his road. What was his overcoming hope? As he stayed absolutely and divinely oriented, Christ knew where he came from, where he was and especially where he was going. Those survival strategies helped him accomplish his Father's will in spite of the most brutal circumstances the enemy and his evil armies could muster! I love how Ken Gire in one of my favorite devotional books, *The Divine Embrace*, describes this strategy on our road to a destination called Paradise - our one true hope - because that's where Jesus is preparing our eternal home with him in his neighborhood.

> But until the day when we go to that place or the day Jesus returns to take us there, we must live our lives *under* the rainbow...where the road ahead is not paved with yellow bricks. Sometimes it has no bricks at all, only the sharp-edged remains of our shattered dreams. What we find under the rainbow is not an easier road to travel but traveling mercies *for* the road, however long or hard it may be. One of those mercies is that along the way we are given glimpses of the one we love only from afar. Something happens to us in those moments. A shift in focus. We find that our eyes are no longer on the steepness of the road or the sharpness of the rocks beneath our feet but on him who has gone before us. [14]

IF YOU'RE NOT IN THE BOOK OF LIFE, YOU FACE AN ETERNAL "MAYDAY"

Does Anyone Really Hope for Hell?

A nationwide poll about belief in life, death, heaven, and hell conducted in 2003 by the Barna Research Group of California,[15] showed that although the lifestyles, values, and self-perceptions of most adults have undergone significant change, the vast majority continue to believe that there is some life after death. Interestingly enough, the poll indicated that 81% of Americans firmly believe in some type of life after death, with 9% considering it a possibility and only 10% believing that death brings absolute finality. However, one in every four adults (24%) admitted that they have "no idea" what will happen after they die. Overall, 76% believed that heaven exists, while slightly less said that there is such a thing as hell (71%). Of those not going to heaven or hell, the remaining fringe group claimed they would either come back in another life form (5%) or simply cease to exist (5%).

While there was no dominant view of hell by the survey participants, two particular perspectives were popular. Four out of ten adults (39%) believed that hell is "a state of eternal separation from God's presence" and one-third (32%) said it is "an actual place of torment and suffering where people's souls go after death." A third viewpoint by one in eight adults (13%) was that "hell is just a symbol of an unknown bad outcome after death." Obviously, the results of the poll emphasize that staying oriented and knowing where you're going is an important survival strategy and it clearly appears many people do not have a clear orientation of their eternal destination. There's much more worldly wishing going on than eternal hoping! But the real eye-opening result of the survey of people who believed they would go someplace after death indicated that only half of 1% anticipated going to hell upon their death. No one hopes for hell!

Since no one expects to end up in hell, is it surprising that non-Christians and Christians alike express doubts about a literal hell? Only one third of the Barna Group poll thought hell was literal as described in the Bible and almost all thought they were going someplace else anyway so they weren't particularly interested. No wonder so many shy away from any discussion or discourse on hell. As a matter of fact, even the mainstream Christian church struggles with the concept and applicability of the realities of hell. *The Los Angeles Times* newspaper ran an enlightening article in 2002 entitled "Hold the Fire and Brimstone," which reported that while heaven is still a very popular subject, preaching about hell stands at an all time low in American churches.

> In churches across America, hell is being frozen out as clergy find themselves increasingly hesitant to sermonize on Christianity's outpost for lost souls...Hell's fall from fashion indicates how key portions of Christian theology have been influenced by a secular society that stresses individualism over authority and the human psyche over moral absolutes. The rise of psychology, the philosophy of existentialism and the consumer culture have all dumped buckets of water on hell.[16]

Several Christian ministers and scholars interviewed by the *LA Times* for the article attempted to explain and offered many excuses why their churches and other churches currently downplay hell: "It's just too negative." "It's not sexy enough." "Churches today feel the need to be appealing rather than demanding." "Once pop evangelism went into market analysis, hell was just dropped." "There's been a shift from focusing on what happens in the next life to asking, 'What is the quality of this life we're leading now?'" "It's a failure of nerve by churches that are not wanting to take on a non-popular stance." "What we've done is make things comfortable for people with padded pews and air-conditioning and a promise that we won't say anything that will offend you."[17] The devil, of course, rejoices in such views because they're preaching his favorite doctrine: "You will not surely die, so don't worry about hell." Paul warned Timothy of godlessness in the last days: "For the time will come when men will not put up with sound doctrine. Instead, to suit their own desires, they will gather around them a great number of teachers to say what their itching ears want to hear. They will turn their ears away from the truth and turn aside to myths" (2 Timothy 4:3–4).

Shortly before his death in 1912, General William Booth, founder of the Salvation Army, prophetically warned that in the twentieth century preachers would present "...Christianity without Christ, forgiveness without repentance, salvation without regeneration, politics without God, and heaven without hell."[18] The *LA Times* article confirmed the accuracy of Paul's warning and General Booth's admonition to Christians about losing their orientation of where they're going! The General believed in a literal hell that was eternal in nature, so much so that he dedicated himself and his entire life to rescuing people from this future plight. General Booth warned: "There is a Hell! A Hell as dark and terrible as is the description given of it by the lips of Jesus Christ, the Truthful. And into Hell men are departing hour by hour."[19]

Anyone reading the New Testament will notice that Jesus spoke time and again about a place of eternal punishment. As a matter of fact, he talked more about the dangers of hell than the delights of heaven. Since Jesus spoke about hell more than any other person in the Bible, many believe that God the Father wanted his Son to personally address this extremely difficult issue so no one would believe hell was just some human invention or myth. In his Sermon on the Mount, Jesus explicitly warned his followers about the horrors of hell a half-dozen times. Consider these passages of Scripture that record just a few of the Lord's teachings on hell and eternal punishment directly from the lips of Jesus Christ, "the Truthful" as General Booth called him.

- "...But anyone who says, 'You fool!' will be in danger of the fire of hell" (Matthew 5:22).
- "If your right eye causes you to sin, gouge it out and throw it away. It is better for you to lose one part of your body than for your whole body to be thrown into hell" (Matthew 5:29).
- "Do not be afraid of those who kill the body but cannot kill the soul. Rather, be afraid of the One who can destroy both soul and body in hell" (Matthew 10:28).
- "As the weeds are pulled up and burned in the fire, so it will be at the end of the age. The Son of man will send out his angels, and they will weed out of his kingdom everything that causes sin and all who do evil. They will throw them into the fiery furnace, where there will be weeping and gnashing of teeth" (Matthew 13:40–42).
- "If your hand or your foot causes you to sin, cut it off and throw it away. It is better for you to enter life maimed or crippled than to have two hands or two feet and be thrown into eternal fire. And if your eye causes you to sin, gouge it out

and throw it away. It is better for you to enter life with one eye than to have two eyes and be thrown into the fire of hell" (Matthew 18:8–9).

- "Woe to you, teachers of the law and Pharisees, you hypocrites! You shut the kingdom of heaven in men's faces. You yourselves do not enter, nor will you let those enter who are trying to. Woe to you, teachers of the law and Pharisees, you hypocrites! You travel over land and sea to win a single convert, and when he becomes one, you make him twice as much a son of hell as you are" (Matthew 23:14–15).
- "Then he will say to those on his left, 'Depart from me, you who are cursed, into the eternal fire prepared for the devil and his angels'" (Matthew 25:41).
- "Then they will go away to eternal punishment, but the righteous to eternal life" (Matthew 25:46).

In the New Testament, hell is primarily the translation of three words, *Hades*, *Sheol*, and *Gehenna*. It means the place or abode of the dead, the unseen world. Jesus most often chose the word *Gehenna of Fire* as his ultimate depiction of hell. It referred to the Valley of Hinnon, south of Jerusalem, a garbage dump where filthy waste, dead animals, and the bodies of executed criminals were cast out and burned continuously in a public incinerator where it's said that the maggots and worms feasted day and night. It was probably the most despicable symbol of human destruction and suffering that the Jews in Jesus' time could relate to.

In addition to seeing and smelling this horrific dump, the hearers of Jesus' description remembered from their Hebrew history that the Canaanites who worshiped Baal and the god Molech used this same *Valley of Ben'Hinnon* to sacrifice their children in a fire that burned day and night producing endless, agonizing shrieks from those burned alive. No doubt they completely understood the horrors of the terrible place of destruction and ultimate punishment that Jesus described as hell.

Jesus spoke of hell as a place of everlasting fire like a furnace of unquenchable flames, a place of everlasting punishment, where its victims are tormented in both their bodies and souls because they rejected him. Some believe the fires of hell are only symbolic. Even if it isn't really fire, something in hell will be like fire that will never be quenched. Ryle made a great point that no matter what the descriptions of hell are–either literal or figurative–hell will be much worse than anyone can possibly imagine!

> It is vain to talk of all the expressions about it being figures of speech, the pit, the prison, the worm, the fire, the thirst, the blackness, the darkness, the weeping, the gnashing of teeth, the second death, all these may be figures of speech if you please. But the Bible figures mean something beyond all questions, and here they mean something which man's mind can never fully conceive. O reader, the miseries of mind and conscience are far worse than those of the body. The whole extent of hell, the present suffering, the bitter recollection of the past, the hopeless prospect of the future, will never be thoroughly known except by those who go there. [20]

Perhaps the most horrifying aspect of hell is its eternality: "eternal fire" in Matthew 25:40–41; "eternal punishment" in Matthew 25:46; and "forever and ever" in Revelation 19:10. *"Forever and ever"* means without end, extending into infinity. The scriptures tell us that the worm that gnaws the internal conscience of men in hell never dies. "Their worm will not die, nor will their fire be quenched" (Isaiah 66:24). Jesus repeats Isaiah's warning of the everlasting internal and external painful consequences of sin, of being "thrown into hell…where 'their worm does not die, and the fire is not quenched'" (Mark 9:47–48). If the worm never dies, then those being tormented by the worm will never die. Internally the worm gnaws and externally the fire burns! Charles Spurgeon warned about the foreverness of hell in a sermon preached in a field on September 4, 1855.

> They are forever–forever–forever–lost! On every chain in hell, there is written "forever." In the fires, there blaze out the words "forever." Up above their heads, they read "for-

ever." Their eyes are galled, and their hearts are pained with the thought it is "forever." Oh! If I could tell you tonight that hell would one day be burned out, and that those who were lost might be saved, there would be a jubilee in hell at the very thought of it. But it cannot be–it is "forever" they are "cast into utter darkness."[21]

Many who claim to believe the Bible seem to be having serious reservations about such a horrible eternal punishment, and non-Christians reject the notion of an eternal judgment by God altogether. Since people believe they are not going to hell after they die, is that really such a big shocker? Over and over again, the Word of God declares a coming judgment for all people, "But unless you repent, you too will all perish" (Luke 13:3). Clearly, Scripture teaches that there will be a judgment after death, "Just as man is destined to die once, and after that to face judgment…" (Hebrews 9:27). Paul tells us that those who serve the Lord will receive an inheritance from the Lord as a reward, but there's bad news for those who don't serve God no matter who or what they are, "Anyone who does wrong will be repaid for his wrong, and there is no favoritism" (Colossians 3:25).

The Bible also teaches that there will be unending, eternal judgment for those who do not know God and who do not accept and obey Jesus' gospel. "This will happen when the Lord Jesus is revealed from heaven in blazing fire with his powerful angels. He will punish those who do not know God and do not obey the gospel of our Lord Jesus. They will be punished with everlasting destruction and shut out from the presence of the Lord and from the majesty of his power" (2 Thessalonians 1:7–9). Those who have not repented for their sins receive what the Bible describes as "the second death." "But the cowardly, the unbelieving, the vile, the murderers, the sexually immoral, those who practice magic arts, the idolaters and all liars - their place will be in the fiery lake of burning sulfur. This is the second death" (Revelation 21:8).

There's going to be a final judgment for every human being who has ever lived, both believers and unbelievers. All persons will one day stand before Jesus Christ and be judged for their deeds.

When we looked at the survival strategy of staying on the line, we learned that all believers will stand before the Lord at the Judgment Seat of Christ and be judged according to what they've done to establish what rewards they will receive when they enter into heaven. However, for everyone else who has chosen not to accept God, at the Great White Throne Judgment as described by John in Revelation 20:11–15, God will make the final judgment of all non-Christians from the entire history of earth prior to casting them forever into the lake of fire forever.

> Then I saw a great white throne and him who was seated upon it. Earth and sky fled from his presence, and there was no place for them. And I saw the dead, great and small, standing before the throne, and books were opened. Another book was opened, which is the book of life. The dead were judged according to what they had done as recorded in the books. The sea gave up the dead that were in it, and death and Hades gave up the dead that were in them, and each person was judged according to what he had done. Then death and Hades were thrown into the lake of fire. The lake of fire is the second death. If anyone's name was not found written in the book of life, he was thrown into the lake of fire.

The books that are opened contain God's records of everyone's deeds whether they are good or evil, but those at that Great White Throne Judgment will not have their names in the Book of Life and they will be dispatched to eternal punishment with no more chances for forgiveness or survival.

Jesus presented several vivid word pictures of hell as a place of outer darkness, unquenchable fire, everlasting punishment, conscious and unbearable torment day and night, where there will be weeping, wailing, and gnashing of teeth completely separated from God. These images are particularly striking in their somber tone and vivid depiction of suffering in hell, indicating that those in hell actually experience a conscious torment impacting all their senses. Even though being separated from God for eternity is no real threat to unrepentant sinners who choose not to be with God now, the knowledge that they made an eternal mistake will consume them with a burning loneliness that cannot even be imagined in present time.

These images of hell by Jesus sound exactly like the hopeless feeling of being lost in a fire: surrounded by complete darkness, lungs aching for one more breath, breathing in scorching particles of choking toxins, eyes burning and watering with no visibility, so much heat you feel like you will explode, and every lifeline expended (air, radio, hoseline, etc). You're struggling on your own without anyone to help you, and your "mayday" cries for help bounce back unanswered. Here's an excerpt from the testimony of a firefighter who became trapped in a horrifying fire that claimed the lives of two other firefighters on his crew. Captain Mike Spalding of the Indianapolis Fire Department compared his terrifying and life-changing experience to being "Trapped in Hell."

> As we were following the hoseline out, the smoke got darker, got real dark. It got to the point where I had my flashlight on, plus I had my helmet light on, and they didn't do a thing. It was just pitch black. And then conditions abruptly changed...The heat just came in like a blast furnace. In the darkness, I could see little orange flickers around me. The heat was unbelievable. Unbelievable. I felt like my throat was going to catch fire...my ears were telling me it was hot. I heard my ears sizzle like bacon on a skillet. I was driven to the floor. I was low, but I was driven flat on the floor. And I grabbed my radio. I tried to make some calls for help. I pushed the emergency button, because I knew enough that I knew we weren't going to get out of there without help. The heat from this flashover was like a blast furnace, and that causes you to turn into an instinct-driven animal...The pain from the heat and the feeling of being trapped is overpowering. If I was on the ninth floor, I would have jumped. I was down on the floor. I knew that we had to get out. I made a quick sweep of my hand. I felt no John, no Woody, no hoseline. Everything

> was just orange flickers in the blackness, this pitch blackness. So I dove into the blackness...There was nothing I could do. I had lost my radio mike, the heat was suffocating. I was trapped and I knew this was it.[22]

I believe this may accurately illustrate the torment of an eternal hell that those not listed in the Book of Life will face. The worst imaginable conditions that never get better and where they will cry out forever for help in the excruciating darkness, yet no one, including God, will ever come to rescue them. Over and over they will scream out an eternal mayday. The classic preacher Jonathan Edwards once spoke of people being in everlasting trouble unable to find even a moment of relief in hell.

> Nor will they ever be able to find anything to relieve them in hell. They will never find any resting place there; any secret corner, which will be cooler than the rest, where they may find a little respite, a small abatement of the extremity of their torment. They never will be able to find any cooling stream or fountain, in any part of that world of torment; no, nor so much as a drop of water to cool their tongues. They will find no company to give them any comfort, or do them the least good. They will find no place, where they can remain, and rest, and take breath for one minute: for they will be tormented with fire and brimstone; and they will have no rest day nor night forever and ever.[23]

IF YOU'RE IN THE BOOK OF LIFE, YOU ARE SAVED IN HOPE!

Christians Are Heirs Having the Hope of Eternal Life!

Those who believe they're going to heaven have varying beliefs of what that truly means. The Barna Group's survey of the afterlife indicated that while 43% of respondents said that their Christian beliefs would take them to glory, 15% declared that they would get to heaven because they "have tried to obey the 10 Commandments."

Another 15% expected to gain admittance because "they are basically a good person." Among the others responding to the survey, 6% believed that God is letting everyone in, because he loves all people and will not let them perish.[24] Eternal survival demands knowing where we're going by staying oriented to the truth of the One who has prepared a home for those who love and know him, as well as a terrible destination for those who don't. Sadly, more than half of those who think they're going to heaven and not hell may be in for the ultimate shock of their eternal lives. In spite of the apparent human confusion, it all depends in which "book" your name is written!

The Book of Life, also known as the Lamb's Book of Life, lists the names of those who will live with God forever in heaven. God knows his own children, and he has written their names permanently in his book of life. It is this book of life that determines whether a person will inherit eternal life with God or receive everlasting punishment in the lake of fire. No matter who you know or who you are, there are no tickets available from any other source or at any price. Although Christians are held accountable for their actions, they are forgiven in Christ and their names were written in the "book of life from the creation of the world" (Revelation 17:8).

Speaking of the heavenly city, our eternal home, the Bible tells us, "Nothing impure will ever enter it, nor will anyone who does what is shameful or deceitful, but only those whose names are written in the Lamb's book of life" (Revelation 21:27). Here's the ultimate survival question. How do you get your name written in the Book of Life? Simple—by believing in the Lord Jesus Christ as your Savior. The moment people place their faith in Jesus as their Savior, their names are written in the Book of Life, never to be erased (Revelation 3:5). You must be saved to enter heaven's gates. Pastor and author John MacArthur defines "saved" as a survival verb that determines those in the Book of Life.

> Saved speaks of rescuing someone in imminent grave serious and even permanent danger or disaster. In the spiritual sense, however, which is its main usage in the New Testament it has the idea from being saved from sin, being

rescued from sin, from sin's power, from sin's penalty, being preserved therefore safe and unharmed from divine wrath, from judgment, from hell, from eternal punishment.[25]

Christian hope constantly keeps us oriented to where we're going because in it we have been saved. It is the promise of God's perfection, which we see revealed only in his Son, Jesus Christ. In this hope, all Christians have been saved. But in the present time, hope is still a distant future, but according to God, it remains a reality not yet possessed. "For in hope we have been saved, but hope that is seen is not hope; for who hopes for what he already sees? But if we hope for what we do not see, with perseverance we wait eagerly for it" (Romans 8:24–25, NASB). Paul indicates that if you actually possess the thing hoped for, it ceases to be hope. Why? Because Christian hope is based on a holy truth and a divine fact yet to be possessed. However, we must be patient and we must wait so we can persevere in the knowledge that this hope is a certainty. Believers have complete assurance that God will do all that he has promised because "in hope we have been saved."

When we were lost, we were "without hope" (Ephesians 2:12), but saved in Jesus Christ we have that constant "living hope" that encourages us day by day.

> Blessed be the God and Father of our Lord Jesus Christ, who according to His great mercy has caused us to be born again to a living hope through the resurrection of Jesus Christ from the dead, to obtain an inheritance which is imperishable and undefiled and will not fade away, reserved in heaven for you, who are protected by the power of God through faith for a salvation ready to be revealed in the last time.
>
> 1 Peter 1:3–5 (NASB)

Only Christians share in a "living hope" that grows more wonderful every day.

Truly, if "we are saved by hope" as Paul tells us, we certainly should always be able to give some account of it! This is our action plan to accomplish this survival strategy: "Always be prepared to give an answer to everyone who asks you to give the reason for the hope you have" (1 Peter 3:15). Christians must be able to express why we expect to go to heaven when we die. Ignorance should never be the characteristic of Christians because we must absolutely know what we believe as his "expert" witnesses.

If you've ever read John Bunyan's abiding allegory, *Pilgrim's Progress*, you probably remember the character named Ignorance. A ferryman named Vain-Hope brings Ignorance across the River of Death on a ferry so he doesn't have to cross on his own as required. Unfortunately, just like many of those in the survey expecting to go to heaven, Ignorance believes that he will be received into the Celestial City because of doing good works. But Ignorance is refused entrance at the Celestial City and thrown through one of the doorways to hell at the direction of the King of the Celestial City.

Not knowing exactly what your hope is based on will be a poor excuse no matter how close you get to heaven's door. Like Ignorance, many people, even good people, may get to their journey's end, take the easy way and get ferried by Vain-Hope over the River of Death to the gate of heaven, only to find to their everlasting sorrow that there is no admission for them into the Celestial City.

Paul wrote a letter to Titus and began by telling him about the knowledge of the truth that leads to godliness, "...a faith and knowledge resting on the hope of eternal life, which God, who does not lie, promised before the beginning of time, and at his appointed season" (Titus 1:1–3). He says the hope of eternal life rests strictly on God's promise. Then, in chapter 3, Paul clarifies that becoming an heir in the hope of eternal life is only the result of God's mercy and grace and because Jesus saved us.

> But when the kindness and love of God our Savior appeared, he saved us, not because of righteous things we had done, but because of his mercy. He saved us through the washing of rebirth and renewal by the Holy Spirit, whom he poured out on us generously through Jesus Christ

our Savior, so that, having been justified by his grace, we might become heirs having the hope of eternal life.

Titus 3:4–7

Not only have we been cleansed ("washing of rebirth") and made new ("renewal by the Holy Spirit"), but we have also been "justified," declared righteous by God in his infinite grace. The goal that he accomplished in all this was to make us his heirs who would inherit eternal life. By God's promise, eternal life is something that we now possess by inheritance but we have not yet experienced its joy. That's exactly our hope! We know where we're going!

Many people argue that a good and loving God would never condemn those he loves to eternal death in hell. However, the God of grace and mercy has provided an eternal option through his Son. "For God so loved the world that he gave his only begotten Son, that whoever believes in him should not perish but have everlasting life" (John 3:16). Jesus gave no indication of any other roads that may lead to God as preached universally by many religions today and endorsed by some Christians. He forcefully and clearly stated that he is absolutely the only eternal life option for all people. "I am the way, the truth, and the life. No one comes to the Father except through me" (John 1:6).

Eternal life comes only through a personal relationship with God. We cannot know the Father unless we know the Son. "And this is eternal life, that they may know you, the only true God, and Jesus Christ whom You have sent" (John 17:3). Only those who have the Son of God have eternal life. "And this is the testimony: that God has given us eternal life, and this life is in his Son. He who has the Son has life; he who does not have the Son of God does not have life" (1 John 5:11–12). Without a doubt, our true hope rests entirely and only on Jesus Christ, who stands as the only true and secure foundation of eternal hope.

EVERYONE GOES HOME!

"Come Further Up, Come Further In!"

Eternal heaven is where Christians are going. It's the end of our narrow and often difficult road to life and so it must be our everyday, eternal perspective and holy anticipation. We must always stay oriented on heaven—our eternal home. C.H. Spurgeon preached about seeking and preparing for those things that are to come—the permanent and not the temporary.

> Oh seek to know on earth the peace of heaven, the rest of heaven, the victory of heaven, the service of heaven, the communion of heaven, the holiness of heaven: you may have foretastes of all these; seek after them. Seek, in a word, to be preparing for the heaven which Christ is preparing for you.[26]

The eternal significance between heaven and hell is our hope. At eternity, all hope will come to an end. Perhaps that is why Dante, in his work *The Inferno*, imagined the words written over the gate entrance into hell, "Leave every hope behind, ye who enter." Isn't this (no hope in the eternal) how non-Christians live their lives? Their hope rests mainly on the temporary–the sure thing! But if you think about it, even though we were saved by hope, there will be no hope in heaven either, "For in this hope we were saved. But hope that is seen is no hope at all. Who hopes for what he already has?" (Romans 8:24). In heaven there will be no need for hope because we'll have it all! In life, true and divine hope distinguishes Christians from unbelievers. In death, hope again distinguishes Christians from unbelievers, who hopelessly and forever discover their vain hope. James Meikle sums it up for all Christians:

> O eternity! Once the comfort of our longing expectations–now the transport of our enlarged souls! For we are ever with the Lord, seeing His unclouded face, wearing His divine name, drinking at the streams of His pleasures, eating of His hidden manna, sitting beneath the Tree of life, basking under the beams of the Sun of righteousness, singing hallelujahs to Him who loved us, who washed us from our sins in His blood, and brought us here to be with him forever![27]

Our Christian hope should become the same as every firefighter's–everybody goes home! And God tells those who have believed in him and accepted his Son that home will be forever with him in a neighborhood so amazing that no human can come close to expressing the glory of heaven or what God has in store for us. "As it is written: 'No eye has seen, no ear has heard, no mind has conceived what God has prepared for those who love him'" (1 Corinthians 2:9). But, I really love how C.S. Lewis pictures heaven as our eternal home that goes on forever in his final book of the Chronicles of Narnia, *The Last Battle.*

> And for us this is the end of all the stories, and we can most truly say they all lived happily ever after. But for them it was only the beginning of the real story. All their life in this world...had only been the cover and the title page: now at last they were beginning chapter one of the great story which no one on earth has read: which goes on forever: in which every chapter is better than the one before...It was the unicorn who summed up what everyone was feeling. He stamped his right fore-foot on the ground and neighed, and then cried: "I have come home at last! This is my real country! I belong here. This is the land I have been looking for all my life, though I never knew it till now. The reason we loved the old Narnia so much is because it sometimes looked a little like this. Bree-hee-hee! Come further up, come further in!"[28]

With high hopes and great expectations beyond all my human imaginations, I must stay oriented to where I'm going. Because of this eternal survival strategy, I confidently anticipate as my eternal hope that Christ Jesus will welcome me at the gates of his heavenly neighborhood and say, "Well done my good and faithful servant! Come further up, come further in!" And, I will be Home at last!

> And I heard a loud voice from the throne saying, "Now the dwelling of God is with men, and he will live with

them. They will be his people, and God himself will be with them and be their God."

Revelation 21:3

Every Christian Goes Home!

ENDNOTES

"MADYDAY" I'M FALLEN

1 *Phoenix Fire Department, Final Report: Southwest Supermarket Fire,* March 12, 2002, 18–19.

2 John Salka, "Firefighter Survival Tactics–Learning how to Stay Out of Trouble," Firehouse.com, 1.

3 Timothy E. Sendelbach, "Managing the Fireground Mayday, The critical link to firefighter survival," Firehouse.com, 6/26/04.

4 Burton A. Clark, "You Must Call Mayday for RIT to Work: Will You?" *Fire Engineering Magazine,* June, 2003.

5 Houston Fire Department, *Four Leaf Tower Report,* Recommendation #15, July 5, 2002.

1. STAY ORIENTED! KNOW WHERE YOU CAME FROM.

1 Jerry Smith, "A Firefighter's Worst Nightmare," *Emergency Grapevine,* 8/16/05.

2 Reverend Lee Woofenden, "Created in God's Image," Sermon given in Bridgewater, Massachusetts, September 23, 2001, www.leewoof.org/leewoof/2001/9–23–01-NJ.html.

3 Dr. Phillip E. Johnson, "Evolution and Christian Faith," a sermon given at the Evangelical Free Church of Hershey, PA, May 13, 2001. Professor Johnson has also written many outstanding books on the creation issue.

4 Richard Bozarth, "The Meaning of Evolution," *American Atheist Magazine,* 1979-Sep, 30.

5 *Vine's Complete Expository Dictionary of Old and New Testament Words* (Nashville: Thomas Nelson Publishers, 1985), 51.
6 Richard N. Ostling, AP Writer, AP News Story: "Debate over 'Intelligent Design' grows," *Denton Record Chronicle*, August 19, 2005.
7 Frank R. Zindler, "'Creation Science' and the Fact of Evolution," *American Atheist Magazine*, October 1987.
8 *Life Application Study Bible. New International Version* (Wheaton, Illinois: Tyndale House Publishers, Inc and Grand Rapids, Michigan: Zondervan Publishing House, 1988), note on Eccl 3:11, 1354.
9 Roy Abraham Varghese, "The supreme science–Academics viewing the universe through a narrow scope should rethink assumptions." *The Dallas Morning News*, December 16, 2004, 35A.
10 Ravi Zacharius, *Jesus Among Other Gods* (Nashville: Word Publishing, 2000), 66.
11 Kelly Hollowell, J.D., Ph.D., "The Complexity of Inner Space," Science Ministries, www.christianity.com,
12 Discovery Institute, "A Scientific Dissent from Darwinism," www.discovery.org.
13 Dr. Henry F. Schaefer, *U.S. News & World Report*, December 23, 1991.
14 Dr. Henry F. "Fritz" Schaefer III, "The Way of Discovery: A Personal Journey of Faith," www.origins.org/articles/schaefer_wayof discovery.html, December 14, 2002.
15 Will Pounds, "What is Your Name?" www.abideinchrist.com/messages/ex3v14.html. 1999.
16 Louie Giglio, "Changing Wishers Into Worshippers," Big Change Conference, Irving Texas, National simulcast by Church Communication Network (CCN), March 20, 2004.
17 Louie Giglio.
18 Dr. Henry F. "Fritz" Schaefer III, "The Way of Discovery: A Personal Journey of Faith."

2. KNOW & UNDERSTAND YOUR ENEMY. THAT'S WHERE THE TROUBLE COMES FROM.

1 Karl von Clausewitz, *On War*, Book IV, The Combat, Chapter III, The combat in General, translated by www.sonshi.com/clausewitz4–3.htm.

2 Carl von Clausewitz, *On War*, translated by O.J. Matthijs Jolle (New York: Random House, The Modern Library, 1943), 30.

3 Gary E. Seidel, "Ultimate Firefighting," *Fire Engineering Magazine*, March 2000, 86.

4 Sun Tzu, *The Art of War*, Translated from the Chinese by Lionel Giles (Mineola, New York: Dover Publishing, 2002), 51.

5 Billy Graham, *Angels*, Second Edition (Dallas-London-Vancouver-Melbourne: Word Publishing, 1986), 68.

6 George Barna, *Virtual America* (Ventura: Regal Books, 1994), 116–117.

7 Barna Research, "Beliefs: Trinity, Satan," www.barna.org, 2004.

8 Barna Research, "Teenagers' Beliefs Moving Farther From Biblical Perspectives," The Barna Update, www.barna.org, October 23, 2000.

9 Gustav Niebuhr, "Poll Indicates Diminished Role of Devil," *New York Times*, May 10, 1997.

10 Keith Green, *"No One Believes in Me Anymore,"* a song, EMI April Music/ASCAP, 1977.

11 Dan Vander Lugt, *What in the World is Satan Doing?* (Grand Rapids: RBC Ministries, 2000), 4.

12 "Quotes from Gen. Boykin speeches." NBC News. www.msnbc.com/news/980841.asp, October 15, 2003.

13 Cynthia Tucker, "Boykin's beliefs give aid, comfort to the enemy." Newspaper column distributed by Universal press Syndicate, December 29, 2003.

14 Bill Berkowitz, "Boykin's Satanic Convergence," www.workingforchange.com, October 22, 2003.

15 Lisa Myers, "Top terrorist hunter's divisive views." *NBC Nightly News*, October 15, 2003.

16 Lisa Myers.

17 Keith Green.

18 Martin Luther, "A Mighty Fortress is Our God."

19 Quoted in: Paul Laughlin, *Remedial Christianity: What every believer should know about the faith, and probably doesn't* (Polebridge Press, 2000), 168.

20 Dan Vander Lugt.

21 Curtis Bond, "It Seems to Me…A Hot Potato," http://dunamai.com/pastors_desk/hot_potato.htm, 2004.

22 Harold S. Kushner, *How Good Do We Have To Be? A New Understanding of Guilt and Forgiveness* (Little Brown and Company, 1996), 24.

23 James Emery White, *Embracing the Mysterious God: Loving the God We Don't Understand* (Downers Grove, Illinois: Intervarsity press, 2003), 27–28.

3. BE PREPARED. GET READY!

1 Sandy Clark, ed. *The Firefighter's Handbook, Essentials of Firefighting and Emergency Response* (Albany: Delmar Publishers, 2000), 681.

2 Herb Vander Lugt, *Right and Wrong, A Case For Moral Absolutes* (Grand Rapids: RBC Ministries, 1995).

3 Doug Thompson, "A disposable commodity called truth," Column from *the Rant, Capitol Hill Blue,* July 11, 2002.

4 Melinda Lancaster, "The Armor of God," www.caroljackson-ministries.org/armor, 2000.

5 Melinda Lancaster.

6 Geoffrey Bromiley, *Theological Dictionary of the New Testament* (Grand Rapids: William B. Eerdmans Publishing Company, 1985), 849.

7 Bromiley, 703.

4. STAY ORIENTED! KNOW WHERE YOU ARE.

1 John Salka, "Firefighter Survival Tactics–Learning how to Stay Out of Trouble," firehouse.com, p. 2.

2 Gary E. Seidel, "Ultimate Firefighting," *Fire Engineering Magazine*, March 2002.

3 Allen Levi, "*The Moon is Round,*" song copyright 2001. Used by permission, www.allenlevi.com.htm.

4 Allen Levi, "The Moon is Round," www.allenlevi.com/moon-isround.htm, December 2, 2000.

5 C.S. Lewis, "Time and Beyond Time," *Mere Christianity* (New York: HarperCollins, 1952, renewed 1980), 167.

6 Kitty Ferguson, *The Fire in the Equations: Science, Religion, and the Search for God* (Grand Rapids: Wm B. Eerdmans, 1994), 225.

7 Lambert Dolphin, "The Complexities of Time," www.ldolphin..org/time.html.

8 David Harsha, "What is Time?" from *Come to the Savior*, www.gracegems.org/03/time.html.

9 Michael W. Smith and Wes King, "This is Your Time," song, 1999.

10 C.S. Lewis, *The Great Divorce* (New York: HarperCollins, 1946, renewed 1973), 140.

11 Kitty Ferguson, 225–227.

12 Gregory Koukl, "Bad Arguments Against Calvinism," *Stand to Reason*, www.str.org.

13 Philip Yancey, *The Jesus I Never Knew* (Grand Rapids: Zondervan Publishing House, 1995), 78.

14 C. H. Spurgeon, "Following the Risen Christ," a Sermon delivered on March 28, 1880.

15 Lemmel, Helen. *"Turn Your Eyes Upon Jesus,"* song, Public Domain.

16 Geoffrey Bromiley, *Theological Dictionary of the New Testament* (Grand Rapids: William B. Eerdmans Publishing Company, 1985), 178–179.

17 Dr. Phillip McGraw, "Life Law #1: Do You Get It? www.drphil.com/articles.

5. MONITOR CONDITIONS. STAY OUT OF TROUBLE!

1 John Salka, "Firefighter Survival Tactics–Learning how to Stay Out of Trouble," www.firehouse.com, 4.

2 International Fire Service Training Association (IFSTA), *Essentials of Fire Fighting, Fourth Edition* (Stillwater: Fire Protection Publications, Oklahoma State University, 1998), 33.

3 Ray C. Stedman, "Tactics of Terror," Discovery Publishing: Peninsula Bible Church, 1995.

4 Ray C. Stedman.

5 Dietrich Bonhoeffer, *Creation and Fall: Temptation* (Macmillan Publishing Co, Inc., 1959), 116–117.

6 John Calvin, *Works,* Printed for the Calvin translation society, 1844, 289.

7 Tony Evans, *The Battle is the Lord's, Waging Victorious Spiritual Warfare* (Chicago: Moody Press, 1998), 180–181.

8 David Wilkerson, *Two of Me: The Struggle with Sin* (World Challenge, 1995), 2.

9 Doug Rosenau, "Turn Right Between Desire and Action," Part six of an eight-part series on Sexual Integrity, http://www.djchuang.com/sex/ski117.htm.

6. STAY LOW. PRIDE GOES BEFORE DESTRUCTION!

1 *The Firefighter's Handbook*, "Essentials of Firefighting and Emergency Response" (Albany, New York: Delmar–Thomson Learning, 2000), Chapter 4.

2 C.H. Spurgeon, "Pride and Humility," Sermon at New Park Street Chapel, August 17, 1856.

3 Paul T. P. Wong, International Network on Personal Meaning (INPM), www.meaning.ca/articles/presidents_column/humility_nov03.htm.

4 Ed Young, *Fatal Distractions* (Nashville: Thomas Nelson Publishers, 2000), 12.

5 Billy Graham, *Storm Warning* (Dallas: Word Publishing, 1992), 166.

6 Richard Taylor, *Restoring Pride: The Lost virtue of Our Age* (Amherst, New York: Prometheus Press, 1996), 30.

7 Robert Reasoner, "The True Meaning of Self-Esteem," National Association for Self-Esteem.

8 Dr. Nathaniel Branden, "Answering Misconceptions About Self-Esteem," National Association for Self-Esteem, 2000.

9 William Thomas, "The Virtue of Pride," The Objectivist Center,

www.objectivistcenter.org/text/wthomas_virtue-pride.asp?, 10/1999.

10 William Thomas.

11 Howard E. Butt Jr., "The Art of Being a Big Shot," Layman's Institute, Dallas Texas, 1963.

12 Trent C. Butler, ed. *Holman Bible Dictionary* (Nashville: Holman Bible Publishers, 1991), 1136.

13 C.H. Spurgeon, "Pride and Humility."

14 C.S. Lewis, *Mere Christianity* (Westwood, NJ: Barbour and Co., Inc., 1952), 107.

15 Jackie Storer, "Aitken: Pride was my downfall," *BBC News*, July 17, 2002.

16 Charles Spurgeon, "Morning & Evening: Evening, March 6," copyright 1996–2002, Heartlight, Inc.

17 Covenant and Conversation, "Thoughts On The Weekly Parsha" From The Chief Rabbi, "Beha'alotcha - Humility."

18 Covenant and Conversation.

19 C.H. Spurgeon, "Pride and Humility."

20 Rick Warren. *The Purpose Driven Life, What on Earth Am I Here For?* (Grand Rapids: Zondervan, 2002), 148.

21 C.S. Lewis, 107.

22 Isaac Watts, "When I Survey the Wondrous Cross," 1674–1748, public domain.

23 *Life Application Study Bible. New International Version* (Wheaton, Illinois: Tyndale House Publishers, Inc and Grand Rapids, Michigan: Zondervan Publishing House, 1988), 2219.

24 Leon Morris, *The Gospel According to John* (Grand Rapids: Wm. B. Eerdmans Publishing Co., 1971), 141.

25 Ray Stedman, *God's Loving Word, Exploring the Gospel of John* (Grand Rapids: Discovery House Publishers, 1993), 101–102.

26 Ed Young, 27.

7. STAY ON THE LINE! IT'S ALL ABOUT BEING CONNECTED.

1 B. Klaene and R. Sanders, *Structural Fire Fighting* (Quincy, MA: National Fire Protection Association, 2000), 366.

2 Ray Stedman, *God's Loving Word* (Grand Rapids, MI: Discovery House Publishers, 1993 by Elaine Stedman), 401.
3 David Harsha, *The Star of Bethlehem, A Guide to the Savior* (Argyle, New York: September 1863), http://www.gracegems.org/BOOKS/star05.htm.
4 Andrew Murray, *Absolute Surrender*, www.worldinvisible.com/library/murray/absolutesurrender.htm
5 Gary M. Burge, *John - The NIV Application Commentary* (Grand Rapids, MI: Zondervan Publishing House, 2000), 416.
6 J.C. Ryle, Commentary on John 15:1–6, "The Vine and the Branches," http://www.gracegems.org/Ryle/j15.htm.
7 Bruce Wilkinson, *Secrets of the Vine* (Sisters, Oregon: Mulnomah Publishers, Inc, 2001), 59–60.
8 Charles Spurgeon, Morning and Evening: Evening, May 18, "Afterward," Hebrews 12:11, www.heartlight.org.
9 Bruce Wilkinson, 32.
10 Rick Howard and Jamie Lash, *This Was Your Life–[Preparing to Meet God Face to Face]* (Grand Rapids, MI: Chosen Books, 1998), 9–10.
11 Rick Howard and Jamie Lash, 29.

8. STAY TOGETHER! THERE'S STRENGTH IN NUMBERS.

1 William R. Mora, Captain, San Antonio Fire Department, *U.S. Firefighter Disorientation Study:* 1979–2001, July 2003.
2 NIOSH Fatality Assessment and control Evaluation Investigative Report #F2004–05, "Residential Basement Fire Claims the Life of Career Lieutenant–Pennsylvania," January 5, 2005, 6.
3 Dennis Smith, from his speech at the National Fallen Firefighters Memorial Service, October 8, 2000.
4 Harry R. Carter Ph.D., "The Sacred Bond," firehouse.com.
5 Rick Warren, *The Purpose Driven Life, What on Earth Am I Here For?* (Grand Rapids, MI: Zondervan, 2002), 134.
6 Harry R. Carter Ph.D.
7 Dr. Henry Cloud, *Changes that Heal* (Grand Rapids, MI: Zondervan, 1992), 47.

8 Henri J.M. Nouwen, *Reaching Out: The Three Movements of the Spiritual Life,* 1975, 110.
9 T.S. Eliot, *"Choruses from 'The Rock,'" part II, in The Complete Poems and Plays:* 1909–1950 (New York: Harcourt, Brace & World, 1971), 101.
10 Dietrich Bonhoeffer, *Life Together*, trans. John W. Doberstein (New York: Harper & Brothers, 1954), 30.
11 Dietrich Bonhoeffer, 17–18.
12 Eugene H. Peterson, *A Long Obedience In The Same Direction* (Downers Grove, Il: InterVarsity Press, 1980, 2nd Edition 2000), 178.
13 Eugene H. Peterson, 179.
14 Eugene H. Peterson, 181.
15 Carol Fullerton, Ph.D., James McCarroll, Ph.D., Robert Ursano, M.D., Kathleen Wright, Ph.D., "Psychological Responses of Rescue Workers: Fire Fighters and Trauma," *American Journal of Orthopsychiatry* 62*(*3*),* July 1992.
16 Rob Jackson, "Foundations for Life, How to Develop Effective Accountability," *Pure Intimacy,* Focus on the Family, 2004.
17 Rob Jackson.
18 Francis A. Schaeffer, *The Great Evangelical Disaster* (Wheaton, Ill: Crossways Books, 1984, Tenth Printing 1995), 163.
19 Dietrich Bonhoeffer, 23.
20 Dietrich Bonhoeffer, 66–67.

9. STAY CALM! IT IS WELL WITH MY SOUL.

1 Sandy Clark, ed. *The Firefighter's Handbook, Essentials of Firefighting and Emergency Response* (Albany: Delmar Publishers, 2000).
2 Jerry Smith, "A Firefighter's Worst Nightmare," *Emergency Grapevine*, 8/16/05.
3 Marta W. Aldrich, "Law enforcement leader fights crime with faith, preparation," United Methodist Church online ministry, www.UMC.org, September 29, 2005.
4 Allan Schwartz, "Anxiety, Worry, and Stress, Oh My: the Bugaboos of Modern Life," *Psych Central*, 9/1/2000.

5 William Ward, quoted by John Mason, *Know Your Limits–Then Ignore Them* (Tulsa, OK: Insight Publishing Group, 1999), 189.
6 Earl Nightingale, *The Essence of Success*, "The Fog of Worry."
7 Earl Nightingale.
8 Steve Trivett, "Deal with stress and stay calm,' Coaching Skills–Info Notes (11), www.thechangezone.com.
9 Dr. Dorothy McCoy, "Trauma And Worry," *Pioneer Thinking*, February 22, 2006.
10 Billy Graham, "The Cure for Anxiety," *Decision Magazine*, July/August 2004.
11 Rich Mullins, a song, *"Hold Me Jesus,"* Edward Grant, Inc (ASCAP), 1993.
12 Luther Bridges, a song, *"He Keeps Me Singing,"* public domain, 1910.
13 Ray Stedman, *God's Loving Word* (Grand Rapids, MI: Discovery House Publishers, 1993 by Elaine Stedman), 180.
14 Mary A. Baker (words) and Horatio R. Palmer (music), a song, *"Master, the Tempest is Raging,"* public domain, 1874.
15 Bertha Spafford Vester, *Our Jerusalem, an American Family in the Holy City*, 1881–1949 (Garden City, N.Y.: Doubleday and Company, Inc., 1950), 3.
16 Bertha Spafford Vester, 9.
17 Bertha Spafford Vester, 7.
18 Bertha Spafford Vester, 29.
19 Bertha Spafford Vester, 33.
20 Bertha Spafford Vester, 33.
21 Bertha Spafford Vester, 33.
22 Library of Congress Exhibition, The American Colony in Jerusalem, www.loc.gov/exhibits/americancolony, March 4, 2005.
23 Bertha Spafford Vester, 41.
24 Bertha Spafford Vester, 45.
25 Horatio G. Spafford (words) and Philip P. Bliss (music), a song, *"It Is Well with My Soul,"* public domain, 1873.
26 Bertha Spafford Vester, 47.
27 Bertha Spafford Vester, 49.
28 Bertha Spafford Vester, 56.

29 Viktor E. Frankl, *Man's Search for Meaning* (Boston, Mass: Beacon Press, 1959, 1962, 1984, 1992), 75.
30 Elisabeth Elliot, "The Freedom of Attitude–It is Well With My Soul," Interview on *Gateway to Joy*, April 6, 2000.

10. STAY ORIENTED! KNOW WHERE YOU'RE GOING.

1 Lewis Carroll, *Alice's Adventures in Wonderland* (New York: Dover Publishing, 1992), 41.
2 John Calvin, *The Institutes of Christian Religion*, 2.2.18–21 (translation J. T. McNeill, 1960).
3 Mel Tillis and Danny Dill, *Detroit City*, a song, Cedarwood Publishing, BMI, 1963.
4 Joseph Stowell, *Eternity - Reclaiming a Passion for What Endures* (Chicago: Moody Press, 1995), 45.
5 J. C. Ryle, "Our Hope," 1877.
6 www.webster-dictionary.net/definition/hope.
7 Friedrich Wilhelm Nietzsche, *Human, All Too Human* (University of Nebraska Press, 1884), 58.
8 Bertrand Russell, *Mysticism and Logic* (London: Longmans, Green and Co., 1918), 43–44.
9 John Piper, "What is Hope?" a sermon preached on April 6, 1986.
10 J. C. Ryle, "Our Hope," 1877.
11 Joseph Stowell, *Eternity*, 35 and 41.
12 Jim Collins, www.jimcollins.com/lib/goodtogreat/ch4_p83.html, 2002.
13 Jim Collins.
14 Ken Gire, *The Divine Embrace* (Wheaton, Illinois: Tyndale House Publishers, 2003), 32–33.
15 The Barna Group, "Americans Describe Their Views About Life After Death," www.barna.org, October 21, 2003. All statistics and information copyrighted by The Barna Group.
16 Mike Anton and William Lobdell, "Hold the Fire and Brimstone," *Los Angeles Times*, June 19, 2002.
17 Mike Anton and William Lobdell.

18 ThinkExist.com Quotations. "William Booth quotes." ThinkExist.com quotations Online, June 1, 2006.

19 Harold Begbie, *The Life of General William Booth, The Founder of the Salvation Army* (New York: Macmillan Company, 1920), 406.

20 J.C. Ryle, "Fire, Fire", www.gracegems.org/SERMONS/fire.htm.

21 Charles Spurgeon, "Heaven and Hell," a sermon preached in a field, King Edward's Road, Hackney, September 4, 1855

22 Mike Spalding, "Memoir of a Firefighter Trapped in Hell," VFRE Presentation, www.vfre.com/knapp-delisio/memoir.htm.

23 Jonathan Edwards, *The Works of Jonathan Edwards, Volume* 2 (Edinburgh: Banner of Truth, 1974), 884.

24 The Barna Group, "Americans Describe Their Views About Life After Death," www.barna.org, October 21, 2003.

25 John MacArthur, *"He Saved Us,"* a sermon © 1997 by Grace to You.

26 C. H. Spurgeon, "Following the Risen Christ," a Sermon delivered on March 28, 1880.

27 James Meikle (1730–1799), *Solitude Sweetened*, from Grace Gems: pilgrim@gracegems.org.

28 C.S. Lewis, *The Last Battle* (New York: HarperCollins, 1956), 196, 210–211.